PROGRESS IN SELF PSYCHOLOGY
Volume 1

PROGRESS IN SELF PSYCHOLOGY
Editor: Arnold Goldberg, MD

PROGRESS IN SELF PSYCHOLOGY
Volume 1

Edited by
ARNOLD GOLDBERG

THE GUILFORD PRESS
New York London

©1985 The Guilford Press
A Division of Guilford Publications, Inc.
200 Park Avenue South, New York, N.Y. 10003

Printed in the United States of America

LIBRARY OF CONGRESS CATALOGING IN PUBLICATION DATA
Main entry under title:

Progress in self psychology.

    Includes bibliographies and index.
    1. Self—Collected works. 2. Ego (Psychology)—
Collected works. I. Goldberg, Arnold, 1929-
BF697.P75 1985   155.2   85-21875
ISBN 0-89862-300-6

Contributors

Howard A. Bacal, MD
Thornhill, Ontario, Canada

Michael Franz Basch, MD
Chicago, Illinois

Bernard Brandchaft, MD
Beverly Hills, California

Douglas W. Detrick, PhD
Portola Valley, California

Arnold Goldberg, MD
Chicago, Illinois

John M. Hall, MD
Cincinnati, Ohio

Jule P. Miller, MD
St. Louis, Missouri

Jerome D. Oremland, MD
San Francisco, California

Anna Ornstein, MD
Cincinnati, Ohio

Paul H. Ornstein, MD
Cincinnati, Ohio

Morton Shane, MD
Los Angeles, California

Sanford Shapiro, MD
La Jolla, California

Robert D. Stolorow, PhD
Los Angeles, California

Charles B. Strozier, PhD
Springfield, Illinois

Paul H. Tolpin, MD
Chicago, Illinois

Marjorie Taggart White, PhD
New York, New York

Samuel L. Wilson, MD
Santa Monica, California

Bonnie Wolfe, PhD
Los Angeles, California

Preface

After Heinz Kohut died in October of 1981 and the shock of his departure had somewhat subsided, those of his colleagues who were interested in and part of the life and work of this remarkable man, had to consider at length what self psychology would be without him. I once said to him that there was no real creativity in self psychology apart from his work, and at that time he had felt it necessary to apologize for that situation. I now suspect that there could be no real creativity in the field as long as his presence and his own brilliant mind continued to impress and produce so much. In truth it has taken most of us years to understand and appreciate what he gave to psychoanalysis, and the time for new ideas was simply not right. With this book we hope that perhaps that moment is imminent.

There is little doubt in the minds of Kohut's friends and associates that the legacy most significant to him was his work, and his most fervent wish was to have his ideas promulgated and widely disseminated. There was more than one time of either dismay and bewilderment on his part when forced to defend and explain something that he had never written or said, or when asked to respond to a question that he had written upon extensively. But since I was among the naive and untutored questioners, I can only agree that the demon of forgetfulness and misunderstanding never seems to rest for long. We needed and will continue to need forums for discussion, places to exchange ideas and learn, and some vehicle to help new thoughts to grow. To those ends, our first decision was to have annual conferences.

We have held conferences on self psychology all over the country (and outside as well) that have ranged from single presentations to more complex three-day meetings with panels, workshops, and seminars. Most of the conferences have been collected in one volume or another and much of the material in this present book comes from the sixth annual conference held in Los Angeles in 1983. However, we were dissatisfied with reporting the proceedings of a conference in a volume that did not reach publication until some time later, and we also realized that many people actively working in self psychology simply did not attend or submit papers to conferences, so the next step seemed to be to launch a journal, and we held discussions

on this for some time. Actually these began before Kohut's death and floun-
dered not from lack of his own interest, which was markedly positive, but
from simple financial truths. Thus our compromise: an annual volume that
will include the best of our conferences along with selected papers from as
wide a source as possible. Our title is that of progress, and we are convinced
that self psychology can and will thrive despite the loss of its founder.

This volume begins with Charles Strozier's work on a Kohut biography.
This is followed by Jule Miller's account of supervision with Kohut. The
biographical sketch coupled with this glimpse into the man at work are
fitting beginnings to our book. It seems appropriate to have these memories
reawakened as a transition to the work ahead, which will no longer bear
Kohut's signature. This book goes on to Chapters by Basch and Ornstein
and Ornstein with a discussion by Goldberg on a topic at the center of the
problem of technique: interpretation. In the planning of the conference we
hoped to focus on whether and how the interpretations offered by self psychologists differ in kind or substance from those of others. It is no surprise
that the issues of technique so dominated our discussion that we came to
no conclusion but rather raised further questions. The third section again
serves as a transition from Kohut to succeeding generations of self psychologists. We take a chapter of his last book (Kohut, 1984) entitled "The
Self Psychological Approach to Defense and Resistance" and subject it to
varied appraisals and responses. I think the heart of the controversy "Is it
really different or is it just old wine in new bottles?" lies in these penetrating
discussions.

A host of new names appear in the next two sections of our book. In
the clinical section we meet John Hall, and his presentation of a case fulfills
the most exacting requirements a reader may make of a case presentation.
It explains just what the analyst did or did not do, when, and why. I think
Heinz Kohut would have been especially pleased with this product from
someone who had no personal contact with him, which helps prove that it
was the ideas and not the person that counted. Bonnie Wolfe and Sanford
Shapiro present briefer clinical papers designed to explore the setting of
our clinical practice and highlight the continued expansion of our work in
treating perversion. To complete this section, Wilson provides an interesting
clinical view on the common condition of self-pity.

The more theoretical final section of this volume has a chapter by a
familiar contributor, Robert Stolorow, and more new names: Bacal, White,
and Detrick. All these chapters hold promise of new theory shedding new
light on old subjects as well as showing things never seen before. They are
testimony for our hope that much awaits us in exploring the psychology of
the self, as there is no finished business in psychoanalysis.

It is difficult at this point to predict what will happen to the work of
Heinz Kohut and self psychology. It may be gradually incorporated into

the body of knowledge that is psychoanalysis and thereupon subtly but inevitably change that amorphous entity. The old words will never be the same again. The definitions of self, object, ego, representation, have so evolved that a wave of protest has arisen asking us either to stop using certain words or to go back to their "real meaning," whatever that may be; but this is the mark of scientific progress, and self psychology will aid that evolution.

Perhaps self psychology will never be invited into the house of orthodox psychoanalysis, but will always be branded as intruder. This fate too would not be so dreadful, since the work of keeping an invader at bay manages to change the invaded as well. Heinz Kohut's hope was that self psychology embrace and encompass all that was good in psychoanalysis. However, no one wants an arrogant newcomer to try to take over, so the common reaction to the brash claims of self psychology has been that it does not know its proper place.

These three fates of self psychology (1) continued isolation as alien; (2) gradual assimilation into the main body of psychoanalysis; or (3) domination of all analysis, are really fanciful political and sociological issues. One or another may dominate at various times in various places for a long time to come. The historian who looks back on psychoanalysis may even be at pains to say just how and whether self psychology had an impact on the field of psychoanalysis. The important thing is that the science not be too severely effected by these political winds in order to continue to learn and to progress.

The growth of new ideas is a peculiar combination of social and intellectual factors. It is comforting to think that ideas flourish because of their inherent truth or reasonableness and will thereby thrive in a variety of climates; but there is a contrasting and somewhat cynical stance, that creative efforts need the proper combination of appeal to the audience and encouragement of the creator to develop at all, and they are correspondingly molded by the people who surround the originator. Heinz Kohut developed within psychoanalysis and tried mightily to influence the major figures in his development such as Heinz Hartmann and Anna Freud. He worked with a group of admiring and appreciative colleagues who allowed and perhaps encouraged his emancipation from the constraints of orthodox psychoanalysis. Now self psychology emerges with a whole new set of pressures, influences, and critics. It has to stake out a position that bears the mark of Kohut and allows appreciation without forming its own orthodoxy.

Unfortunately, we will not know the proper place of self psychology for many years, and we shall arrive at that destination after a long trip of many short steps. This book is one such step, and we sincerely hope it is in the right direction. The future is uncertain but unavoidable, but we hope it is progressive as well.

The preparation of this book was financed by funds from the Harry and Hazel Cohen Research Fund. Mrs. Chris Susman provided secretarial and editorial assistance.

Arnold Goldberg, MD

REFERENCE

Kohut, H. (1984). *How Does Analysis Cure?* A. Goldberg, ed., with P. Stepansky. Chicago & London: University of Chicago Press.

Contents

PROGRESS IN SELF PSYCHOLOGY
Volume 1

MEMORIES OF HEINZ KOHUT

1

Glimpses of a Life: Heinz Kohut (1913–1981)

CHARLES B. STROZIER

I assume the task of telling some of Heinz Kohut's story with great trepidation. Readers of this volume are not only well aware of and interested in his work but number among them friends and colleagues who knew him much better than I. Many go back years, if not decades, with Heinz Kohut. They have their memories and pictures of him stamped. I can only hope my work contributes to and enhances the memories of those who were really close to him, just as my primary source lies in what several of his friends have already told me of him, material that I have shamelessly appropriated and that I hope in the coming years will be expanded considerably. For let me make clear that another source of my trepidation is that I am nowhere near the end of my work on this project. I need much more time to interview Kohut's family and friends, his colleagues, his admirers and critics alike, former patients, everybody and anybody who knows anything and is willing to share memories and thoughts with me. Furthermore, Kohut's life blended into the larger story of the Chicago Institute since the war and, to some degree, the whole history of psychoanalysis since Freud. Before he was 50, Kohut was labeled—and he bore proudly—the title "Mr. Psychoanalysis." Unlike cult figures like Erikson who left mainstream psychoanalysis for the universities and who wrote better prose, Kohut faithfully and diligently kept the psychoanalytic flame alive, serving on innumerable committees in Chicago and in the American Psychoanalytic Association and gaining the respect of everyone in the field from Anna Freud to Heinz Hartmann to colleagues closer to home in Chicago who had long known he was special. His publications before 1971 were relatively few and, though always interesting and even remarkable, they were, as he himself later noted, safe. Keep in mind that as late as *The Analysis of the Self* in 1971 Kohut was still using obscure terminology like "narcissistic libido" to express some really new ideas. This larger aspect of a volume I am preparing—the way Kohut's life was a part of psychoanalytic history—will occupy a good deal of my time researching.

Kohut is also an intimidating figure to write about. I make no claims
to any special closeness to Kohut. I was not his patient, he no longer taught
at the Chicago Institute when I was a candidate there, and I seldom saw
him socially; but I was touched by him. In 1979 I helped organize a conference
on political leadership at which he was the central figure. After that we
worked on a book together and, in his last year, I conducted a series of
taped interviews with him. He also expressed his enthusiasm for several
papers he heard me give. I was in a sense the new kid on the block at the
very end as he declined physically and at a time when many of his relationships
with contemporaries had soured. In writing my biography, I hope I have
enough distance to be objective, sufficient experience as a biographer to be
effective, and enough sensitivity to discipline my subjectivity. I'm not
indifferent to the largeness of Kohut. He was indeed an idealizable figure
who elicited from the psychoanalytic community both abject devotion and
contemptuous disregard (and, as in Freud's biography, the most interesting
relationships he had are with those who moved from devotion to disregard).
Yet he was always taken seriously; he was always considered special.

Not surprisingly, Kohut was apparently treated specially as a child.
He was born on May 3, 1913. His father, Felix Kohut, who died in 1936,
was very successful in the paper business and was a highly cultured man.
He was truly gifted at the piano and before the first world war changed his
life was heading for a career as a concert pianist. Heinz was also able to
play the piano, but it was a seldom demonstrated talent. During all of World
War I, Felix Kohut served on the Russian front, where his wife and baby
Heinz used to visit him at times. Otherwise, from the time Heinz was 1
until he was 5, his father was away and he and his mother lived with her
parents outside of Vienna. Heinz was particularly close to his maternal
grandfather who, however, died before the end of the war. Felix, geograph-
ically removed in Heinz's early years, seems, after his return, to have been
quite remote characterologically. Fathers and their substitutes were elusive
for the infant Kohut.

Heinz's mother, Else Lampl, who lived to see him serve as president
of the American Psychoanalytic Association in the 1960s, is frankly an
obscure figure for me right now (and I fear may always remain so). She
seemed to be oppressively close at times, then apart and distant at others.
"Difficult" is the adjective several people I've interviewed have used to
describe her, though I don't yet understand what exactly made her difficult
and what she was like when Heinz was young. He often described his
childhood as sad and said he felt intense loneliness because of the social
functions that took his parents away most evenings. In one of my own
interviews with Kohut, he once referred to his "crazy mother" but it was
said lightheartedly and he then went on to relate a touching anecdote of the
congratulatory telegram she sent on his election as president of the American
Psychoanalytic Association. There was something deep and abiding between

Heinz and his mother, whatever the residues of ambivalence. Furthermore, if I may be permitted a conjectural aside, I cannot believe anyone who approached life with such zest and enthusiasm and who was always treated by others as unique and inordinately talented was not somehow treated specially by and close to his mother.

Be that as it may, Heinz was an only child whose education was remarkable, even by the rigorous standards of the Viennese elite. He was at first kept from formal schooling for the first 2 years, and had instead a tutor from the school work with him at home. He then went through the local elementary school and the Döblinger Gymnasium, from which he graduated in 1932. There he had the best of a classical education, including history and 8 years of Latin and 6 of Greek. He also studied French, the knowledge of which was further enhanced in several summers *au pension*, wide reading, and a full year in Paris as a young man. He never studied English when young. Later, in the United States, when he had to do a fast study of English, he immersed himself in *Alice in Wonderland*, from which he could always lovingly quote long passages. Heinz seemed to treasure especially the years in the gymnasium. He was at or near the top of his class and active in many things, cultural *and* athletic—he was good at track and field and he boxed well. In the last year of his life he spoke warmly to me of his teachers at the gymnasium and the wonderful enthusiasm they brought to their instruction. For example, half a century later he described in vivid detail the way a history teacher had evoked the French Enlightenment by painting a picture in words of the gardens at Versailles, their order and elegance.

From about the time he was 8 to 14 years of age, there was also an extraordinary tutor with whom Heinz was in constant contact. Heinz's mother hired this young man, who was probably a university student, for the sole purpose of stimulating her son intellectually. He would show up most afternoons and take Heinz to the opera, the art gallery, to walk the Ring, and talk and play intellectual games. Heinz talked to friends about this tutor for the rest of his life. He clearly left an indelible impression. Yet no one seems to remember his name and Heinz himself after his childhood lost track of him.

At 19 Kohut entered the University of Vienna and its Medical Faculty. He was a consistently good student, who at times creatively bent the rules to adapt a large institution to his own needs. Thus, in 1936 he simply took off without permission for Paris, where for a year he gained some extra medical training and experience working in various Parisian hospitals. One has to suspect, however, that visiting the treasures of the Louvre was as much a part of his intentions in living in France as was gaining an understanding of French medicine from the inside. In any event, he succeeded to stay without losing any time or credit at the University of Vienna. He simply had some friend present his little book to the professors for periodic signature to prove his attendance at lectures where of course he had not been present. Most people would probably not be able to pull off such a trick *and* not miss a step academically. Heinz was different.

As a student in the 1930s—he graduated with his medical degree in November 1938—Kohut became interested in psychoanalysis. One brief and not very successful therapy gave way to analysis with August Eichorn who was close to Freud and provided a direct link to the founder of psychoanalysis. Kohut never knew or met Freud, but there is a famous story he liked to tell of visiting the train station when Freud left for England on June 4, 1938. Freud, in a wheelchair, along with his wife, her sister Minna, Anna, Dorothy Burlingham, his dog Lun, and an entourage of patients and servants boarded the Orient Express bound for Paris. As the train left the station, Freud looked out the window and there stood Kohut with a friend. Kohut tipped his hat. Freud tipped his hat in return and the train rolled off down the track. It is a story that stresses continuities and Viennese connections in a crumbling world. Kohut's fond telling also suggests to me a special sense of mission that he felt about psychoanalysis as a young man.

Within a few months Kohut followed Freud to England, though, lacking Freud's political clout, he was without a passport or the visa he needed to go to the United States. He was therefore placed by the British in a camp for emigrés. There he stayed for the first half of 1939. As a doctor, Kohut enjoyed special privileges in the camp, which the British, civilized as they are, tried to make as pleasant as possible. The inhabitants, for example, took on the local village in a chess match—and defeated them roundly. Still, the camp was a draining experience and sometime that summer Kohut got pneumonia and secured permission to reside with his uncle, Hans Lampl, in London. This uncle had been a very successful businessman in Vienna and had escaped with enough assets to ride out the war in England. He was later to return to Vienna and resume his successful career.

In early 1940 Kohut got his visa and secured passage on a convoy to the United States. Once here he came immediately to Chicago, determined to escape war in Europe and build a new life. He chose Chicago, it seems, largely because an old and dear childhood friend from Vienna, Sigmund Levarie, had established something of a beachhead there as an instructor in the department of music at the University of Chicago. Kohut may also have been influenced by the presence in Chicago of two other noted analysands of Eichorn—Kurt Eissler and Paul Kramer. Upon arrival with barely 25 cents in his pocket, Kohut quickly applied for citizenship—which he was awarded 5 years later—and managed to get an internship at a small, southside hospital. As usual, he impressed everyone he met and the moment he finished his internship he came to the University of Chicago for a coveted residency in neurology. He served in this capacity with distinction. Neurologists at the university still talk of the loss to "real science" when Kohut left neurology for an assistant professorship in neurology and psychiatry in 1944 and then exclusively in psychiatry in 1947. He was apparently marked to be chairman of the section in neurology as soon as they got him through his residency. His boards, for example, were astoundingly good.

One wonders, of course, why Kohut chose to start with neurology and why he then left it for psychiatry. There is no doubt he agonized over his shifting interests; but from everything I can gather, Kohut also seemed to be consciously modeling himself on Freud. Kohut had already had one analysis and, not long after arriving in Chicago, began his second with Ruth Eissler. He read and talked about Freud constantly. The train scene in 1938 suggests a sense of identification with Freud and the psychoanalytic movement. Furthermore, Kohut wanted to be not just a neurologist but, like Freud, a good one. There was, in other words, an early sense of purpose in Kohut, an inner fire and lofty ambition to be Freud's successor, long before those thoughts had any basis in actuality.

In these war years Kohut lived in a room on the sixth floor of Billings Hospital and soon developed a network of close friends and colleagues. He worked hard in the hospital, of course, but he also regularly attended the opera and spent many afternoons wandering through the Art Institute. He also found the Museum of Science and Industry fascinating and spent many weekends there. For a cultured Viennese that museum, which so celebrates American capitalism, must have epitomized the culture of his adopted country. He went out often to modestly priced restaurants, played bridge with friends, laughed, and talked of the Viennese Ring as though it was on the other side of the Midway. He was pudgy then—the running of 7-minute miles and weight loss only came in the early '50s—and he was noted for his meticulousness by friends. His room was always neat as a pin and his clothes were carefully tailored. He rounded out his costume with gloves, which he started wearing at the very first sign of winter. His hair, brushed straight back in the European style, was always in place. Kohut and another well-kept central European on the sixth floor of Billings—Thomas Szasz—were both regarded as unusual by their parochial colleagues when they slept with a hair net; but that was how you kept it looking so good. In everything, he was very well organized. When he read a book, for example, he would carefully set it up in front of him and arrange different colored pens (for underlining) on either side in absolutely perfect order. It looked, said an old friend, as though he were going to eat the book.

Kohut in fact became something of a legend on the floor. People noticed and remembered him. One thing that stood out was his humor and playfulness. He loved, for example, to tell jokes of the sophisticated Count Rudi from Vienna, and his country cousin, Graf Bobi, from Budapest. He would take great delight in telling these jokes, which, if the listener knew German, he would enliven by using Viennese and Budapest accents. Kohut's playfulness had long been a part of his character. Even in the gymnasium he had been a master of tricks like arranging for someone to blow a trumpet under an open window to drown out the lecture. Play, it seems, helped nourish his creativity and possibly relieved some of the tensions from hard work and compulsiveness.

Then, as later, Kohut's talents and interests were diverse. He was in analysis, constantly reading Freud and other writers in psychoanalysis, working on a daily basis as a neurologist, preparing for specialty boards at which he excelled, attending the opera, going to museums, eating out, seeing friends, reading widely and deeply in all kinds of literature (he was particularly fond of Thomas Mann), listening to and thinking about music, and so forth. Some talents and interests—like playing the piano—simply had to be suppressed. He was also a fine singer and, in the words of someone who knows about these things, he could have been an actor. How did he manage it all? Obviously, he was talented in special ways; but he also was a master both of limiting himself and of highlighting the experience of the moment. Then—and later—he hardly had the time to go to as many cultural affairs as he would have liked. When he did it was a big event, something he prepared for, which completely absorbed his attention. After a concert, for example, he could recall every second of the performance and describe in detail its ups and downs.

Kohut had great charm and seemingly boundless enthusiasm. His wide knowledge was impressive. In everyone's eyes, he was marked for greatness. When a little later he graduated from the Institute for Psychoanalysis (in 1948), he was immediately brought onto the faculty and staff, which was a rare honor. Within 3 years he, Joan Fleming, and Louis Shapiro had reestablished orthodoxy in the curriculum and ferreted out the Alexandrian heresy of shortening psychoanalysis. Yet in the '40s Kohut sometimes over-powered and offended. He had trouble suppressing his disdain for the thin cultural background of most Americans. Furthermore, when he talked, you listened. It was brilliant stuff, but his self-centeredness could isolate people and cause wounds that lasted a lifetime. One very perceptive person who knew him well then, noted how curious it was that no one ever hurt him more deeply than Kohut and yet his brilliance, charm, enthusiasm, and humor continued to be irresistible.

Once established in the Institute, Kohut never left it. He kept his ap-pointment at the University of Chicago until 1950, but his concerns now lay elsewhere. He had, it seems, four goals. First, he wanted to become an excellent psychoanalyst, to heal in the unique way pioneered by Freud. Now, of course, it is difficult to assess the real quality of any psychoanalyst as a clinician. The evaluative criteria are unclear, the process secretive, and the therapeutic results often ambiguous. There is a lot more to learn about this aspect of Kohut's life. One of my personal goals is to interest talkative former patients in sharing with me their experience in therapy with Kohut. Be that as it may, I have picked up some interesting information on Kohut the clinician that is worth relating. Colleagues who worked with him over the decades seem to have no doubt he was a superb analyst. He was one of those few people whom other senior analysts consulted on their own cases. Patients who ended up in more than one consulting room talked of Kohut's extraordinary empathy and patience. Furthermore, his case presentations showed him to be completely on top of his cases. He was finely tuned to where a patient was in analysis and what direction the flow of associations was taking. There was undoubtedly an occasional failure, but Kohut gained renown as a successful analyst. Why? One time a former patient was giving a paper and doing a good job at it. Kohut was absorbed in the presentation and beaming happily. It was said then, and probably could apply generally, that he truly loved his patient.

The second goal Kohut seemed to set for himself was to become an informed and effective teacher. There is no doubt he managed to keep a class enthralled, no matter how far afield he went or how long the digression. He liked to begin with a question and then talk at it for the next hour, thinking on his feet, so to speak, sharing with students the creative process. His charisma carried the day and inspired excited listeners to read and think on their own. The medium was, in a sense, the message. The only problem was that some prosaic minds at the Institute felt candidates should know some specific things about Freud from a course on psychoanalytic theory. They therefore established a second course, called a discussion group, back to back with Kohut's lectures, to go over the reading before hearing Kohut.

The same teaching style later carried over to his public lectures at which he could as easily enthrall hundreds as he had done earlier with a dozen students. His marvelous ramble, however, had much more order than many realized. Sometimes, Kohut actually read a paper; but in general he talked, as Freud had, without notes at all. For run-of-the-mill presentations, he would seclude himself for an hour or so beforehand, and stride back and forth thinking. For the big talks, however, he made elaborate preparation. At the first self conference in 1978, for example, he talked without apparent direction but with clear inspiration on a panel entitled, "Psychoanalysis and the Sciences of Man." A couple of years later in going through some unpublished material he asked me to edit, I came across a 70-page draft paper he wrote *before* the self conference entitled "Psychoanalysis and the Sciences of Man."

Thirdly in his career, Kohut sought to achieve leadership of the psychoanalytic community and provide direction for its future development. For much of the '50s and well into the '60s, Kohut labored on many committees, especially those of the American Psychoanalytic Association. As usual, he took this work very seriously. For example, his excellent paper, published in 1960, "Beyond the Bounds of the Basic Rule," which discusses applied psychoanalysis, began as a committee report. Kohut turned an otherwise mundane report into a classic statement on method in applied psychoanalytic work. There is no doubt he was good at such work and in the end he rose to the presidency of the American. However, there is some question whether administration best expressed his creativity. He was in some ways too large a personality. In later years he liked to say half-jokingly that everything he knew of narcissism he learned from committee work, which is a gross exaggeration (that's why it's funny) and biographically misleading. There were also some sharp disappointments in the achievement of this leadership goal, most notably when he was outmaneuvered by Leo Rangell for the presidency of the International Psychoanalytic Association in 1969; and when, in 1978, he was not reelected to the Council of the Chicago Institute amid a great deal of intrigue, and some would say envy, on the part of some colleagues.

It was, however, in achieving his final goal as a researcher and original thinker in psychoanalysis that Kohut was, in the end, the most successful. I will briefly sketch here the development of his thoughts and put his ideas in a biographical context. In retrospect, the continuity in Kohut's thought seems to outweigh the apparent shifts in terminology. He began writing on applied psychoanalysis and surely never lost that interest. The 1959 paper on empathy defines the methodological basis of the psychoanalytic enterprise as a science. Those ideas never changed, only enlarged. It is not a radical intellectual shift to think of the self as being at the center of psychological life rather than to think of narcissism as one line of development, the way Anna Freud would have had it. Such a shift in language is far less important than the discovery of selfobject or, as he first called them, narcissistic transferences. The notion of the selfobject was there in Kohut's mind long before he removed the hyphen; it can be found in one of his earliest papers on Thomas Mann's *Death in Venice*.

Nevertheless, there do appear to be two major stages in the intellectual biography of Heinz Kohut that correlate with other changes in his personal and professional life. Of course the two stages overlapped; any delineation of stages in a life course has a large measure of artificiality to it. Yet we live by timed rituals and we mark passages by symbols that, once created, come to control other things. For Kohut it seems there was a major turning point in 1965, when two things happened: he reached the end of the line in his leadership goal; and, in the same year, before a meeting of the American, he outlined his thoughts on narcissism that inaugurated the original work that occupied the last 16 years of his life.

Before 1965 Kohut was Mr. Psychoanalysis, the most eminent spokesman for classical Freudian thought, conservative, and widely respected by Anna Freud, Heinz Hartmann, Kurt Eissler, and others. Until the mid-'60s the unquestioned respect of such figures seemed central for Kohut, but the effort it took to maintain may have choked his creativity. But whether that is true or not, it soon became painfully clear to Kohut that orthodoxy could not easily contain his developing thought. Anna Freud thus minimized the importance of *The Analysis of the Self* in 1971 and after that quietly withdrew from Kohut's ideas. Kurt Eissler, his old friend and colleague, whose wife had analyzed the young Kohut, told him in the early '70s that he didn't understand a thing Kohut was doing. Kohut was crushed. Such withdrawal of support at first genuinely confused (and upset) Kohut and he never fully reconciled himself to it. But it is worth remembering that his bold new ideas were losing him the respect of those he most admired and that he was increasingly and sometimes viciously attacked. It is now an almost stale criticism of Kohut that he understood narcissism so well because he was himself so grandiose. No great thinker is humble; and it took real courage and fortitude to move away from a tradition—at least as perceived by those responsible for orthodoxy within that tradition—that was so completely a part of Kohut's soul.

His language also gradually shifted from the arcane terminology of ego psychology to a clearer set of terms more his own, ones obviously more appropriate for his ideas. This language change came in fits and starts. The 1966 paper on narcissism is a model of clarity and stays largely free from jargon, while the first book, in 1971, returns to the old terms to carry the new ideas. Then the rage paper in 1972 began a long series of publications that, in an unbroken way, move toward a new language for self psychology, toward terms like "selfobject" that are so simple and yet so richly evocative. I do not want to overdo this point of a new language; still, our words are vital symbols of our thought. One cannot think freshly without discovering a new way of saying things. It is central to the creative process in psycho-analysis—and in many other areas of science as well.

As a footnote, I also want to point out that before "Forms and Trans-formations of Narcissism" in 1966, Kohut had published a total of only six full-length, substantive articles in psychoanalysis, though he had published a paper while still in medical school and several neurological papers in the early 1940s. Of the psychoanalytic papers, two dealt with his psychological theory of music, one is the essay on *Death in Venice*, and one is the essay on method in applied psychoanalysis. Thus, fully two-thirds of his major publications dealt with applied psychoanalysis. A fifth article was the long synthesis, "Concepts and Theories of Psychoanalysis" written with Philip Seitz, and *only* the last—the 1959 empathy paper—broke new ground in psychoanalytic theory. The rest of his writing was not the kind of stuff that turns the world upside down: there were 22 reports, panel discussions, book reviews, and obituaries, and two published addresses as president of the American Psychoanalytic Association, the first as he assumed office, the second when he left. The total number of printed pages for *everything* he wrote before 1966 (when he was 52) in Paul Ornstein's edition comes to only 295 pages. The point I hope is obvious: one gauge of Kohut's expansive creativity since the mid-'60s is the marked increase in the amount of sustained, serious writing he produced.

Finally, the mid-'60s marked a major change in Kohut's circle of friends: they got younger. Old and dear friends remained just that, but complicated and competitive relationships with peers gave way to a wholly new circle of younger colleagues who self-consciously grouped themselves around Kohut as, beginning in 1902, the first circle of admirers came to study with Freud. The Jung of the group—John Gedo—played a crucial role in getting it organized. It met in Kohut's home, beginning in the late '60s, to go over emerging chapters of the *Analysis of the Self* and first consisted of Gedo, Arnold Goldberg, Michael Franz Basch, David Marcus, Paul Tolpin, and Paul Ornstein. Later, Marian Tolpin, Anna Ornstein, and Ernest Wolf joined, and Gedo left. Some others have played a role in the group, which while Kohut was alive had three peak periods of activity—before each of his two books, and during the preparation of the Casebook that Dr. Goldberg edited.

The purpose of this group was to discuss Kohut's work in a supportive way. Kohut, like Freud earlier with his group, was the master; they, the students. They were the best and brightest of the younger members of the Chicago Institute; they now joined in his enterprise. Despite division, controversy, and some hurt feelings, the group endured, and both helped Kohut keep productive and feel recognized, and on their own began increasingly to extend his ideas in their own publications and, with the self conferences that began in 1978 and are now in their sixth year, to widen the circle of influence from Chicago to the nation. Over the years, snide remarks have been made about the fawning attitude of the group toward Kohut and his dominance over the members has been castigated. But he was, like Freud, the one with new ideas. It is to the group's credit that they recognized and appreciated it. As Arnold Goldberg told me,

> The thing about Heinz is that he had something. Like him or dislike him, you just don't often find that kind of person. . . . And he knew he was special. Most of his critics weren't playing the same game he was playing. He was playing hard ball. They were into the 16-inch stuff. There was just no one in his league.

To conclude on that playful metaphor, we are, it seems, at a critical stage in the history of self psychology and indeed of psychoanalysis generally. Kohut had an acute and poignant sense of the importance of the annual conferences in pushing forward self psychology. He never missed one while he lived. He even dragged himself from his sick bed to attend the last, 4 years ago in San Francisco. He came on Sunday morning then, looking pale and tired, but he pulled himself majestically erect to lecture on empathy. After he finished the large audience stood and broke into long, moving applause. Somewhat embarrassed, he motioned enough. "Thank you," he said in parting. "I want to take a rest now." He died 4 days later.

2

How Kohut Actually Worked

JULE P. MILLER

There is widespread curiosity among those who are interested in self psychology about how Heinz Kohut actually worked in the clinical situation. Both students and senior colleagues frequently ask questions such as, What did Kohut consider a fragmentation? How did he work with dreams? How did he deal with frank oedipal or preoedipal material? What are some specific examples of the repair of empathic failures leading to transmuting internalization?

While Kohut has written a great deal and has answered these questions, at least in part, the answers are scattered throughout the body of his work. *The Psychology of the Self: A Casebook*, edited by Arnold Goldberg, is a valuable contribution and answers many of these questions. Nonetheless, many analysts and candidates remain intensely curious about Kohut's actual specific teachings. This chapter attempts to answer some of these questions.

I was fascinated by my reading of *The Analysis of the Self*, wrote to Kohut, and arranged to begin consultations with him in November 1978. I saw him for a total of 23 double-length sessions between then and July 1981. Our work was interrupted from time to time because of his several severe illnesses and our last meeting occurred less than 3 months before his death. I believe I had a view of the final stages of the development of his thinking.

At the time I began my consultations with him, I was an experienced analyst, having been practicing for nearly 16 years. I presented in some detail the last 2 years of a successful 5-year analysis. We followed this patient through the termination phase, and most of the examples I will give in this chapter are drawn from that work. I also presented to him the first 2½ years of a beginning analysis and, also, made various "spot" presentations of interesting clinical instances.

The patient on which this chapter is primarily based was a highly successful man in his 30s when he first consulted me. He was married and the father of several children. The patient was the eldest of four siblings; the two siblings closest to him in age were brothers. His symptomatology was primarily that of diffuse, restless anxiety, contentless depression, and troubling homosexual fantasies and feelings. These homosexual fantasies were usually precipitated or intensified by frustrating life experiences. In his growing-up years there had been sporadic episodes of gross homosexual activity. However, there had been no overt homosexual activity for several years prior to the beginning of the analysis; nonetheless, his homosexual fantasy life and homosexual impulses remained active. He had an on-going but constricted sexual life with his wife.

Both Kohut and I regarded the patient as a narcissistic personality disorder, and thought that the predominant transference in the analysis was an idealizing one. I will mention first an incident that occurred relatively early in the analysis, which I reported to Kohut during our initial meeting. I sneezed unexpectedly and the patient was startled. He was temporarily dislocated psychologically and, when recovered, he recalled his father's tendency to sneeze suddenly and loudly at the dinner table. He said it reminded him of "the explosion of an atomic bomb." In my comments to the patient, I dealt with this partly in terms of the intrusiveness of my sneeze, but mainly in terms of his special sensitivity, which, it seemed to me, determined the extent of his reaction.

Kohut's response was that he would have handled this incident differently. He would have focused less on the patient's sensitivity and more on the intrusion of my sneeze into the orderly analytic atmosphere. He said that, after all, in analysis we invite the patient to regress. This patient was regressed and was prone to fragmentation to begin with, and, as a consequence, he was close to a "minifragmentation" at this time in the analysis. It would have been more profitable to point out the connection between the intrusion into the analytic atmosphere of my sneeze and the way he reacted to that intrusion rather than to focus on his sensitivity. Such a focus could seem critical to the patient and, therefore, hinder genuine analytic exploration. This incident illuminated for me two aspects of Kohut's thought, first, that a fragmentation can be a rather minor event, as well as a major one, and secondly, his emphasis on the naturalness of the patient's response—in this instance that it was natural that a patient in analysis respond in a startled way to an intrusion on the orderliness of the analytic process. Under other circumstances and with more material, Kohut might also have made genetic connections between this episode in the analysis and comparable experiences of unexpected dislocation in the patient's formative years.

Then I reported a recent session in some detail. Early in the hour the patient said he had mistakenly come an hour early for his appointment, had opened the door to the waiting room, and was startled to see an old man sitting there. The man seemed to be dull, depressed, and apathetic. The patient was shocked to find this person in the waiting room, which he had expected to be empty, and he experienced a sense of panic and dislocation. After several moments his self-experience shifted, and he said that he felt like me. He felt that he was tall; he was answering the door, and the other person in the waiting room looked short and insignificant to him. However, this shift soon passed, and he again felt anxious and dislocated. He then had a strong desire to go to a nearby bookstore and look at books containing homosexual pictures and stories, which was his principal type of homosexual gratification at this time. In the bookstore he looked at pictures of muscular men in leather, men with huge penises, and various scenes of S&M. He found the entire experience highly exciting. He said this experience in the waiting room was one of "extraordinary importance." He said that he wished he had a Polaroid picture of himself opening the door an hour early and seeing the other man so that he would have a clear recollection of the scene, because he felt that it epitomized his essence as a person. The patient said, "I feel this very strongly, but I don't understand it." He wondered if the old man could be linked to his father or to me. An association to the scene was that he was reminded of his mother being carried out of the house on a stretcher when he was approximately 5 years old. She was having difficulty with a pregnancy, had begun to bleed, and her leaving for the hospital was an emergency. Among my comments I included mention of his feeling dislocated at the surprise of finding someone in the waiting room. I added, however, that in a sense he had set up the situation by coming an hour early (he was well aware of the time) and then had reacted, in part, by blaming me as if I had deserted him and had been involved in causing his dislocation. I suggested that he might have arranged to precipitate a reliving of a shocking and confusing childhood experience.

In considering this hour, Kohut agreed with the first part of my formulation. He believed that the patient had experienced a mild form of fragmentation with a sense of shock, anxiety, and dislocation, which he had mastered momentarily by an attempted identification with me. When this proved unsuccessful, he had then turned to a type of homosexual stimulation in an attempt to restore the cohesion of his self. This had been largely successful as he was much more pulled together by the time he returned to the building for his analytic session.

Kohut disagreed with my interpretation that the patient had arranged this incident. He said that although it might be correct, he felt it was an unnecessarily complicated initial formulation. He then enunciated a basic principle: one should take analytic material first in a "straight" manner, as if it means what it seems to mean. If this does not prove productive, then one can consider inverting it or manipulating it in various other ways. Kohut felt the tendency of analysts to look first for a hidden meaning and to ignore the simple and more manifest meaning was a mistake. In this specific instance he added that he would have been inclined to believe that this patient was extremely eager to see me. Like a young child, eager to see his father, he had come early to his session. Once he opened the door and found the other patient sitting there, the sequence was much as I had described it, but the patient's motivation should be regarded first as one of an intense, childlike wish rather than as an attempt to "set up" a situation of disappointment. Interpretation should be directed primarily along these lines.

This was a strange conception to me, since I came from a more traditional analytic climate. Later I had a chance to test the efficacy of this formulation. Following my consulation with Kohut, the patient again brought up the incident, which he considered of "extraordinary importance." This time I was able to modify my interpretive understanding. I emphasized his strong wish to see me and his coming early as an expression of that wish, rather than as an attempt to "set up" a frustration. He was visibly relieved at this second formulation, and it was followed by a flood of material, including the comment that this felt much more right to him than what I had said previously, which he had acknowledged made intellectual sense but which he could not feel. I believe, in retrospect, Kohut was correct in stating that I had underestimated the importance and intensity of the patient's wish to see me at this particular time in the analysis. For example, several sessions after the hour reported above, the patient could not make his appointment because of an unexpected and vitally important meeting. As soon as the meeting was over, the patient sped down to my office hoping to have the last 2 or 3 minutes of his session and in this way to see me and "touch base" before the end of the hour.

The next hour I will discuss is one that occurred about 1 month later. Kohut used this hour to illustrate how he would handle "classical" analytic material. This was a Tuesday hour, the first hour after the patient and I had missed our appointment on the preceding Friday because I had cancelled. The patient came in saying he was exhausted and depressed. This feeling had begun several hours earlier. He mentioned casually that it might be connected to our having missed our usual appointment on Friday. Then, after some other material, he reported a dream. The dream followed an unusual sexual episode in which his wife was on top of him and moved about masturbating herself to orgasm while fully clothed. It was an exciting and spontaneous episode for them both. That night the following dream occurred, which was divided into two episodes. In the first episode, their small stationwagon, parked in the driveway, burst into flames. The rear end was on fire. The patient had a hose with which he was watering the yard at the time, and he put out the flames with the hose. He thought this dream was primarily sexual, although he added that it might have some connotations of anger. The second episode of the dream was a fragment in which a number of people were involved. A woman had a can with a certain shape, and he was supposed to insert his penis into this can. She was holding it in her hand. The rest of the dream was vague. The patient said this dream reminded him of an earlier dream in which he was supposed to insert his penis into a disposal.

Later in this hour the patient talked about being hungry. At first he mentioned this in connection with a movie in which a young man ate prodigious amounts of food. He mentioned being hungry several additional times. I said that he might be hungry because he had missed the hour on Friday, and he agreed with this. Later the patient said he was hungry enough to eat a horse. Still later, he added that he was so hungry he could eat the picture on my wall, pointing to a certain painting, and then he added that he could almost eat the couch. There was a pause, and I said he seemed to be getting closer to me. He laughed nervously. After a pause he had an image of sucking quite ferociously and then more passively someone's penis and then someone's breast. He said it was not necessarily me but that he supposed it probably was me. He then associated to the machine that was used to pump his mother's breast when he was a child so that his father could deliver her expressed milk to feed one of the patient's younger brothers who was hospitalized. He then commented that he was now feeling less fatigued and more energetic in the session.

At this point in my reporting of this session, Kohut interrupted to say that he wanted to give me his thoughts. He said, "In a certain way, it is all there." The patient missed an appointment with me, had a weekend, and then came in having had a dream of sexual excitement the night before, which was probably, more specifically, a dream of homosexual excitement, indicated by the rear end of the car bursting into flames, which he extinquishes with a hose. Then there was a reference to castration fear, the associated dream of the penis and the disposal, and finally to orality, with the patient feeling hungry and fantasizing about eating a picture in my office and then eating my couch, which could have to do either with the ingestion of my penis or actual oral incorporation of me.

Kohut said that, in a sense, this was a consistent sequence of classical material; however, he did not say "Aha!" as he might have in the past as if this were the essence of the hour. He no longer regarded this sequence as the crux of the patient's psychopathology, but rather as an extremely important "intermediate sequence," and said that it could have been so interpreted in essentially classical terms. Whether it should have been so interpreted, broadly and in its totality, would depend on the state of the transference and the analysis. He added that a classical interpretation of this kind can be made when the material is this clear in the analysis of a narcissistic personality disorder or, for that matter, in the analysis of any other type of condition, assuming that the other indicators of appropriateness of interpretation are favorable.

Kohut stressed that he regarded such sequences as "intermediate sequences." He believed that the most basic material is not the oral material, the anal material, the homosexual imagery, or the castration fears; most basic is whatever material has to do with the maintenance of the cohesiveness of the self or, conversely, with the production of a rupture in self-cohesiveness. Therefore, from his point of view, the most central aspect of this session was that the patient had developed an idealizing transference relationship to me and saw me as the good father that he did not have while growing up. My cancelling the Friday hour and not being available over the weekend constituted a narcissistic injury that precipitated a fragmentation of the patient's self. When he met with me again, that breach was healed. This, in Kohut's opinion, was the deepest level, the anchor, fore and aft, for the intermediate sequence of classical material.

In an important sense, the homosexual material, castration material, and the rest, represented a kind of regressive or degradation response to the narcissistic injury. So, in a complete interpretation one would include this narcissistic injury, the break in the self–selfobject relationship, as being of central importance. One might also interpret, however, the "intermediate sequence" as a part of the patient's response to the interruption of the selfobject relationship in an essentially classical manner.

In the kind of figure–ground reversal that is typical of the psychology of the self in the larger sense, Kohut felt that the interruption of the ongoing transference was the most important level to be addressed. The classical intermediate sequence was in the nature of a regression or a fragmentation sequence and was less significant. He drew upon one of his favorite analogies by commenting that if one took a complex organic molecule and fragmented it, one would get simpler chemical elements that would not necessarily be more important in a functional sense, but might well be less important although more elemental.

In a subsequent hour this point of view was expanded. Once again, I was going to cancel an analytic session because of a trip. The patient was upset about this, and he talked of how much he was going to miss me and of how he tended to feel dislocated if he had a number of free hours during the course of the day. (He was going to have a number of free hours on several days because of my absence.) The patient talked about how before the analysis or early in the analysis he would have filled this time with homosexual activities in bookstores; however, this was now much less appealing to him and less effective in helping him to feel good. I commented that his attachment to me had been intensified by our continuing analytic work so that he was now looking to me for a good deal of emotional sustenance and was, indeed, quite upset over my forthcoming absence and felt dislocated by it. The patient said that was certainly true and said that he felt like the spaceman in the movie *2001*, who, while floating in space attached to the spaceship by a lifeline, was cut loose and left to die and to drift forever in space. The patient added that he felt like this man floating in space without support. I linked this again to my forthcoming absence and to his feeling of abandonment and injury, and the patient seemed to feel a bit better as a result of these remarks.

In commenting on this section of the hour, Kohut said he thought my remarks to the patient had been good, but he wanted to add something that he felt, while not essential, would definitely have made my interventions richer and more effective. Kohut's concept was that in a complete interpretation, the analyst should consider more than a central portion that represents the main part of the current transference repetition; the analyst should also be sensitive to the leading edge and the trailing edge of the material in question. For example, Kohut might have commented in this instance that what was being repeated with me was the patient's wish for an idealizable selfobject or a strong father. When he learns that I am going to leave him unexpectedly, he is disappointed and angered, and he responds with the abandoned spaceman image and related feelings. This was the middle part of the interpretation, according to Kohut, and I had stayed at that level. He thought it could have been expanded to include the leading edge and the trailing edge. The trailing edge includes more genetic material when it is available either through the patient's direct expression, the patient's associations, or the analyst's empathic ability to discern likely genetic configurations. It involves the beginnings of the patient's need for an idealizable selfobject in order to repair his defective sense of self, the kinds of feelings and experiences in his formative years that prepared the way for this deficit and subsequent need. At the other edge of the formation, the leading edge, one would consider the evolving and developing aspects of the transference relationship, as well as other factors of the patient's progress—how he handles conflict, what new or different tactics he uses to manage it. For example, the patient might be responding in a more open, understanding way and with less acting out; then one would acknowledge and incorporate these developments in the most complete interpretation of such a sequence of material. Obviously, Kohut added, one would not always make such an extensive or broad interpretation. But at those times when it was indicated, one would include the leading edge, the main body of self–selfobject material, and, also, the trailing edge, which is the genetic basis for the entire sequence.

In this connection Kohut added a theoretical aside. He said that in his opinion this patient had developed a strong idealizing transference toward me. Very often in such instances—he believed this case was one—the wishes of the patient were compound. On the one hand, the patient wished to be mirrored, appreciated, singled out, and admired by the idealized selfobject; at the same time, he also wished to merge with the idealized selfobject and through such merger to share or gain the selfobject's power.

Another session around this time further illustrated Kohut's interest in taking material "straight" first, as well as his initial generally positive approach to what the patient says. In this session the patient, who happened to know of my personal interest in a certain celebrity, told me excitedly and in great detail some personal and private information about this person. In other words, he was providing me with important gossip that he believed I didn't know. (He happened to be correct.) I understood this in several ways, but primarily as competition with me, showing me an area where his knowledge was superior, especially where he felt more of an "insider." The patient felt deflated by my comments. He added that he could not deny that there was a certain cogency to them, but he said, "What you said punctured my balloon."

To this, Kohut said he thought the competitive element was present but of secondary importance in this particular session. What he heard much more clearly was a positive enactment of the transference situation: the patient as an excited, pleased little boy running to tell his father something he knew the father did not know, which would please and delight the father. Kohut thought that it was the pride in giving me valued information and the expectation of appreciation from me that was the main dynamic in this instance, and he would have interpreted along such lines. Kohut believed the patient's feeling of deflation was due to my missing this primary element and concentrating on the secondary element, competition.

In this connection, Kohut spoke once again of the value of trying to see analytic material in simple terms, as it is presented. The patient's presentation may well reflect simply and directly the repetition of certain longings or situations from childhood. Too often the analyst begins by assuming a complex encoded message that must be manipulated in order to be understood. Kohut believed that occasionally such manipulation was required, but that one should begin with a straightforward empathic appreciation of the material. Of course this applies to material expressing rage and hatred toward the analyst or others as much as it does to longings for closeness or other affects. This does not mean that Kohut did not make much use of the reading of metaphor, but the metaphor was usually read directly rather than as inverted or complex. He felt such types of complex encoding existed but usually were not as important as other issues.

Kohut stated that he did not hesitate to indicate when a patient was making progress or when he thought that something had come up in the analysis that indicated growth. He added that he thought it was important not to interpret in a completely neutral tone of voice at all times. If one is commenting on the patient's achievement or on some positive bit of progress, the tone should indicate, at least to a slight degree, some element of enthusiasm or pleasurable positive sharing with the patient. He believed a completely neutral tone at such times could be stultifying and have negative effects. In connection with the instance just mentioned, Kohut added that if a patient feels deflated, then we probably have done something wrong, and we need to review our interventions or lack of interventions carefully. If it turns out that the content of our deflating comment seems accurate, it may be that our timing was wrong so that the total effect of the intervention was dislocating. In this sense Kohut took seriously Freud's dictum that in some way the patient is always right.

At this point Kohut stressed again his tendency to work with relatively broad interpretations that followed the main line of the material and dealt with the main line of the patient's psychopathology. He was less interested in side issues and details. In particular, Kohut said that he avoided interpreting slips of the tongue, puns in dreams, and the like. Kohut said that to do so is tantamount to focusing on details; the patient often feels caught, exposed, and fragmented by such interpretations, because they repeat the kind of focusing on details that is often a pathological feature of the patient's childhood experience with his parents. Kohut believed that if the issues indicated by such a slip are important, it is more effective to wait until they become part of a broader presentation in a session and can be interpreted in a more useful way.

The next two sessions provided examples of the kind of experience that Kohut believed would precipitate in this patient a fragmentation of modest extent, the patient's reaction to it, and some technical issues. The patient began by saying he felt better after the preceding hour. He had been having a nice morning and had decided to have lunch and then take a swim. Like his father before him, the patient frequently took a swim after lunch. When he got to his swimming club, he found to his surprise that the swimming pool had been drained. (It had been closed for repairs.) He felt shocked at this sight. He was, once again, temporarily dislocated in his feelings and thought immediately of going to a bookstore to look at homosexual pictures. He thought also of going to a bar and having a drink, which disgusted him. (The patient drank only rarely.) He later added that if there had been a private place available, he would have gone there and masturbated. In this connection, he commented on how vulnerable he was to sudden disappointment and to sudden and unexpected changes in the structure of his day. He mentioned that the structure seemed very important and supportive to him and that he had difficulties if there were open hours in the day, especially on the weekend if it was not fully planned. Later in the session he talked again about what swimming meant to him. His father swam and was still a member of a swimming club; when he was swimming he was absorbed in activity and could not think about anything. He loved the feeling of the warm liquid surrounding him, "as if I were in a womb." I related his experience of dislocation to his disappointment at the pool being closed and empty, because it interfered with his wish to be like his father and, also, with his wish to recreate a regressive, womb-like atmosphere.

In the next session the patient made a significant amplification of the prior session. He said that when he had the trauma of missing his swim and thought about going to the bookstore to look at homosexual pictures, he had omitted telling me about certain other fantasies and actions. The fantasies included the idea that he would abandon all restraint, give way to the intensity of his homosexual longings, and masturbate publicly in the bookstore; and, if he did so, his semen might flood the entire store. He also mentioned the fantasy of wanting to be like the "Incredible Hulk," a monstrous and extraordinarily powerful person whose existence was triggered, the patient believed, by anger. I asked him why he had not mentioned this the day before. He replied that he wasn't sure whether it was because he was not aware of it or because he had simply chosen not to discuss it. He said of course he had done none of those things; instead of going to the bookstore that featured homosexual material, he went to an ordinary bookstore where he spent part of the afternoon browsing but feeling impotent and apathetic. I responded that he seemed to need to see himself in one of two rather extreme ways, either as occupying center stage in an exhibitionistic fantasy, or in an apathetic and impotent condition.

Kohut viewed the patient's response to the empty swimming pool as a fragmentation based on rather evident dynamics. He concurred with my initial formulations and interpretations to the patient. However, he disagreed with my additional comment about the patient's need to experience himself in one of two extreme ways. Kohut said he wasn't sure whether that was correct but, in any event, felt it added little that would be helpful to the patient. He would have pointed out instead the positive gain the patient had made. Whereas previously the patient would have yielded to the temptation to go to the homosexual bookstore to restore his sense of well-being through indulging in homosexual gratification, on this occasion he resisted and went to the ordinary bookstore and spent the afternoon with his usual reading even though he felt impotent and apathetic. Kohut added that he would probably have said something to endorse the patient's ability to tolerate the feelings of displeasure and anxiety due to his disappointment about the empty swimming pool. Kohut further added that there is no point in pretending, with a patient who comes to you for help, that you are not interested in helping him. If such a patient takes a step forward, it often should be called to his attention and affirmed. Of course, this is not always desirable, and when it is, it should always be done so that the patient will not feel "locked into" the progress.

In an hour several months later a dream provided us with an example of what Kohut has referred to in his writing as a "gross identification" with the analyst. He believed this was usually a sign of progress and would be followed by more refined identifications and then by minute transmuting internalizations of appropriate aspects of the analyst's functioning. He seemed to feel that this was in large measure a natural and essential part of the analytic process, that it should be facilitated when necessary by appropriate interpretation, but that excessive interpretation could interfere with it. In the hour in question, the patient began by mentioning an unusually positive sexual encounter with his wife the night before. This was followed by a dream that the patient laughingly said had to do with a merger of our two buildings. In the dream he was in the library of the Psychoanalytic Institute where I have my office. In the middle of this library there were two stacks of books that were actually part of the new library in his office building. The patient was in the Institute library for a while, and then he went down the hall passing the office of another analyst. He noticed that this office was filled with books. The patient said that in the dream it seemed that I went to my office in this same general area, and he found himself wondering where my office actually was and whether he could find it. He said that perhaps it was somewhere on the same floor.

Kohut said this was a typical dream of gross identification—parts of the patient's library are now inside my library, which could be viewed as a kind of merger with me. Kohut said this was an example of the kind of gross identification he had written about and is usually a sign of a deepening of the analytic process. He said that it was often followed by anxiety, which may have been represented at the end of the dream when the patient was uncertain about where my office was and whether or not he would be able to find it.

Kohut felt the anxiety occurred because such a dream represented a merger of identification between patient and analyst; at the same time, the patient may feel in danger of losing the analyst as a selfobject. This loss may be a direct one, as a consequence of the identification, or it may be of a more indirect kind based on the patient's fear that, in becoming like me, he would compete and clash with me and provoke retaliation. So, the central aspect of the dream consisted of the patient's identification or merger with me and with a secondary fear of losing his self–selfobject relationship with me as part of that identification.

In this connection Kohut described a very similar kind of dream that a patient of his had after several years of analysis. Kohut said when this dream occurred, he had pointed out the identification or merger to the patient and indicated that he thought it reflected an increasing analytic engagement. He said he did not interpret it beyond that point. Kohut did not suggest that it might be an attempt to deny hostility toward him, he did not ask for associations other than those that were spontaneously offered, nor did he engage in any other maneuvers that might have been counter-productive and interfered with the spontaneously developing enrichment of the analysis. On the contrary, Kohut understood this gross identification as the first step in the unfreezing of a very deprived and frozen person. Kohut went on to say that in the course of this analysis, which had a good result, the gross identifications became finer and partial identifications more specifically related to the analyst's function as a selfobject. Selected and appropriate aspects of these finer functional identifications were later internalized, providing part of the patient's previously missing psychic structure. This process is an important aspect of what Kohut refers to as transmuting internalization.

The patient then talked about the beginning of this particular session. He had arrived early and did not feel like being "out and about" in the building but felt more comfortable sitting in my waiting room, close to me. At this point Kohut said he felt these additional associations followed the lines he had indicated about this being an initial improvement dream with a subsequent reaction. The patient had expressed an identification or closeness with me that then stimulated certain anxieties about a possible loss of our relationship, so that he wanted to sit in my waiting room early so as to feel as close to me as possible.

In an hour approximately 1 month later, the patient touched on some similar themes. After this session I was going to be absent for nearly a week. The patient responded with a two-part dream. In the first part he was in a room, writing at a secretary desk similar to one his father was planning to give him, a valuable antique, and, he said to me, "You were there. You were leaving. I was very upset. Then I was on all fours crawling toward you, screaming for you not to go and crying, but you left anyway." This was the end of the first part of the dream. At first the patient tried to distance himself from it by saying it was overdramatic, like an opera. Then he said that the scene when he was on all fours seemed to express a desperation. Next he reported the second half of the dream, which was possibly part dream and part fantasy. In this dream he owned a homosexual clothing store, and men came in to buy brief underwear and so forth. He would kiss these men and then take them into a back room, make love, and have orgies. His associations to this were that this homosexual scene felt dull to him; it was not as exciting as such scenes had been previously. However, he did recognize in it the familiar sequence in which I leave and he then has some type of fantasized homosexual experience. When I argued that in his telling of the dream, this scene had seemed to be exciting to him, he said that if this were the case, he was not aware of it. He insisted that the dream scene was dull and uninteresting compared with the excitement that used to accompany such dreams and fantasies.

Kohut, of course, took exception to my argument with the patient. He felt it was another instance of my complicating things unduly and not looking at the positive side of the patient's experience. Only after very careful consideration should the analyst decide that the patient "really" feels just the opposite or turn upside down or inside out what the patient has said. Kohut said that he would understand this sequence as follows. The patient is distressed with my leaving as a child would be, seeing his father go. The connection between the analyst and the father is expressed by the antique desk, something the father is giving him that is very valuable. He experiences a relationship with the analyst-father, and then it is threatened. I am leaving even though he behaves like a child crawling on the floor and screaming, "Daddy, don't go." The homosexual fantasy that followed this break in the transference, the patient felt was somehow less pleasureable than before. This was evidence of the patient's growth and progress in the analysis. Kohut believed the sequence should have been understood and interpreted this way.

The clinical episode described above, including the dream and clarifying interpretation was probably an instance of optimum frustration with resolution through interpretation leading to transmuting internalization and the acquisition of a "bit" of psychic structure. Kohut believed that this result was illustrated by a number of the clinical episodes described here, but structure building was likely more pronounced in other episodes, generally not included in this chapter, in which my understanding of the material, in Kohut's opinion, was more accurate and comprehensive than in the examples given. (Clinical episodes in which Kohut's view differed from mine seemed more clearly to illustrate his thinking and his work. Therefore, these were the examples I selected for this chapter.) Kohut added, however, that despite certain less-than-optimum interventions in the episodes described here, the analysis seemed to be going well.

During the early part of the fourth year of the analysis, the idealizing transference became intense and manifest. The patient talked with feeling about how he regarded me as tall, handsome, highly insightful, extraordinarily helpful to him, and able as an analyst. He once blurted out, "Why you're even better than Dr. X" (referring to an eminent local analyst). The dreams in this period followed suit, indicating an intense idealization, but of a more mature form than previously. For example, whereas earlier, when there was a break in the analysis (even for only 2 or 3 days), the patient might have had an explicit homosexual dream, with associations invariably including and usually centering on our reunion, and on his pleasure at and longing for our being together again, in the phase of the analysis now being discussed, the sexualization was much more minimal and the idealization intense, but of a more mature form.

For example, following an interruption of several days, the patient dreamt that he was attending a concert. It was a large concert hall, and when he found his seat, he realized he was sitting close behind the "great conductor," a man of fame and musical eminence. It filled him with intense pleasure to enjoy the proximity and, by implication, shared eminence of the great conductor whom he associated without hesitation to me. Interestingly, this period of the transference made me extremely uncomfortable. I found myself tempted to divert the growing power of the idealizing transference. I felt embarrassed and uneasy. It was difficult to understand this through my own introspective efforts, although I was well aware, from reading, that the patient's idealization was likely stimulating unresolved areas of my own repressed grandiosity.

This was my first experience with an intense idealizing transference, possibly because in the past I had deflected them before they became too intense. In many years of practicing analysis, I have not experienced a transference relationship that made me so uncomfortable. Certainly the most intense rage or scathing criticism from a patient did not make me nearly as uncomfortable as did this idealizing transference. I have no doubt that my interest in narcissistic phenomena and the work of Kohut in general is related to a degree of vulnerability in this area; nonetheless, with help from reading Kohut's work and from my consultations with him, I was able to permit the transference to expand, to intensify, and to persist. As working through progressed, periods of deidealization became more frequent, and later they too were intense. Nonetheless, they seemed more "familiar" to me and were, from a subjective point of view, neither so novel nor so difficult for me to manage.

In this general period of time, my patient had two sequences of dreams that gave Kohut a chance to talk about his ideas about the desirability of the analyst's promoting the patient's healthy tendencies rather than focusing on regressive tendencies. In one dream, there were two groups of people in a bar. The patient had the choice of joining one of the two groups. One was a group of women; the other a group of homosexual men. The patient hesitated in his decision, and is not clear what group he joined. In another dream several weeks later, the patient was seated at a table in a bar with some women, laughing and talking. He looked around and behind him was a group of heterosexual men seated at another table, drinking and perhaps playing poker. He felt ashamed and embarrassed because he was sitting and talking with women instead of heterosexual men. Various associations followed, including such comments as because of the interests of his family, he knows more about antiques, fine silver, and china than do most men, and this contributed to his feelings of effeminacy. However, he soon returned to emphasizing his discomfort in the dream of sitting with the women. My response to the dream was to wonder with him why he felt uncomfortable about sitting with the women.

Kohut thought this was an error. He said I picked the wrong branch in the material. This was the first dream in this series in which the patient had a meaningful choice between sitting with women and joining heterosexual men. Kohut thought a more productive comment would have stayed with the positive tendencies and pointed out the choice. In the earlier dreams his only choice was to sit with women or to sit with homosexual men, but in the later dream he had a choice between sitting with women and joining the heterosexual men. This indicates a progression that Kohut would have pointed out. My focusing on what made him embarrassed implied encouragement and endorsement of that position. Kohut said this was an example of forcing a patient into an unhealthy regression that occurs rather often in classical analysis. Interestingly, in the next analytic hour with this patient following the consultation with Kohut just described, the patient said he had been surprised at my emphasis in interpreting his dream. He said it was as if I were trying to push him backwards into homosexuality or, at least, not helping him free himself from a kind of identification with women.

In this same general phase of the analysis, our discussions led to an overview of the psychopathology of the case. In an informal, summarizing fashion, Kohut said that he felt the patient was someone who had defects in mothering that were partially due to mother's depression and partially to her illnesses and absences, usually at the times of the births of several younger siblings. He thought that as a result of these traumas, the patient turned away from his hope for a close nurturing and mirroring relationship with his mother toward a relationship with an idealized father. Kohut believed this attempt also failed, which accounted for much of the patient's symptomatology. When he began the analysis, his homosexual fantasies and urges involved many wishes for eroticized closeness to, contact, and merger-identification with various idealizable men. Another of his symptoms needed more complex explanation. In the patient's wish to penetrate men anally, he is identifying with the disappointing, aggressive father. Also, he symbolically gave to these men (whom Kohut felt represented the patient's younger brothers) the masculine substance that he had wanted to receive from his father. In other words, in penetrating them anally, he was injecting his homosexual partners, linked unconsciously with his younger brothers, with the masculinity he never got from his father.

Kohut added that on first hearing this sounds close to the classical conception of this type of perversion. The difference, which he thought crucial, is mainly one of emphasis. Kohut would say that what the patient really wanted from his father, but did not get enough of, was a good father-son relationship. He wanted an opportunity to idealize his father, share with him, and feel mirrored by him. If he had had enough of such experiences, he would have had a chance to acquire a sufficient sense of masculine identity through transmuting internalizations in childhood. Instead, there was a fragility to his sense of masculinity and the patient used a symbolic and sexualized way to attempt to cure himself, and acquire the needed solid masculine identity. In other words, the perverse symptoms and the acts and drives that were associated with them were primarily degradation products and of secondary importance. The central issue was the patient's wish for a structure-building father–son relationship that was not adequately provided during his formative years. By reopening these issues in analysis and working through the idealizing selfobject transference, it is hoped and expected that a significant degree of this needed structure-building by transmuting internalization will occur, as in this case.

Shortly thereafter, a brief episode occurred that illustrates some of the ways Kohut viewed defense interpretation. The patient had presented some material that caused me to say that he seemed to want to pick a fight with me, and that I thought he wanted to pick a fight because in that way he could avoid his inner life experience. I believe this was essentially correct. Kohut agreed, but objected to the form in which I made it, because he felt the patient would experience it as if he were being blamed, and this would make the intervention less effective. Kohut might have said, "You would like to pick a fight with me because that is the way you have kept yourself from feeling empty over the years, kept yourself from feeling bored, and made meaningful contact with people important to you." In this way Kohut would combine the defense interpretation with its genetic aspect. Of course, the analyst must be able to sense what that genetic aspect is and present it in such a way that the interpretation will seem less critical or accusatory to the patient and, therefore, be more likely to be productive of genuinely revealing material.

As the idealizing tranference was worked through, as deidealization became more prominent, and as the intensity of both these phases of the transference began to fade, the patient began to talk of termination. In one session the patient said he had decided to terminate in June, 5 months away. In the next session he reported a dream. In this dream he was in an elevator. As the elevator reached the fifth floor, the cord holding it broke. As the elevator came hurtling down, he snatched a baby out of its mother's arms. He braced himself in an attempt to cushion himself and the baby against the crash. I gave a genetic interpretation of this dream, saying I thought it had to do with the trauma he experienced at age 5, when a sibling was born and his mother became very ill and he was isolated from her for a long time. I thought the baby represented him, and he was trying to cushion himself against the trauma more effectively than his mother had been able to cushion him in his childhood.

Though Kohut agreed, he did not think my interpretation was optimal at this particular point. He reminded me that in the preceding hour the patient had for the first time selected a specific month, approximately 5 months away, in which to terminate. He had talked about termination a good deal, but this was the first time in which he had actually mentioned a specific month. Kohut said he would understand the dream as indicating that the patient experienced this planned termination as representing a sudden loss of support, like the breaking of the cord holding the elevator, so that the plunging elevator could also be understood in a more immediate way, as an anticipation of the sudden shock of loss of contact with me following termination and the wish to protect himself from this. The projected termination was approximately 5 months away, and at that time it would be the end of 5 years of analysis. In this particular clinical situation, Kohut preferred the immediacy of the transference interpretation to the genetic one that I had offered, although he felt both were correct.

In general, Kohut was a "classicist" in that he tended to focus first on the transference relationship and, later, when the material seemed propitious, to link this up with genetic material in an increasingly broad and explanatory manner. In connection with the session just described, Kohut said,

> You know this patient tends to fear a sudden loss of support and that he is sensitive to such loss. Perhaps this should be pointed out to him again. You also need to remember that he is, for the first time, more fully entering the heterosexual world both in terms of the frequency and the quality of his heterosexual activities and in terms of his inner feeling about himself. He is relatively new in this position. He needs time to adjust to it. He needs time to cushion the shock of termination.

Kohut then stated that for these reasons he is generally willing to give a person plenty of time to terminate and is willing to permit resumption of the analytic work if the date which is initially set proves to be too early. He was also willing, in appropriate cases, to graduate the frequency of hours, to taper off during the termination phase, rather than to insist that all patients proceed with the full analytic schedule and then stop suddenly.

Closer to the end of the analysis, my patient reported a long dream, on a portion of which Kohut's comments were particularly interesting. In this dream the patient was in an old-fashioned hospital, with a high ceiling, white walls, and a white enameled bed. There were paintings on the wall, and he and another patient were looking at them. Suddenly the other man said, "My god, these are real." The patient looked more closely and became very excited. They were real paintings, by the old masters. "There is a Degas, there is a Renoir, there is a Monet . . . ," he said, "My god they are worth a fortune. They are worth hundreds of thousands of dollars apiece." He was elated that these old masters were genuine, because, since they belonged to the patients, they also belonged to him. As mentioned, this was only a small part of the dream, and there were extensive associations to the dream.

For the purpose of this chapter, most interesting among the patient's associations was his linking of the genuine and extraordinarily valuable art work in the hospital to some of the fine paintings and antiques possessed by his parents, and to several items in my office (an Oriental rug and an antique porcelain vase). The patient admired these items for their fine quality and linked them with the art work in the dream. (In fact, both of these pieces are of fine quality, but there are many other items in my office that are quite ordinary. The patient had, therefore, selected these two particularly fine items from a rather large undistinguished inventory for the purposes of the dream.) He also associated to the idea of the "old masters," noting that it seemed to have a double connotation, referring both to the paintings and to the masters who did the paintings.

Kohut had a good deal to say about the dream and the extensive associations. Of particular interest, however, were his comments in relation to the genuineness of the paintings. Kohut was struck both by the patient's excitement at the discovery of the genuineness and by the genuineness itself. He said he felt this, taken in context, meant the patient thought he had gotten something real and of great value from me, and, also, that he had gotten something of substantial value from his parents. The old masters were genuine, so the results of his analytic work seemed genuine to him and he was more fully in touch with some genuine and substantial experiences with his parents that helped to account for the considerable measure of health that he had always possessed.

Kohut took no notes during our consultative sessions, which typically lasted 1½ hours. At the beginning of the next session he would read notes he had made after I left. Even in his period of severe ill health, I was impressed with the accuracy and completeness of these notes. Kohut summarized the material that had come up in our discussion. He also indicated what he thought I had handled well, and what had been less than optimum or where I had gone astray in his opinion.

Two other points occur to me: Kohut did not like the use of questions and felt they should be employed very sparingly in analysis. He said you cannot analyze a person by asking him questions and that while there is a legitimate place for questions on occasion, the main burden of understanding the patient rests with the analyst. It is the analyst's job to listen and to comprehend the patient's feeling state and the meaning of that state empathically. The analyst cannot abrogate this responsibility by asking the patient to tell him what is going on in his mind.

Kohut's work was distinctly interpretive in cast. If I had any criticism of his clinical work when I was studying with him, it was my opinion that he was too interpretive and that more should have been left unsaid. I am not sure that I feel this way any longer; perhaps I was envious of his ability to grasp and order the meaning of the material. In any event, I do not mean to say that he was a very active analyst; on the contrary, I had the impression that he practiced a traditional form of "expectant" analysis. On the other hand, Kohut strongly emphasized the importance of interpretation as he described it in his later writings, namely, as an understanding of the patient such that the patient realized the analyst knew how he felt and, subsequently and overlapping, as the explanatory phase in which the analyst pointed out the origins and meanings of the behavior, feeling states, and fantasies to the patient. His interpretive efforts were focused primarily on the transference and on related genetic areas, although he also felt that judicious use of extratransference interpretation and the examination of the patient's current relationships outside the analysis were not only legitimate but often essential.

INTERPRETATION AND SELF PSYCHOLOGY

3

Interpretation: Toward a Developmental Model

MICHAEL FRANZ BASCH

When Kohut (1971) discovered that the resolution of selfobject transferences other than oedipal ones permitted patients to mature who had heretofore seemed unanalyzable, he expanded the therapeutic horizons of psychoanalysis as well as of psychotherapy generally.

Kohut said that we work by explaining to the patient what it is we have first understood. The emphasis on empathically understanding what a patient is saying or trying to say was a necessary corrective to the doctrinaire approach of those analysts who essentially advocated, even if they did not practice, the idea that the analyst was an objective observer, as opposed to a participant, removed from his feelings and reactions to the patient. However, we are in danger of forgetting that being understood is not the same as understanding, and in itself is not sufficient to bring about an analytic result. Analysis requires a judicious balance between empathy and interpretation, between understanding and conveying our understanding to the patient.

Interpretation is defined as explaining or giving a meaning. When the patient is explaining himself to us and/or to himself without impediment, there is no need for us to speak. We interpret when we believe that we have come to understand something about the patient that he or she cannot fathom or organize without our help. Something is in the way and we have to remove the obstacle, technically called a defense, and we hope to accomplish that with our explanation.

Just as we try to listen empathically—to hear what the patient is saying from the patient's point of view—so our interpretations must address the patient where we find him: that is, we must address ourselves in a meaningful way to the particular defensive operation that was cognitively possible for the patient at the time that the original trauma or traumas to the development of the self occurred that seem to be reflected in his present difficulties in the analysis.[1] In other words, we must address the patient in a language that he can comprehend if we hope to be heard.

1. Trauma is to be understood as referring to the patient's perception and registration of events seemingly instrumental in generating a pathological outcome; this includes the distortion, embellishment, and/or misinterpretation of these events in the patient's conscious and unconscious fantasy life, both at the time of their occurrence and later.

Defense, as Freud (1915) said, is always against affect. This insight, like so much of his clinical work, was entirely correct but before its time, and its significance could not be fully appreciated until developmental psychology and other branches of science could catch up with his prescience. However, when it came to the metapsychology of affect, to explaining its nature, Freud's hypotheses have not held up. Basing himself on the clinical examination of the psychoneuroses Freud postulated that affect is simply the conscious aspect of instinctual discharge; this has led generations of analysts to look for the hidden instinctual conflict, sexual or aggressive, that was being covertly expressed through every affectively toned association or behavior manifested by the patient in analysis. Kohut was to discover implicitly through the rigorous application of Freud's method that affect was not necessarily linked to instinctual conflict. Affective expression constituted a much broader signaling system indicative of the vicissitudes of tension control generally, and it reflected problems within all the lines of development, including, of course, as one such subgroup, the secondary problems of instinctual conflict generated when the significant selfobject failure in a patient's life had occurred during the oedipal period. Today we know a great deal about affect and its place in human development that was not known in Freud's time. I have documented this elsewhere (Basch, 1976) and will only briefly touch upon some facets of that topic in this chapter.

From the beginning of life, affective reactions are the basis for the ordering function of the brain. The programs or scripts that we develop to avoid pain and maximize harmony, both within the self system and in its relation to the world, are all based on the affective connotations and implications that attach to our experiences. Together affect and cognition make up thought. When we interpret to a patient we are using the adult's cognitive capacity as leverage to change his mind, that is, to come to a different decision about an affective constellation that at one time made sense, but that is now not only no longer necessary but positively harmful to his or her well-being. I will try to demonstrate that we can make a correlation between interpretation, defense, and development that will be both theoretically sound and practically useful.

The psychiatrist and infant researcher Daniel Stern recently published a paper on what he calls "affect attunement" (1984). He described his observations on cross-modal communion, one form of affective communication between mother and child. An infant was silently reaching for something just beyond his grasp, and at the moment he stretched, his mother said "uuuuh. . .uuuuh!," participating vocally in the child's muscular effort. In this way the mother conveyed directly to the infant on the sensorimotor level that she shared the experience, that he was understood and that he was not alone.

Similarly, when we pick up a baby who is crawling on the floor intending to cradle her in our arms we do not simply swoop down and silently elevate her. We say "U-u-up we go!" Drawing out the vowel so as to mimic the arc in which the child is traveling, ending with "p" as she finishes her journey against our chest encircled by our arms, thereby sharing vocally with her the kinesthetic experience she was having as we picked her up.

Stern cites the experimental evidence that shows that children are prepared, especially from 6 months on, to receive and correctly interpret cross-modal messages, that is, to translate auditory intensity into light intensity, or what is felt into what is seen, and so on. For example, a bumpy pacifier that it has never seen is introduced into a baby's mouth, after a few minutes it is taken out and put side by side with a smooth pacifier and the child is permitted to look. It will look longer at the bumpy pacifier indicating by its interest that it recognizes the object it has had in its mouth (Meltzoff & Borton, 1979).

Through affective attunement the mother is serving as the quintessential selfobject for her baby, sharing the infant's experience, confirming it in its activity, and building a sensorimotor model for what will become its self concept. Affect attunement leads to a shared world, without affect attunement one's activities are solitary, private, and idiosyncratic. You recall Freud's dictum to the effect that it is the parent's superego, not their ego, that is communicated to the unconscious of the child; not what parents would like the child to believe but what they unconsciously do believe. How can such communication take place? How can our unconscious be so accurately conveyed to the child's? The baby discovers his genitals and delightedly explores them. His mother, let us say, is a psychologically minded, enlightened person who, seeing this, tries to make sure she does not traumatize the baby and refrains from openly forbidding his behavior, instead, as the books advise, tries to distract him. However, although she has not openly expressed her anxiety she has not joined his activity with her eyes, voice, or bodily movements, as she would ordinarily do if he were playing with his toes, or hands, or any other part of the body, except perhaps the anus, and so, like all the rest of us, this baby lays down sensorimotor memories to the effect that there are all sorts of activity that are shared, but that there are some that are beyond the pale, not accepted, somehow wrong, and to be hidden. By the same token, if, for whatever reason and on a broader scale, affect attunement is not present or is ineffective during those early years, the lack of shared experience may well create a sense of isolation and a belief that one's affective needs generally are somehow unacceptable and shameful.

Patients with merger needs, like Kohut's (1971) Miss F, experience contact as intrusion and want us only to echo their words and moods, the closest they can come to obtaining affect attunement, indicating by their need that tension control through affective communion had failed in significant ways during their development. The long period of affective mirroring that these patients need, as described by Kohut, permits them to overcome the unconscious anticipation of the rejection of their affective needs and the shame that they experience whenever they dare to reach out in that direction;

only when that has been accomplished will the patient's resistance to examining his selfobject transference be resolved.[2]

The patient in the merger has been described as very difficult to tolerate because he vitiates our individuality, threatens *our* narcissistic needs for validation, communion, and reinforcement of self-esteem. I do not think that this is necessarily so. Our primary satisfaction comes from understanding and doing our job. We are able to deal with equanimity with the anger and erotism of patients in the oedipal transference because we understand what is happening and, though we experience the neurotic patient's affect empathically, we do not feel we are its victims, so, I have reason to believe, a theoretical understanding of the patient in the merger—not just that he is in a merger, but why on developmental grounds this may be so—can protect us from reacting inappropriately to the experience of being a nonperson for these patients—an amorphous object, there, like the genie in Alladin's lamp, to serve and having served, disappear until called for once more.

Closely allied to the defense of withdrawal due to lack of affective attunement is the defense that Freud called primal repression. Not an issue in the treatment of psychoneurotic patients whose developmental problems occurred later, it is often seen in patients with narcissistic personality disorders.

Freud suggested that primal repression involved "thing presentations" (percepts) that, because they were associated with negative affect, had never been connected with appropriate "word presentations" (word memories), and were therefore unavailable to the thought process. As I have discussed elsewhere (1977) though Freud erred in equating thought with words, his concept can be translated into our developmental language, without losing its significance. Primal repression can be understood as a defense against painful affect or overstimulation that operates by barring the elevation of sensorimotor memory to the preoperational, symbolic level of cognitive development, effectively blocking reflection upon and recall of the experiences involved.

It is not unusual to see patients who cannot identify their feelings or describe emotions. It is as if aspects of their affective development (Basch, 1983a) had stopped at the autonomic level of stimulation and sensorimotor experience. Their inability to feel feelings, that is, relate affects to the self-concept, predictably makes their relationships shallow and unsatisfying, and often this is the problem that brings them for treatment. It usually turns out that these patients grew up in an environment that either eschewed or positively interdicted affective experience of any intensity and variety.

---

2. H. A. Bacal's chapter "Optimal Responsiveness and the Therapeutic Process" (Chapter 16, this volume) suggests, correctly in my opinion, that the analyst must first serve as a "transitional selfobject" for the patient during the "creative aspect of the transference" before the archaic selfobject transference will take place and lend itself to interpretation.

When dealing with problems of affective attunement in the primitive merger, empathy and interpretation were one and the same, or, more accurately, during the preverbal, presymbolic, nonreflective period of sensorimotor development only response in action is registered. When we deal with patients at that stage our echoing of their experience is all that is meaningful, any attempt at explanation is experienced as an unwarranted intrusion. However, at the level of primal repression, which may be pictured as taking place at the interface between the sensorimotor and preoperational phase of cognitive development, empathy and interpretation are not conflated. Though primitive, we are now dealing with a reflective self, capable of objectifying its experiences, and we want to engage the patient on that level with our interventions. However, one does not begin with attempts at genetic interpretations, but, rather, with interpretations of process. This means first clarifying with and for the patient what he is experiencing and only then what it might mean, especially in relation to the here and now. These are the patients who show evidence of having reacted to something in the analyst's personality, or in the analytic situation, but except for displaying increased tension in their behavior vis-à-vis the therapist, feel nothing. Here, as Kohut taught us, we must be empathically attuned to what has happened, to use our knowledge of the patient to put ourselves in his shoes and imagine what he might be experiencing without being able to become aware of it. Our interpretations here are in the form of hypotheses that encourage the patient to search himself for somatic reactions or vague bits of ideation that will gradually let him experience affect symbolically, undoing the arrest in development that Freud called primal repression.

In 1927, based on clinical observations that he recounted in the paper entitled "Fetishism," Freud postulated the defense that the editor of the *Standard Edition* called "disavowal." In papers between 1927 and his death in 1939, Freud often came back to disavowal and attached increasing importance to it (Basch, 1983b). Disavowal has, for the most part, been unjustly neglected and/or misunderstood by psychoanalysts because (1) it does not play a primary role in psychoneurotic symptom formation, and (2) it cannot be easily fitted into the structural model or explained by a metapsychology based on the notion of instinctual discharge (Basch, 1974, 1981, 1983b). Practically speaking, disavowal involves self-deception, it is the defense that corresponds to and explains what Kohut (1971) called the "vertical split."

As the amorphous, physiognomic (Church, 1961; Werner, 1948) conceptualization of the child's preoperational world gives way to what Piaget has called the concrete level of operations, logic and language begin to divide experience discursively. Sequential ordering of time, space, and intensity become a possibility. Now the child is able to use symbols to separate self from other conceptually, and to see himself as set apart from the rest of the world. As Kohut pointed out, so-called psychic structures, predictable ways of functioning, when they are still new are fragile and require appropriate selfobject input and support to establish themselves and mature properly. If the basis for the self-concept is already enfeebled, or if the necessary validation or mirroring of the burgeoning self is not forthcoming, disavowal will come into play.

Disavowal, like all other defenses, is basically a normal aspect of cognitive development but used in the interest of protection rather than maturation. Let me put this in context by once again looking at affect and its significance for development. Affect is the amplifier and motivator that leads to action. The more selective we become in the mobilization of affect the more sophisticated and effective our goal directed behavior becomes. Initially, affect is an inherited autonomic response system (Basch, 1976). The infant is at the mercy of whatever stimulation comes his way. He responds totally and as often as he is stimulated, positively or negatively, until exhaustion and withdrawal into sleep take over. Obviously this cannot be permitted to go on for very long; the function of cognition is that of a stimulus barrier, it serves to delay affective response and to enable the organism to react selectively and with measured intensity. What we have learned to call the self is an important step in that direction, perhaps the most important one for creatures like ourselves whose adaptive response to stimuli of various sorts is for the most part not preprogrammed genetically. Once we can contrast self and other, self and the rest of the world, two kinds of programs can be written, those that pertain to the maintenance of the self system and therefore recruit affect, and dispose us to action, and those programs that register and correlate information that does not have immediate meaning for our self. So, for example, hearing a siren in the distance we record it as a perception and continue on our way, however, if we happen to be in the unfortunate position of needing an ambulance, that sound has a great deal of meaning for our self and mobilizes a flood of affect. Neurologically, we are talking here about the difference between semantic and episodic memory (Tulving, 1972), semantic memory being the store house of knowledge in the general sense, while episodic memory stores those events that have meaning for our concept of self, and are significant for our self-esteem. This division is in the interest of our psychic economy, insuring that we respond only to what concerns us, and then only in modulated fashion, mobilizing affect and the corresponding intensity of activity only to the extent that we judge self-esteem and cohesion to be involved in a given instance. Ordinarily there should be free communication between these two sets of memories; what is not important for integrity at one time may become so when circumstances change, and, *per contra*, what was terribly significant for our self-esteem may, with the passage of time and further maturation, fade in its importance.

The defense of disavowal erects a barrier to that freedom of exchange between semantic and episodic memory. Unlike psychotic denial, disavowal permits recognition of reality and access to the memory of a traumatic event, but prevents translation into episodic memory. In this way, the affective significance that a particular event would and should have for the self is blocked. This protects the person from what is unconsciously perceived as a potentially overwhelming flood of affect and a subsequent fragmentation of the self organization. For example, in Freud's 1927 paper, he reported two cases of patients who had each lost a parent in early childhood. He thought at first that they had denied the loss, but then realized that they were perfectly well aware of the reality of that event, but had disavowed its meaning. Disavowal says, "Yes, it happened, but, since it has nothing to do with me, why get upset?" We are all acquainted with patients who indicate through dreams and errors of everyday life that our upcoming vacation is having an impact on them, but who steadfastly reject our suggestion that this is so and try to shame us for thinking we are so important. Where is and how can we overcome the block to the mobilization of affect in these cases of disavowal?

Roughly, but with sufficient neurological justification, we may think of factual knowledge as processed by the left half of the brain, affective experience by the right. The connection between the two is made by language, by what Vygotsky (1934) called "inner speech." Speech not used for communication to others, but used to integrate the semantic with the episodic. Functionally speaking, that process of integration of affect and experience is or forms the concept of self. The more we talk about something the more it becomes part of our self. That is why teachers, who talk and mobilize affect as they do so, usually learn more than students, who listen without affective participation.

What is disavowed is not talked about; the self-deception of disavowal is maintained by blocking the working over and working through to affect made possible by speech. The resolution of disavowal requires that the analyst listen carefully for what the patient leaves out, glosses over, mentions only in passing, treats as trivial, and so on. The resolution of disavowal involves the analyst in active questioning, exploration of inconsistencies, and possible confrontation of the patient with the significance of his nonverbal or minimally verbal behavior. It necessitates not only the analyst's activity but at times may place him in the position of challenging the patient. This does not mean that the analyst is one whit less empathic in dealing with disavowal than with any other defenses. On the contrary, empathic understanding of the patient's disavowal of meaning guides him as he first creates an anxiety provoking situation for the patient and then shows him that he can first speak, then think, and finally confront his feelings about previously interdicted areas with good results. Disavowal is the defense against shame at the level of concrete operations when logic no longer permits more primitive evasions. Disavowal forestalls the loss of connection with the selfobject that an endangered self anticipates. It is unavoidable that that sense of shame behind the disavowal will have to be mobilized in the analysis and then dealt with by patient and therapist.

Secondary repression is the defense of the essentially well-established self that encounters a threat to self-esteem when there is a significant failure in selfobject support during the oedipal period, a time of development when self-esteem is threatened by having to cope with realistic limitations to power and ambition and the recognition of vulnerability. The strong, cohesive self of the future psychoneurotic cannot readily resort to the self-deception of disavowal, such a person, confronted by selfobject failure during the oedipal phase of psychosexual development with its recrudescence of incestuous wishes, turns to secondary repression, a barrier to advancing thought from its infantile, idiosyncratic, fantasy-dominated stage (Freud's primary process, Piaget's preoperational phase) to the level of logical relationships and their manipulations (Freud's secondary process, Piaget's concrete operational phase) (Basch, 1977). If, however, at some later date secondary repression then fails to contain infantile sexual demands or memories, then symptoms develop to form a second line of defense. As disavowal kept memories from affect, blocked left hemispheric activity from involving the right one, repression does the opposite. In repression the early memories associated with the right hemisphere and strong affect are made unavailable and thereby prevented from communication with the left hemisphere and discursive, verbal embodiment.

Symptoms, as Freud said, are compromise formation. Unable to contain affect and action, the neurotic symptom disguises the true memory by displacing it onto related but not identifying memories or ideas. Unlike the technique in disavowal where the analyst must be active in order to get the patient to talk and mobilize affect, in neurosis there is already a pressure of affect, and here the empathic analyst, as Freud taught us, need only not interfere with the transference, that is the displacement of those affect-laden unconscious wishes unto his person. In consistent terminology, the selfobject function of the empathic analyst of a psychoneurotic patient is to serve as a target for the already mobilized affect of the patient. Unlike the case with disavowal, here the less active the analyst is the better it is. The important thing is not to interfere with the emergence of the affect as the neurosis is "transferred" to his person and made available for genetic interpretation, linking the present wishes and fears to those first experienced with important figures of the past.

Of course, with the possible exception of the merger transference, what we can look at in isolation for didactic purposes seldom presents itself in such neat fashion in the actual analytic situation. Usually the analyst is presented with shifting resistances, not uncommonly within the same session, and must accommodate his or her interpretative style to suit what is coming into focus. The practice of psychoanalysis that uses as its reference point the development of the self system is broader and more inclusive than the psychoanalytic practice based on instinctual reductionism. We now use Freud's method to treat patients whose transferences not only bear an earlier developmental stamp than that of the psychoneurotic, but, more important, whose problems are not directly related to psychosexual development. If the nature of the problem is different, then the defense and the resistance are going to be different also, and our strategy of interpretation must take that into account. That, in turn, requires an integration of what is now known about normal development with what, thanks to Kohut, we are now able to hear from our patients.

Obviously, much more can and needs to be said about the correlation between what empathy and introspection reveals to the psychoanalyst using Kohut's clinical theory, and what research in developmental psychology can teach us about the processes that lead to the formation of the self organization, the supraordinate ordering principle of human life. I have tried to illustrate the advantage of pursuing this course by at least beginning to show how our concept of interpretation and its technical application benefits from such an approach.

ACKNOWLEDGMENT

The author wishes to thank Drs. Arnold Goldberg and Joseph Sandler whose discussion of an earlier version of this chapter provided several valuable clarifications that were incorporated.

REFERENCES

Basch, M. F. (1974). Interference with perceptual transformation in the service of defense. *The Annual of Psychoanalysis*, 2:87–97.

Basch, M. F. (1976). The concept of affect: A re-examination. *Journal of the American Psychoanalytic Association*, 24:759–777.

Basch, M. F. (1977). Developmental psychology and explanatory theory in psychoanalysis. *The Annual of Psychoanalysis*, 5:229–263.

Basch, M. F. (1981). Psychoanalytic interpretation and cognitive transformation. *International Journal of Psycho-Analysis*, 62:151–175.

Basch, M. F. (1983a). Empathic understanding: A review of the concept and some theoretical considerations. *Journal of the American Psychoanalytic Association*, 31:101–126.

Basch, M. F. (1983b). The perception of reality and the disavowal of meaning. *The Annual of Psychoanalysis*, 11:125–153.

Church, J. (1961). *Language and the Discovery of Reality*. New York: Random House, Vintage Book Edition.

Freud, S. (1915). The unconscious. *Standard Edition*, 14:159–204.

Freud, S. (1927). Fetishism. *Standard Edition*, 21:152–157.

Kohut, H. (1971). *The Analysis of the Self*. New York: International Universities Press.

Meltzoff, A., & Borton, R. (1979). Intermodal matching by human neonates. *Nature*, 282:403–404.

Stern, D. N. (1984). Affect attunement. In J. D. Call, E. Galenson, & R. L. Tyson, eds., *Frontiers of Infant Psychiatry* (Vol. II). New York: Basic Books.
Tulving, E. (1972). Episodic and semantic memory. In E. Tulving & W. Donaldson, eds., *Organization of Memory*. New York: Academic Press.
Vygotsky, L. S. (1934). *Thought and Language*. Boston: MIT Press. (Paperback edition, 1962).
Werner, H. (1948). *Comparative Psychology of Mental Development* (rev. ed.). New York: International Universities Press.

4

Clinical Understanding and Explaining: The Empathic Vantage Point

PAUL H. ORNSTEIN AND ANNA ORNSTEIN

INTRODUCTION

Francis Bacon noted several centuries ago that once people become wedded to a certain idea or concept, their minds are no longer open. They will continue to look for evidence, however flimsy it may be, to buttress preconceived notions, and will reject all evidence that contradicts them.

Bacon's idea is broadly valid. It has practically turned into one of the "covering laws" of a depth-psychology-informed social psychology. It holds true for all people, in all human endeavors, including psychoanalysis. At a first glance this should not be surprising, after all, psychoanalysis, as an avenue to self-knowledge and self-healing, evolved naturally out of immanent gifts and propensities inherent in our psychic structures as human beings. These everyday, ubiquitous gifts and propensities for empathy and introspection were, sooner or later, bound to be elaborated into a method: the scientific endeavor of psychoanalysis. On further reflection, however, the idea that Bacon's judgment includes psychoanalysts as well, is greatly surprising. Have psychoanalysts not developed a method whereby their very enslavement to an idea, concept, fantasy, or preconceived notion was to be lifted? Is not psychoanalysis in general—and the psychoanalyst's training analysis in particular—supposed to transform this human propensity for ideological enslavement into a modicum of cognitive-emotional freedom, the achievement of "analyzed man"?

The successes of psychoanalysts on this score have thus far been greatly disappointing even if psychoanalysts do, indeed, have a method for the diminution of ideological enslavement. This polarity between ideological enslavement and ideological freedom in psychoanalysts is also a function of the social-psychological matrix in which the psychoanalytic enterprise is embedded.

Analytically attained openness or ideological freedom was to fashion in us a listening perspective in which our theories would essentially serve as "tools of observation" (Kohut, 1973). When theories are used as tools of observation, they have a properly limited half-life, which is determined by how long they maintain their heuristic and explanatory potential. Such an attitude, if attained and maintained, could perhaps exempt psychoanalysts from Bacon's covering law and better insure psychoanalysis its coveted scientific status.

We will, however, not continue at this point to paint this larger picture of the scientific status of psychoanalysis in further detail, no matter how enticing the task and how useful a fuller picture might actually be. But the issue of openness to new configurations of inner experience is of special importance in the interpretive process, hence this brief preamble should serve as a broad frame for a closer examination of some aspects of the central operational elements of psychoanalysis, namely, the issues of understanding and explaining.

UNDERSTANDING AND EXPLAINING:
TWO STEPS IN THE INTERPRETIVE PROCESS

For a variety of historical reasons, understanding, which should have been alongside explaining as the two distinct steps in the interpretive process, has either been taken for granted or seriously underplayed as a specific and necessary intervention in psychoanalysis—in both clinical and theoretical discussions and writings. Hartmann (1927) and Eissler (1968) explicitly excluded understanding as a significant step in its own right in the interpretive process—for what appear to be ideological reasons. They considered psychoanalysis an "*explaining psychology*," to be sharply demarcated from "*understanding psychology*," which they regarded as nonanalytic and viewed with suspicion. In order to buttress their claim, they needed to consider interpretation (which was equated with explanation) as the sole analytic tool and could not afford to grant understanding a separate clinical or theoretical position.

Loewenstein (1951) and Kris (1951) in their extensive, influential work on interpretation do not address this artificial and unwarranted dichotomy between understanding psychology and explaining psychology. They define interpretation and the interpretive process so broadly and encompassingly, however, that they implicitly accommodate—albeit under a different label— what we call here understanding. But by not placing understanding explicitly into the interpretive process as a separate and clearly defined step, they have overlooked some significant and obligatory functions of understanding as compared to and contrasted with explaining. Not until Kohut (1973) placed understanding and explaining (interpretation in the narrower sense) side by side and accorded understanding a systematic, clinical and theoretical position within the more broadly conceived interpretive process, was this anomaly significantly corrected.

As we have described elsewhere (Ornstein & Ornstein, 1980), Kohut (1973, 1977) demonstrated that psychoanalysis as a scientific psychology consisted of two interrelated layers: (1) understanding psychology—with introspection and empathy as its methods—encompassing meanings, motives, and relationships, and (2) explaining psychology—with inference, concept formation, and theory building as its methods—searching for causal connections. We had earlier joined Kohut in asserting that the two layers together, in a particular relationship to each other, constitute present-day psychoanalysis. Kohut linked the two layers by saying that "psychoanalysis *explains* what it has first *understood*." There is here no sharp demarcation between these two layers of psychoanalysis, but their conceptual separation has both clinical and theoretical advantages.

Up until this correction, interpretation (i.e., explaining) alone was considered to be the key—even if not the exclusive—operation in psychoanalysis. Nothing portrays more vividly the ambiguous epistemological status of psychoanalytic interpretation than when analysts speak of "having interpreted to the patient," or "having given an interpretation"—without further reference to the form and content of the interpretation. This conveys the idea that there is something magical about interpreting per se, that is then considered not magical at all, but is thought to be purely dependent on the form and content of the explicit verbal statement of the analyst. The content, however, is treated here as self-evident and correct, well known and standard. It is as if the activity of interpreting, or of giving an interpretation carried a force and power that other kinds of verbal communications—not regarded as interpretations—could not or did not possess.

The term, interpretation, per se, does not carry the kind of precision and power that such a stance imputes to it. The power interpretations do carry, resides in the overall context of the analytic relationship and experience and can be captured more accurately through a broader definition of the interpretive process and the total setting in which this occurs.

There is also the difficulty that arises from treating verbal communications of the analyst—designated as interpretations—very differently from the verbal communications of the patient—designated as free associations. In this process the analyst is listening for the inevitably present latent meaning or the metamessage of the patient's communications. He expects, however, that the patient will hear his explicit, manifest, and intended message, as if he himself conveyed no metamessages in his communications at all. When the patient does not hear the explicit, intended message—or, more accurately, when he does not focus on it, but detects the metamessages and responds to those instead—certain communicational problems arise. The solutions to these communicational problems are of utmost importance for the proper conduct of an analysis. The analyst's response to the patient's way of treating his interpretations will determine what kind of analytic experience the patient will be allowed to have. Because of the striking difference in the manner in which the two participants' communications are treated, we shall briefly focus on what specific impact these divergent ways have on the patient's analytic experience.

The patient may, for instance, treat the analyst's interpretations as expressions of love, praise, and admiration, or rejection, criticism, and demand; as food to be filled up with; as soothing or calming and to be savored; as painfully penetrating and therefore to be warded off; as holding, caressing, or sexually exciting, and so forth. The possibilities are legion and well known.

The analyst's responses to the patient's way of treating his interpretations may fall into two opposite clusters and a third form of response that attempts to combine the two.

1. From one listening perspective and theoretical position the analyst will essentially convey that the patient's treatment of his interpretations deviates from the "norm" and will obstruct the attainment of insight. The analyst will remind the patient that his words are not to be eaten (or to be taken as praise or as sexual penetration) and that such responses are defensive efforts at defeating the analyst's objectives and aim at perpetuating regressive drive gratifications. Responding in this manner, even if tactfully and kindly and with explanations that seem to maintain objectivity, the analyst rejects the patient's subjective experience of his interpretations. Whatever the immediate impact of this implicit rejection or disapproval, the analyst, nevertheless, feels justified in maintaining this interpretive stance, since in this manner he can pursue the necessary defense analysis. He does this in the service of his long-term analytic goals of conflict resolution through insight. He thereby dismisses the patient's subjective experience of disapproval, although drive-defense interpretations inevitably express disapproval.

Since the disapproval that the patient hears was not intended, the analyst takes it for granted that it was not expressed in his interventions. When the patient insists that he has heard it, this is further interpreted as a distortion. Of course, there is a "distortion" of what was consciously, explicitly, and deliberately intended by the analyst, but this is not the issue. The issue is that from the vantage point of the patient's self-experience in the transference there is no distortion: the patient perceives the unintended message, the kernel of truth around which his transference reactions crystalize. The analyst, by claiming neutrality, hopes to elucidate the genetic-dynamic origin and meaning of the patient's responses to his interpretations. By considering the patient's responses as "regressive," however, the analyst's subsequent interpretations aim at pulling the patient out of that regression to a higher level of functioning, from which the patient's reaction, mode of perception, and communication are seen as a retreat.

To illustrate, a 36-year-old patient in his 5th year of analysis shared a fantasy of himself sitting on the analyst's lap, slowly unbuttoning her blouse and sucking on her breasts. He felt comforted by the fantasy and found himself using it to fall asleep. He added that he could not imagine his mother ever holding him in such a way that he could relax with her; she always appeared to be in a state of agitation.

The fantasy was understood as a "regressive (pregenital) evasion" of the patient's oedipal sexual wishes. The analyst interpreted this by saying that the patient persisted in this resistance to the recognition that he wished to possess the analyst-mother sexually. This interpretation was to help the patient give up the preoedipal attachment to the mother and move on to the oedipal phase, where the analyst—as she stated in her report—would "represent reality that dictated the need for adaptive autonomy." (The transference was obviously seen here as repetition of the infantile, in spite of the patient's statement that he had just expressed a longing for an experience he could not recall having had with his mother.)

This way of listening and responding is restricted by holding on to the view that all psychopathology of analyzable patients can be understood and treated on the basis of the drive-defense model, irrespective of the developmental level to which their origins can be traced. In this context it is also important to differentiate between "regression" versus "fixation" at the root of the psychopathology, since patients with (preoedipal) fixations are not considered to respond favorably to analytic efforts at drive-defense interpretations.

In a clinical situation such as the one just described, the psychopathology is considered to be mainly regressive in origin, and the analyst's communication aims at achieving a split in the patient's ego. Such communications represent a continued appeal to the observing ego, fostering the therapeutic alliance, the secondary process thinking, and so forth—all in order to undo the regression and continue the analytic work toward insight into the pathogenic conflicts. This emphasis seems to bypass (and thereby often discourage) the emergence of those aspects of the patient's archaic self-experience that cannot be understood as the avoidance of certain specific (oedipal) conflicts or as the retreat from more mature object relations. What is of significance here is that the recognition of the preoedipal components of the transference did not change the drive-defense model for their interpretation.

To stress this once more, when the analyst persists with his drive-defense interpretations, in spite of the fact that the patient perceives and responds to the unintended dismissal of his archaic longings as defensive, he directly thwarts the patient's conscious and unconscious longings in the transference, instead of welcoming them as grist for the analytic mill of understanding and explaining. To be even more explicit, the patient's communication in the transference is, by definition, archaic—in the sense in which it expresses revived, unresolved, infantile and childhood issues, including the childhood solution to the problems. Appeals to the so-called therapeutic alliance, to be achieved by the observing part of the adult ego, seem to us to reject the infantile or the child in the patient. Patients almost invariably experience them that way. Such appeals certainly demand of the adult ego a reevaluation and renunciation of infantile drives and defenses. In the face of such a demand how could the patient not draw the conclusion that the analyst disapproves of those archaic longings? Analysis of the transference, in our view, necessitates just the opposite: it is only the empathic acceptance, understanding, and explanation of infantile and childhood longings that will allow their slow transformation and their ultimate integration into the adult psyche.

2. From another listening and theoretical position the analyst fully accepts the patient's mode of response as an expression of his archaic level of experience and he tries to elucidate the meaning of what the patient's way of experiencing his interventions expresses (in the transference and genetically), rather than what it defends against or distorts.[1] From this perspective, the patient's mode of communication reveals his efforts at establishing an emotional connection to the analyst in the service of attaining or maintaining the cohesiveness of his self and ultimately in the service of a belated maturation and growth, that is, structure building. These efforts reveal not only the particular structural deficits that spark the patient's efforts in the transference, but also his specific ways of trying to fill in or replace the missing psychic structures.

The clinical example cited earlier would indicate to this analyst that the patient, who puts himself to sleep with the fantasy of sucking on her breasts, has reactivated his "thwarted need to grow." This fantasy is secured as a transference expression of the patient's longing to acquire his own capacity to sooth and to calm himself in the analyst's presence. In other words, rather than considering the fantasy as a "resistance to growing up," to this analyst, the same fantasy indicates that the analysand has overcome his shame—which served as a resistance—and he is now able to express to himself and to the analyst his most deeply felt longings and desires. Rather than seeing it as a resistance, the presence of the fantasy and its expression indicate progress in the analysis.

This way of listening and responding means that the analyst fully accepts that patients with a psychopathology based on developmental deficits or derailments (so-called fixations) are analyzable, once the patients are able to mobilize the transferences that correspond to their specific form of psychopathology. The recognition of these transferences—the selfobject transferences (the mirror transference and the idealizing transference)—

---

1. We acknowledge that from the external observer's point of view the patient's response to the analyst's interpretations might well be regarded as "defensive" and "distorted". We are not questioning here the validity of these observations, but claim only that for our analytic purposes the observations made from the empathic vantage point are the only decisive ones. We focus our understanding and explaining exclusively on these (cf. Schwaber, 1983).

their archaic as well as their more mature forms, permits the analyst to respond with understanding and explaining, hence entirely within the interpretive process, on that level of psychic organization on which the patient functions in the transference. The idea here is not to undo the regression or fixation directly, or to pull the patient up to a higher level of psychic functioning, but to make contact with and accept whatever he brings to the analyst and in whatever form and on whatever level he does so, with the aim of structure building through understanding and explaining in a climate of optimum frustration. Structure building is here conceived of as a process of belated maturation and growth, as opposed to change through adaptation.

3. From a third, intermediate position (hard to justify both clinically and theoretically) the analyst believes that the two preceding antithetical approaches can be combined into one coherent treatment process. The idea is to do this by not confronting the patient for some time with what the analyst thinks is the regressive-defensive meaning of the patient's behavior and experience. Instead, at least temporarily and tactically, the analyst accepts the more archaic communication—only privately considering it as defensive regression (as if such a private opinion would not find its way into his communications). The analyst's hope is that this prolonged withholding of the otherwise correct interpretation will allow time for the strengthening of the patient's ego (via identifications?) and consequently the therapeutic alliance. This should then permit the analyst to procede with the hitherto withheld, unaltered, drive-defense interpretation.

The above two-step sequence is a schematic outline. The fact of the matter is that in analysis the more archaic and the less archaic levels of communication oscillate or alternate in the flux and flow of the analytic experience. To follow this flux and flow in the manner just outlined, would seem to require of the analyst a frequent and rapid shift to contradictory attitudes, from drive-defense interpretations to noninterpretive interventions, that is, from nonacceptance to acceptance of archaic longings in their own right, thus contributing to the chaotic ups and downs observed in such an analytic process. It is therefore only with gross disregard for the patient's tendency to develop a sustained and cohesive transference, and undue attention to the content of the patient's communications instead, that the two antithetical attitudes can be combined. For how can "accepting the archaic experiences as valid in their own right" be held simultaneously with "viewing the archaic experiences as drive-related defensive regressions"? In such a combined approach the analyst actually views the patient's communication as evidence of regressive defense, not valid or analytically legitimate in its own right, since the latter would spell "fixation" and hence unanalyzability. The analyst withholds the "correct" interpretation to avoid confronting the patient when he judges that the patient's ego could not tolerate such a confrontation. It is obviously the patient's ego then, that needs to be strengthened, rather than the analyst's interpretation to be made more accurate and more useful to the patient.

We shall not pursue here further the comparison and contrast of the three approaches to the analytic process just described. Instead, in what follows, we aim at bringing our ideas regarding the interpretive process up to date, that is, in line with the method of the analyst's prolonged empathic-introspective immersion in the patient's self-experience and the findings and theories derived from it.

THE INTERPRETIVE PROCESS IN THE SELF–SELFOBJECT MATRIX

With our focus on the analyst's activities as these affect the patient's subjective experience, it is important to reemphasize that what is ultimately of significance for the analytic process is *not* what the analyst says, or thinks he says, but what the patient experiences in connection with what the analyst says.

In other words, the analyst cannot afford to lose sight of his own impact on the patient's experiences and with that on the process of analysis. In this connection it should also be noted that the effectiveness of the working together of the analytic dyad—the work that a particular patient and analyst pair can do together—is more important for the course and outcome of an analysis, than is the level of the psychic organization of the patient alone.

It follows then, that the psychoanalytic process is set into motion, or is actually created, by what the patient brings to the analyst and by the analyst's responses to it. We now recognize that an analysis does not automatically mobilize all of the patient's psychopathology; what does eventually become activated also depends on the analyst's responses.

To focus our discussion on the analytic process we should recognize some significant elements in the process: (1) the moment-to-moment interchanges between patient and analyst that lead both participants to grasp the nature of the patient's inner life; (2) the progressively increased centering of the patient's inner life on the analyst as a selfobject; (3) the deepening understanding that patient and analyst achieve in the course of the analysis regarding the meaning of the patient's behavior and experiences; (4) the way in which this deepened understanding affects the moment-to-moment interchanges between patient and analyst and thereby the patient's experiencing of the analyst–selfobject.

It is the most important characteristic of this entire process—which has a spiral rather than a linear momentum—that all of what transpires in it occurs in the self–selfobject matrix and can only be understood in reference to this matrix or more accurately, with the empathic vantage point from within that matrix.

Understanding and Feeling Understood

When we speak of the analyst's activity in terms of a particular level of understanding, we recognize that only the patient who is the object of the effort to be understood can indicate to us whether or not he was actually understood. The patient's reaction of feeling understood, then, attains a special significance in the interpretive process. The analyst's efforts to identify the patient's subjective experiences accurately and the patient's reaction to feeling understood, are both central for the subsequently emerging explanations to become experience-near and emotionally meaningful as well.

A small segment of an interaction of the effort to understand and the feeling of being understood (or not being understood) should serve as an illustration. Mr. K, in analysis for some time, presented the following dream shortly after a prolonged vacation. With two of his brothers present and aiding him, he was running toward an airplane to board it. It was like those last-minute evacuation scenes around Saigon, in Vietnam. He had two obstacles to overcome to make it to the plane in time. In the end he made it. TR, a friend, was at the plane organizing it all.

In his associations the patient emphasized the horrors of his "internal Saigon" from which he was running, without putting much stress on the fact that (manifestly at least) he actually made it. In his effort to summarize what had been said by both of them thus far, the analyst included the question: "In the end you were then rescued, weren't you?" The patient felt deeply hurt and misunderstood. As it turned out, he presented the dream to show—and wanted the analyst to recognize—that in spite of his inner turmoil during the vacation, he felt a "unity" within himself (his two brothers were acting helpfully and in unison with him, indicating that the split-off parts of him were now in greater harmony and connected with his core-self, as he put it); and that he had overcome obstacles, reached the plane and *escaped*. The analyst's use of the word "*rescued*" made the patient feel that he was perceived by the analyst as passive and dependent, in need of a rescuer. It even felt to him that the analyst might have considered himself to be in the role of a rescuer, when in fact he felt that he escaped as a result of his own activity and strength in the analyst's absence.

Here, finding the word "*escaped*" (with its connotation of self-generated activity) was crucial, since it was the one that best described the patient's self state. Understanding, then, on this level means to establish communication, in which finding the expressions that best describe the patient's subjective experiences in the objective. Understanding in this sense is an achievement within the analytic dialogue and comes about through a sustained focus on the patient's self-experiences. The moment-to-moment interchanges between patient and analyst consist of such efforts at understanding.

Explaining and Feeling More Deeply Understood

But when and how does the analytic dialogue include more than the moment-to-moment experiences? Is it in keeping with the empathic mode of listening and interpreting, to offer explanations that the analysand cannot resonate with, although he might, nevertheless, ultimately accept them? In other words, how does the empathic vantage point and mode of interpretation expand the patient's self-awareness? How and when does the analyst include in his interpretations the unconscious, split off, and respressed aspects of the self? There is also the question of how the analyst can, while maintaining an empathic position, include a statement about the patient's defensive operations in his interpretations?

It is in relation to this last question that the maintenance of the empathic vantage point for interpretation is of particular importance. Certain defenses that are themselves unconscious (disavowed or repressed) and defensive personality traits cause suffering that patients and/or the environment have to endure. These have to be understood in terms of their genetic origins in order to be interpreted from within the vantage point of the patient's own experiences. This may be conveyed in statements such as this: "As I listen to you, I am having trouble discerning what it is you are trying to tell me, as if you could make your wishes known only in the vaguest manner, barely hinting at them." Once the analyst understood the patient in greater depth, he can add a genetic "explanation": "I think I can now understand better where the vagueness in your manner of speech may come from. Based on some of your experiences (and these should be specifically stated) you developed a cautious way of communicating, as if you could never be sure how others would respond to what you say—especially, when this concerns something you want for yourself."

However, the introduction of genetic explanations also introduces more explicitly the analyst's theorectical biases. Reconstructions are not predominantly discoveries of preexistent truths, but the creation of the particular, unique, analytic experience. For such a reconstructive interpretation to further the analytic process and the attainment of insight, it has to resonate with the patient's own experiences; it has to evoke in the patient the feeling, that the analyst has captured something of his past that illuminates his present—that it all fits in with the patient's own changing and expanding image of himself, in cross-section and longitudinally. These reconstructions concern themselves with infantile and childhood self states and not simply with events of the past. If these reconstructions are arrived at jointly, if the patient feels that he has participated in their formulation, his own responses to these reconstructions will demonstrate how powerfully they promote the analytic process.

Some of the responses that promote the process are identified as feeling understood *in depth* this time, rather than only in terms of the feeling states that arise in the moment-to-moment interchanges. It is these reconstructive interpretations that add the new dimension to the analyst's understanding and to the patient's feeling of being more deeply understood. Patients frequently respond to meaningful reconstructions in one of the following ways: (1) "Now I am beginning to have a sense for where I came from, who I was, and what explains my feelings and experiences." (2) They show a sense of mastery and an attainment of a unification of disparate, contradictory, or conflicting feelings and strivings: "I can now see how all these feelings belong to me—I am the same person, no matter how I feel." The feeling of being understood, hence of understanding oneself better, can also be enhanced by the patient's active participation in arriving at explanations. This can be fruitfully contrasted with the patient feeling somewhat jarred and surprised when the analyst offers explanations that had not been built up from the detailed exchanges of the analytic dialogue.[2]

Thus, evidence for the progression and deepening of the analytic process is provided by the lessening of the patient's need for the defensive use of repression and disavowal. With this lessening, the split-off parts of the self will be increasingly experienced as part of the total, expanding, and now more unified self, leading to the enhancement and firming up of the cohesion of the self. It is then secondary to this increased self-cohesion that what had previously been repressed and/or disavowed (horizontally or vertically split), is now brought into the orbit of awareness. It should be clear that it is not the bringing into awareness by the analyst that is of primary significance here, but rather the bringing into awareness by the patient himself, since that is the consequence of the strengthened self-cohesion.

The analyst's empathic acceptance of the patient as he or she is (with symptoms, self-recriminations, rages, and the rest) serves as a selfobject function (analogous developmentally to the gleam in the mother's eyes) that becomes transmutedly internalized. In other words, when the analyst

---

2. We realize that no one advocates importing such jarring, abstract, experience-distant reconstructive interpretations into the psychoanalytic process—interpretations that spring forth from the analyst's own theoretical system as his private association and explanation, without properly considering the patient's associations. Yet, the joint effort and the patient's immediate and long-term responses will be of decisive importance. A beautiful example is offered in Kohut's description of "The Two Analyses of Mr. Z" (1979). An aspect in a termination dream is interpreted in the first analysis as the patient's defensive refusal to allow the entrance of the gift-bearing father through a slightly open door, in order to safeguard the regressively colored, but basically oedipal relationship to the mother. The same detail in the dream is seen in the second analysis as an effort on the patient's part, to slow down the reception of the desperately longed-for paternal gifts (the missing masculine substance). Both reconstructive interpretations aimed at capturing the patient's experiences from within the vantage point of his own inner state. Both fitted into the overall context of the larger picture of the whole analysis. Yet, the first interpretation seems to have been reacted to more as a foreign body, whereas the second one seemed to resonate more profoundly with the patient's own grasp of the meaning of his experiences.

accepts the patient's infantile and childhood self, the patient, too, can ultimately accept his own infantile and childhood longings. The central aim of analytic understanding and explaining is just that.

Being a patient, however, involves a variety of self-recriminations and self-punishments regarding infantile needs. When the analyst, through interpretation, also rejects the infantile in the patient, that increases, rather than decreases, self-recrimination and self-punishment. Freud considered this to emanate from the repetition compulsion and from unconscious guilt (the negative therapeutic reaction), which constitute the core of resistance.

When Freud's view of resistance as an expression of the repetition compulsion and of unconscious (superego) guilt is translated into interpretation, it is as if the analyst were saying: "You are resisting in order to hold on to your guilt (and to your self-recrimination and self-punishment), so as to camouflage your wish to hold on to your infantile longings and gratifications (expressed in your sadomasochistic activities)." It is our view, that whenever such a statement is heard by the patient in a drive-defense interpretation, this triggers an intensification of the patient's resistances and most likely unnecessarily prolongs the analysis. At best, it leads to a surface adaptation to the analyst's implicit demands, rather than to emotional growth via structure building.

The Analytic Dialogue and the Deepening of the Treatment Process

The metaphor of climbing a mountain together may be helpful in picturing the analytic dialogue and the role of the genetic reconstructive interpretations within it. Patient and analyst walk the mountains together. At times one is ahead and the other trails behind (the analyst, it is hoped). They are, in their manner of walking, their speed, and so forth, getting to know each other's temperament, ways of proceeding and orienting themselves: their respective modes of expression and communication; the idiosyncratic elements of their style of relating. They are thus constantly in search of each other on this climb: this is the dialogue on the level of understanding. It is the maintenance of contact, the noticing of where the patient is, noting what route he is taking, what obstacles he has to master, and how he feels as he struggles to move ahead. Through many difficulties (repeated stumbling and falling down; losing their way on a side trail) from time to time they reach a plateau where they take a rest and look back at how far they have come. They have arrived at this view through a jointly coordinated effort. They can point to landmarks they have passed together. In the course of the climb itself they do not have this perspective; they are busy getting on with the journey. On a plateau they reach a point where they understand enough to put their understanding into a larger frame.

Putting one's past (and one's current experiences) into such a perspective by connecting past and present meaningfully, is a life-long task in which people engage (consciously or unconsciously) in and out of psychoanalysis. Psychoanalysts have to recognize this tendency more than they have thus far and build on it (rather than center their attention on the resistances against it) in order to elicit optimal participation by the patient in the analytic work.

The analyst's effort to understand and the patient's feeling of being understood, as negotiated through the analytic dialogue, lead to the deepening of the treatment process. This deepening is evidenced by the expansion of the patient's needs, demands, wishes, fears, expectations, and fantasies, which will then move more freely into awareness and become expressed in the transference. When this occurs, it is a dramatic demonstration of the advantages of not pursuing the resistances by direct confrontative interpretations. This "deepening" of the transference inevitably and regularly increases the patient's feelings of vulnerability in the analytic situation—relatively independently of the nature of the preanalytic psychic organization. Although both qualitative and quantitative aspects of this vulnerability will have their specific genetic antecedents, it is this increasing vulnerability vis-à-vis the analyst-selfobject that leads to the frequent and painful disruptions of the transference, which become the pivotal points of the analyst's reconstructive interpretations.

SELF-COHESION AND THE PROCESS OF UNDERSTANDING AND EXPLAINING

As we indicated at the outset of this chapter, a survey of the pertinent psychoanalytic literature quickly reveals how broad, encompassing, and at the same time imprecise the term, interpretation, is. Yet, many a debate about what qualifies as a psychoanalytic treatment revolves around the meaning attached to the concept and to the assumption that interpretation has a clear-cut and precise meaning.

In our earlier contributions we tentatively resolved this dilemma by speaking of the interpretive process, in which we saw various forms of the analyst's verbal communications as components of interpretation and cumulatively contributing to the attainment of insight. It seemed to us that to focus on a particular form of the analyst's verbal communication was less important than what the patient made of it: understanding was only achieved if the patient felt understood and if something about him was truly explained and he actually felt more deeply understood as a result. Thus, whatever the form and content of the analyst's intervention, it always hinges upon understanding and being understood.

But the conceptual separation between understanding and explaining is still necessary and makes good theoretical sense—even though in practice these are almost always intermixed, they blend together and are often indistinguishable from each other, except in their extreme or "pure" form. When communication flows naturally between patient and analyst, focused on the moment-to-moment experiences of the patient, as they walk up to the mountain toward a plateau, bits of understanding and bits of explaining cannot be distinguished from each other by scrutinizing the form and content of the analyst's contributions alone. Furthermore, both understanding and explanation are arrived at cumulatively. What appears as understanding at one point can be part of the process of explaining at another. Similarly, what seems like an explanation at one point might well be a step in the deeper understanding at another.

What Constitutes Understanding in Psychoanalysis?

No effort at grasping one's own or another's inner experience is theory free. But in contrast to explanations that are offered on the basis of explicitly formulated formal theories we hold regarding the nature of health and illness, understanding is relatively theory free. The theories that inform our empathic introspective understanding of the nature and meaning of another's experience are self-knowledge and accumulated commonsense about human nature, both of which are at the basis of every form of communication.

Analytic empathy and introspection undoubtedly go beyond being guided by commonsense and self-knowledge attained through life experience (and not through a psychoanalytic treatment process). When prior psychoanalytic experience and training guide the analyst's empathic-introspective observations, it is perhaps more difficult for the analyst to separate his empathic understanding from his theory-based explanations. Only if the analyst himself felt understood in his own analysis, or if he has successfully overcome the trauma of having only been explained, but not really understood, can he direct his theoretically informed listening to be empathically centered on the patient's experience, to view this experience from the patient's own vantage point, without the need to explain before he has understood. Patients often experience the analyst's need to explain as intrusive, especially when prematurely offered or without the preceding step of understanding.

In the sense, then, in which we use the term, understanding means essentially staying with the patient's own experience without the effort, at first, of making sense of it; establishing and maintaining contact; reflecting back what the analyst has heard, to indicate that he indeed heard it; making his presence known at moments when the patient needs to know that the analyst is close behind and has not lost sight of him on this journey. Some patients can feel their own genuine presence and meaningful participation in the analytic process only after such steps of repeated affirmation or validation through the process of understanding.

What Constitutes Explaining in Psychoanalysis?

Where understanding (when the analyst is "in sync" with the patient's feeling state and experiences and grasps their meaning) shades into explaining is traditionally that point at which causal connections are introduced by the analyst (or by the patient) into the analytic dialogue. The epistemological status of explaining in psychoanalysis has long been questioned (recently more vigorously) by those who view psychoanalysis as primarily a study of meaning, a hermeneutic discipline, in which causal explanations do not apply.

We maintain that "explaining" is a proper term for describing the second step in the interpretive process, if we specify its operational use. What we mean by explaining is the placing of the understanding arrived at by patient and analyst into a developmental-genetic context and the making sense of these experiences explicitly on the basis of the analyst's specific observational tools: his (always provisional) theories. Explaining in this sense aims at grasping the meaning of the patient's experiences in terms of motivation and purpose, all in the context of the self-selfobject unit. Explanation here is "causal" only in terms of elucidating antecedent states whose discovery gives meaning to present experience.

Webster's New International Dictionary (Third Edition) does not differentiate sharply between understanding and explaining, and defines their meanings as overlapping in many ways. Our use of these two terms in psychoanalysis is thus in tune with traditional linguistic consensus. Our insistence, nevertheless, on their conceptual differentiation (cf. Kohut, 1977), as already indicated, has both clinical and theoretical justification, which we will introduce after a clinical example of the combined use of understanding and explaining.

Understanding and Explaining the "Thwarted Need to Grow"

The following clinical vignette demonstrates the combined use of understanding and explaining in the form of a comprehensive genetic reconstruction and the impact this had on the process of analysis.

The patient, in the 3rd year of her analysis (with A.O.) began to describe a sexual fantasy in considerable detail. As she spoke, she suddenly interrupted her narrative and said, "At this very moment, I have the distinct feeling that you really don't care about me right now. I wish I would die." Then she added, "I want to escape you and I want to outrage you, shock you or excite you. Leaving here in the middle of the hour could be such a dramatic, outrageous thing. It is humiliating to have to beg you for your response. I am okay when I am not around you. But what is happening to me here with you? I don't understand. . . ."

The analyst thought that the interruption of the patient's narrative was due to a sudden emergence of shame in relation to the sexual fantasy she was detailing. It was as if she had, to her own surprise, revealed more than what was comfortable for her. The image of feeling suddenly exposed, brought to the analyst's mind a story the patient told her some time ago. As a little girl, 3 or 4 years old, her T-shirt got torn off at a family gathering and she experienced an acute sense of shame, feeling that her family, especially her mother, disapproved of her naked body. The analyst used this memory to convey her understanding of what the patient was now experiencing on the couch: relating her sexual fantasies exposed her, making her feel as if she were standing naked in front of the analyst. The fear of the analyst's response was overwhelming and she wished she would die.

But the episode signified more than the reexperiencing of shame. The childhood memory of shame at her exposed body was a screen memory, related to her feeling throughout her childhood that her body evoked scorn and disapproval, rather than delight, in her mother. In view of the importance that this screen memory had for the patient's current self-perception (that she was not a good looking woman), the analyst commented on the *urgency* with which the patient "exposed" herself by giving the details of her sexual fantasy. The urgency indicated to her, she said, that there was a wish to create a situation in which she could stand naked in front of the analyst. But this was a risky position to be in: would her naked body (represented by the sexual fantasy) be found beautiful *now*?

After the analyst said this, the patient replied, "I very much want you to look at me—but then I want to look at you and see what your eyes are saying: do they say I am beautiful?" The analyst continued: "It was the fear that my eyes (my voice) wouldn't say that and you would rather die than have that happen to you again. Then there was the wish to shock me and outrage me by leaving the office. This sounds like your response to the expected disappointment that I would not find your naked body beautiful. Leaving the office is to express your rage for failing you this way. Now I will feel the painful humiliation too. But the dramatic way in which you would do this, would insure *some kind of response* from me. Not being sure that you can elicit a positive response from me, your "outrageous" behavior would secure at least an intensely negative one. It sounds as if the most important thing about all of this is that I notice you and respond to you intensely."

This latter statement was an interpretation of the patient's life-long mode of protecting herself against feeling humiliated whenever she struggled with strong exhibitionistic wishes. The expression of these wishes, even in the most disquised form would be quickly followed by intense shame, so that she had to re-repress the wish: by doing something outrageous she would give expression to the exhibitionism and successfully re-repress the wish to be admired. The patient's response indicated that she felt further understood as a result of the interpretation; instead of resorting to her life-long defense of being provocative or "outrageous," she spoke freely of her wish that the analyst look at her approvingly and with admiration.

The clinical vignette demonstrates an instance in which "the thwarted need to grow" was reactivated in the analysis. Crucial in her comments was the analyst's recognition of the meaning of the urgency with which the patient "exposed herself" by telling of the sexual fantasy in detail; an urgency that did not represent an irresistible drive that ought to be tamed or renounced, but recognized as a legitimate childhood wish that had now come to the fore.

To summarize this experience, we would say that the patient, as an adult, had an experience in the analysis that was analogous to her childhood experience, but that would now have to have a different outcome. It is as if the patient were saying: "As an adult, it is impossible for me to have an experience here in which I can feel my body admired by you. But that is what I need to get well. Telling you a story and experiencing it as if you were now looking at my naked body, is the closest that I can come to that experience. You can see why I would be anxious about your response — so much depends on that. At first, there was a fear of repetition — you too would find my nakedness unattractive. But then you indicated that you understood what I wanted from you when I told you the story. Your understanding of that helped me realize my wish that you would find me beautiful."

At this moment patient and analyst had reached a new, comfortable plateau on their mountain walk together. The patient felt increasingly confident about the analysis and said, "I feel I am integrating something here with you. It was strange, your interpretation brought a lot of associations . . . primarily to being a little girl. . . . It felt sad. . . . I was amazed by what you said in a lot of ways but that you knew the intensity of it all was the most important; that you knew that I had to have some intense response from you. Your words could have destroyed it all, but they didn't. I feel very connected to you now. It feels as if you like me okay — you don't need to like me above everyone else!"

Similar episodes followed; the telling of fantasies and dreams had to have a shock value; they had to excite and involve the analyst. Many of these instances proved disruptive to the patient and each of them was followed by a new level of integration.

The Analytic Impact of Understanding and Explaining

The preceding clinical vignette illustrates how the analyst's understanding (aided by a recall of a screen memory reported to her earlier) conveyed her acceptance of the patient's experience on the couch. Tipped off by the urgency with which the patient communicated her sexual fantasy, and then by the content of the screen memory, the analyst explained — that is, she

understood more deeply and thoroughly, by placing into its genetic context—
the meaning and motive for the patient's immediate experience. Understanding that the patient wished to evoke in the analyst an intense response
of admiration for her physical beauty, and the extension of this by explaining
what made it so risky for her to "expose" her wish and ask for this admiration
freely, permitted the patient a more direct and less inhibited expression of
the wish to be looked at and found beautiful.

The analyst was then able to combine her understanding and explaining
into a comprehensive reconstructive interpretation, that connected the patient's immediate experience on the couch (the wish to be admired, the
intense shame and humiliation it triggered, and the turning of this wish into
a fantasy of "outrageous behavior" as a compromise) with her life-long,
habitual ways of defending against her intense wish to be admired, which
now had become associated with a sense of shame and humiliation.

This further understanding made it unnecessary for the patient to remain
bound to her compromise solution and she now spoke more freely and
without shame of her wish that the analyst look at her approvingly and with
admiration—thus activating or liberating the patient's hitherto "thwarted
need to grow." When this inherent tendency to complete previously interrupted, derailed, or arrested development—whatever archaic form it may
take initially—is recognized as a legitimate childhood wish and is accepted,
understood, and explained, the process of belated maturation and growth
is analytically enhanced. When it is countered by being viewed as an irres-
istable drive that needs to be controlled, tamed, or renounced, this nonacceptance may further thwart and often actually preclude structure building
and the felicitous outcome of an analysis.

What we have thus far discussed and illustrated about the separate and
combined functions of understanding and explaining, should now be summarized and elaborated on in order to bring these clinical activities in harmony
with psychoanalytic self psychology.

1. The process of understanding forges an analytic contact with the
patient on his or her own terms, in relation to feelings, thoughts, wishes,
needs, fantasies, and demands, and the various ways all of these had to be
dealt with at the moment (that is, in the transference) and habitually (that
is, in keeping with the patient's character). This is a validation rather than
a challenge to the patient as he or she is—a validation that includes the
unconscious motives and the particular mode by which these motives are
protectively defended. The acceptance and understanding of the infantile
wishes (repressed or disavowed) and their defenses lead to the patient's
subjective feeling of being understood in depth.

The feeling of being understood aids the patient in establishing a self–
selfobject matrix (the various forms of selfobject transference) in which
understanding continually reinforces the stability and cohesiveness of the
self. Self-cohesion increases as the split-off parts of the self are progressively

included with the firmed-up core of the self. Increased and sustained self-cohesion leads secondarily to improved functioning in diverse ways and in many areas. Among them are self-awareness and insight, essentially as consequences of progressive structure building. Even at best, the analyst's empathic understanding still creates optimum frustration—since it always remains only verbal communication, no matter how gratifying the feeling of being understood is—and thereby contributes to the process of structure building.

2. The process of explaining deepens the analytic dialogue by connecting the past with the present and thereby offering a longitudinal perspective. By bringing together experiences from various developmental and later epochs of the patient's life, it enhances self-cohesion. It further anchors what has up to then been understood. There is added opportunity here for further empathic acceptance and understanding of infantile and childhood yearnings and their transmuting internalization. Understanding and explanation allow the infantile and childhood wishes to be finally more freely expressed in the atmosphere of unconditional acceptance, which is a precondition for their subsequent transmutation and internalization. This is in sharp contrast with the experience in which the symptomatic patient rejects the sick part of his or her own personality. This very rejection creates self-recrimination and contributes to symptom formation. Thus, every implied or subtle expression of rejection by the analyst places upon the patient a demand for rejection of his infantile longings and thereby creates further splits in the psyche.

REFERENCES

Hartmann, H. (1927). Understanding and explanation. In *Essays on Ego Psychology* (pp. 369–403). New York: International Universities Press.

Eissler, K. R. (1968). The relation of explaining and understanding in psychoanalysis: Demonstrated by one aspect of Freud's approach to literature. *Psychoanalytic Study of the Child*, 23:141–177.

Kohut, H. (1973). Psychoanalysis in a troubled world. In P. H. Ornstein, ed., *The Search for the Self* (pp. 511–546). New York: International Universities Press, 1978.

Kohut, H. (1977). *The Restoration of the Self*. New York: International Universities Press.

Kohut, H. (1979). The two analyses of Mr. Z. *International Journal of Psycho-Analysis*, 60:3–27.

Kris, E. (1951). Ego psychology and interpretation in psychoanalytic therapy. *Psychoanalytic Quarterly*, 20:15–30.

Loewenstein, R. M., (1951). The problem of interpretation. *Psychoanalytic Quarterly*, 20:1–14.

Ornstein, P. H., & Ornstein, A. (1980). Formulating interpretations in clinical psychoanalysis. *International Journal of Psycho-Analysis*, 61:203–211.

Schwaber, E. (1983). Psychoanalytic listening and psychic reality. *International Review of Psycho-Analysis*, 10:379–392.

5

Discussion

The Definition and Role of Interpretation

ARNOLD GOLDBERG

Interpretation, as a word, suffers the fate of its own definition. That the word cannot be confined to a single meaning results both from its place in history, as well as from its carrying so heavy a responsibility. One interprets something at one time differently from at another—thus the role of history; and what something means is the essence of explanation—thus the burden. Psychoanalytic interpretation is doubly victimized since the mere intellectual or decoding aspect of the act of interpretation is never sufficient to fulfill what is asked of a comprehensive analytic definition. Rather, for psychoanalysis, interpretation is considered to be the basic vehicle of treatment; and so something in the definition must account both for what it means, and for what it does. There must be something in the knowing more than we did before or more than the knowing by itself that accounts for the change that we insist is the result of a proper interpretation.

To trace the evolution of the definition of interpretation it is easy to divide the phases of analytic positions. Roughly it moved from the early abcess image: the symptom relieved by discharge occasioned by interpretation, to the much later dialogue image: one that stressed what was given or added to the mix by the interpreter. There are also a host of definitions that situate themselves at points in between the minimally involved surgeon and the maximally involved surrogate parent.

Interpretations were felt to be given to the patient for his or her consideration, to be "done" to the patient for a specific effect beyond his or her control, or to be discovered by the patient as a product of mutual analytic work. In the division of labor the patient associated freely, and the analyst made sense of this material. This simple assignment of tasks, however, has recently undergone something of a radical transformation, which derives from a new-found interest in interpretive science or hermeneutics, as well as from some not-too-recent developments in the philosophy of science that have but recently impinged on psychoanalysis.

The second of the above, the implication of the philosophy of science, is of primary importance since it speaks to a point that many analysts ignore, misunderstand, or deny: The now accepted tenet that all observation is theory laden and theory directed, and that one cannot gather a fact that is not already presupposed or dictated by theory. One cannot in the words of one sage "peek around" the theory to see the data. Yet analysts do seem to think that there are observations that are theory free or prior to theory, as Ornstein says; or else that the method of free association somehow allows one to avoid the imposition of theory in the data (Kris, 1983). It is said that by paying attention to the sequences and patterns of free association one can somehow restrain oneself from making preconceived formulations. The innocence of that position betrays a lack of appreciation that the very notion of sequences and patterns is a theory of sorts. What would that disciplined and restrained analyst say of the listener who carefully noted the repeated pattern of a speech impediment in the patient or who counted the consonants in a given exchange or who observed repeated references to lunar changes? No doubt they might be dismissed as nonanalytic, but the moment that *that* or any similar such statement is made we are launched on a theory that we had hoped to hold at bay.

The very idea of a sequence involves a host of presuppositions and preconceptions such as those spelled out by Freud and felt to be the hallmark of the theory of free association. Granting that we can allow that set of preconceptions as a baseline, can we say that the continued exercise of free association will thereupon make for fairly uncontroversial sets of patterns or sequences? It never seems to work out that way. There is always a choice to be made, and that allows us to return to the earlier issue: hermeneutics. It seems that somehow we do manage to see meaning; and as long as we see something that others do not, we are bringing our theory to bear and so we are interpreting.

The tradition of hermeneutics is long, but unfortunately it is thought of as so devoted to the understanding of theology and history, that some say it stands in opposition to scientific thinking or at least to the so-called natural sciences. But every science is interpretive, and all data everywhere are seen according to the preconceptions of the observer. In the exchange between the analyst and the patient, and in the construction of shared meanings rather than of imposed meanings, we embark on a process of understanding that involves the hermeneutic circle: the back-and-forth filling in toward total comprehension.

What Heinz Kohut offered us was not a new method of data collection, not a new atmosphere for conducting analysis, not a special sort of humanity or kindness, but simply (and profoundly) a new theory. The implications of such a new way of seeing the world may indeed be an increased sensitivity to one's patients, but without the theory such sensitivity is no more than that shared with every like layperson. Thus the interpretations that we make are products of this new theory, and the meanings that we construct with our patients arise from the contributions that the theory allows us to give. Interpretations in self psychology direct themselves to selfobject issues, and they focus the attention of the patient to these struggles. So they are, by definition, biased and preconceived, like any and all observations made by any analyst at any time no matter how hard they may strain to free themselves of such bias. For even *that* position of total freedom from preconceived ideas is, of itself, a special form of preconception.

I have a patient who said that she had a fantasy of getting some extra time from me at her terminating hour. Now there are many ways of decoding that statement and indeed, in a previous analysis, it had been interpreted as indicating a feeling of deprivation the patient professed. She had been clinically depressed, and much of her treatment before had either been devoted to feelings of oral deprivation and/or a profound envy of what others might have: a penis, a man, and so forth. In this, her second analysis, we saw a heretofore unrevealed image of herself as an important and admirable person. Her ambitions were intense and almost painful for her to recognize. They were quickly overlaid with feelings of inadequacy, with lonely memories, and with the old wish for someone to make her feel intact and whole. But the deficiency was not of a penis or of oral supplies, rather it was of an admiring and mirroring selfobject. Her analysis took an entirely different course with this form of interpretive activity, and progressed in an entirely different direction than that associated with the goal of resigning oneself to one's inadequacies. The question is not about the "truth" of this interpretation, but rather how one arrives at it at all.

No sort of prolonged empathic immersion would reveal this material until and unless one is possessed of a theory that allows one to see it as such. The further elaboration of how such a shared theory allows someone to change relates to the kind of developmental issues that Basch has brought forth. Once we see the world differently, we seem to inhabit a new world. This is not merely a cognitive achievement as Basch has demonstrated, but it consists of a new order of affective relationships as well. The twofold activity of understanding and explaining lifts the nature of a relationship from levels characterized by fragile or poorly constructed linkages to those characterized by more stable and enduring ones. We connect to one another in a different manner when we do so with maximum empathy and comprehension.

This is the way the definition and the burden of interpretation is revisited upon us by self psychology. It does not solve the problem as much as it makes a new set of perceptions possible and thus changes the interpreter. Possessed of a theory of self psychology, the psychoanalyst is a changed participant in the analytic process. This may, for some, allow for a heightened self-awareness as, for example, in one's personal scrutiny of empathy and its breaks. It may, for others, simply add an option to a pluralistic way of looking at clinical material. It likewise may alert us all to the profound constraints and restrictions that the study of and commitment to a new theory makes upon us. Every new idea allows us to see more but, paradoxically, to be *less* creative. We cannot be discovering new things so readily when we are proving that our theory is valid. We need an occasional break from our theory to see if it can do as much as we had hoped. That, supposedly, was the impetus for Kohut's own creative work. It was an effort to answer questions raised by a straining of the older theory beyond its capabilities.

But Kohut's theory still leaves questions to be answered. How, for example, are we to consider his restriction of interpretations to empathic failures? He states that disruptions in the self–selfobject relationship are the arena of interpretive activity. The analyst makes sense of the sequence of empathy–empathic break–reestablishment of self–selfobject unit via empathy and interprets this to the patient. As clear as this may be, it seems to describe a process that does not fully encompass the range of interpretive activity of most psychoanalysts. We often interpret dreams that do not seem to show any evidence of empathic failure, lest we stretch the idea to include any state of less than perfect understanding. The answer to this and other questions may launch us on to much further work in understanding interpretation.

We may have reached a temporary limit or impasse in both defining interpretation and knowing how it works. Self psychology does allow for a new entry in the study of the problem, but it would be foolhardy to think that we have done much more than modestly expanded our vision. The definition and role of interpretation seems merely to echo so many of the unsolved questions in psychoanalysis. We need to focus our investigation of the particulars of self–selfobject development in order to see just what selfobject failure means at different points of development and so also to comprehend just what transmuting internalization stands for in a developmental sequence. We need to determine just what the salutary effects of understanding are as opposed to, and in conjunction with, explanation. Shall we confine understanding to empathy and join them in a phrase such as empathic understanding? Or shall we limit our interpretive efforts to an explanation of the above mentioned sequence? Do we cure people by more than interpretation and, if so, just how shall we account for this? Heinz Kohut's last book addresses many of these questions as do the chapters presented in this section. We seem, however, to have a lot more work to do.

REFERENCE

Kris, A. O. (1983). Determinants of free association in narcissistic phenomena. *Psychoanalytic Study of the Child*, 38:439–458.

DEFENSE AND RESISTANCE

6

Summary of Kohut's "The Self Psychological Approach to Defense and Resistance"

MORTON SHANE

In this chapter of Kohut's *How Does Analysis Cure?*, he considers three interrelated questions: first, in general, the place of defense in self psychological theory; second, in particular, whether the analysis of defense, that is, resistance analysis, is still indispensable to analytic technique as conceived by self psychology; and third, and more particularly, how self psychology evaluates the traditional treatment process as an overcoming of resistance in order to make the unconscious conscious.

Kohut ties these three questions related to defense and resistance to a distinction he made previously between 19th-century scientific objectivity, which he sees as defining traditional psychoanalysis, and 20th-century scientific objectivity, which he sees as defining self psychological psychoanalysis. The traditional analyst sees his patient objectively, and seeks to discover discrete mechanisms of a mental apparatus; the self psychologist acknowledges his own impact on the field he is observing, and, using empathic contact with the patient, is able to broaden his perspective beyond this mechanistic view. Traditional psychoanalytic beginnings in hypnosis introduced a mode of thinking ill-adapted to the requirements of complex mental states. It encouraged a metaphor of surgical detachment, viewing the unconscious as an abscess to be penetrated and drained. By and large, according to Kohut, the traditional analyst imitates and models the surgeon who puts aside all feelings, even his human sympathy, as he proceeds to drain the pathogenic abscess in the unconscious. While the introduction of ego psychology influenced the theory of mental illness, it did not influence the technique. There were exceptions, however, to this overall approach of traditional psychoanalysis; Loewald and Stone, for example, introduced a new attitude of understanding and explaining so that stunted psychological development might resume. However, the old conceptualizations persist and remain strong, especially in the areas of defense and resistance, where the traditional model, according to Kohut, is "penetration to the unconscious via the overcoming of resistance." Kohut asks what this model explains and what it fails to explain. To quote him directly:

The explanatory power of the old model is best . . . when it is applied to isolated processes and isolated, circumscribed sectors of psychic life. It is worst . . . when it is applied to the complexities of man . . . [particularly] to man's personality viewed along the time axis of his unrolling life. To be specific: the traditional model explains slips of the tongue and other forms of the psychopathology of everyday life to perfection; it also does well with regard to the interpretation of the majority of dreams — self-state dreams being the exception—as long as they are viewed as delimited units of psychic function; and it is also satisfactory with regard to understanding the symptoms of the transference neuroses as long as they, too, are viewed as delimited units of psychic function or, more accurately, as delimited units of psychic dysfunction. The model is unsatisfactory, however, in explaining personality in general and the psychopathology of personality disturbances in particular—especially disturbances in which the essential psychopathology results from the thwarted development of the self. (p. 181)

The focus on defense mechanisms and unconscious drive wishes, which still describes the traditional model, remains important to the beginning student of psychoanalysis undertaking his first analyses under supervision, just as it had been important when analysis itself was in its infancy. But now the focus of attention for the experienced practitioner has shifted to an attempt to grasp the condition of the self. This is an important point, so I will again quote Kohut:

Defense-motivation in analysis will be understood in terms of activities undertaken in the service of psychological survival, i.e., as the patient's attempt to save at least that sector of his nuclear self, however small and precariously established it may be, that he had been able to construct and maintain despite serious inadequacies in the development-enhancing matrix of the selfobjects of childhood. (p. 184)

At this point, Kohut presents a long case illustration covering a 3- to 4-month period during the 4th year of analysis of a middle-aged lawyer suffering from marital and work dissatisfactions, focusing on three dreams that occurred at the beginning, middle, and end of that period, respectively. This man had previously had an interrupted traditional analysis. The case illustration is designed to contrast the traditional approach to treatment, and particularly to defense and resistance, with the self psychological approach.

I will begin with the verbatim report of the three dreams:

Dream 1. A summer resort. . . . The patient . . . was sleeping not inside the building but on the front lawn. He was ill at ease, uncomfortable, thrashing about restlessly with the result that he became uncovered. People began to walk by. He was dismayed by the thought that they would see him partially uncovered.

Dream 2. The patient had reported at the beginning of the session that during a recent disagreement with his wife he had behaved more maturely than in the past. Specifically, instead of getting enraged as would formerly have been the case, he had cancelled an engagement of his own in order to allow [his wife] to attend a concert with a girlfriend. . . . [He dreamt:] He was honored by the Lawyer's Association and was to get a prize. Although he himself had not heard the announcement that he was to be honored, the man sitting next to him told him about it and also explained to the patient that, as a compromise, he was sharing the prize with someone else. The patient then went to the podium and was given the award; it was a camera. To the surprise of everyone he lifted the camera and took a picture of the audience. The audience was stunned.

Dream 3. His friend John W was with the patient during the analytic session. John was lying next to the patient on the couch. There were other people in the room too. . . . [An older person had] a heart attack. The patient sprang into action . . . [and did] mouth-to-mouth resuscitation. (pp. 185–186)

Kohut then discusses a traditional approach to the analysis of this patient. He first identifies four kinds of resistance pertaining to the case illustration, correlated, according to traditional analysis, with the themes of (1) sibling rivalry; (2) exhibitionism and voyeurism; (3) anal-retentive erotism; and (4) incomplete resolution of the Oedipus complex. The discussion of each type of resistance is ultimately designed to demonstrate that

> the models of traditional analysis, although adequate up to a point, fail to provide a conceptual framework that enables us to appreciate the most important functions of these so-called resistances, whereas self psychology, by contrast, does provide such a framework. (p. 187)

Taking up the first theme, sibling rivalry, Kohut reveals that the patient had only one sibling, a brother 2 years his junior, clearly his mother's favorite, by whom he felt displaced and outclassed in regard to both physical attractiveness and physical adroitness. He defensively withdrew from competition and avoided angry jealousy in relation to his brother, assuming an attitude of superiority, isolation, and nonconformity, especially in the intellectual field. This defensive stance became manifest in both his first and second analyses in regard to his attitude toward analytic work on his dreams. Since analysts are interested in dreams, supplying them is playing up to authority in competition with younger siblings, that is, other patients. The patient would both conform and defy; he would supply a dream fragment, but, rather than work on it, he would instead veer off into intellectual side issues about the general meaning of dreams. Moreover, he felt pressured by the analyst to have dreams, remember them, and analyze them during his sessions. Dreams 2 and 3 contain clear inferences to the traditional theme of sibling rivalry and can be understood from a traditional point of view. In dream 3, the patient shares and is pushed off the analytic couch by a brother figure, and in dream 2, he and a brother figure share a prize. In both dreams the patient seeks a special bond with the analyst figure, making himself victorious in the end. In dream 3, it was he, not the "brother,"

who saved the analyst-figure's life by resuscitating him. In dream 2, he
could be mature and share his prize with a "sibling."

Moving on to the second theme, exhibitionism and voyeurism, and
their defensive inhibition, Kohut relates that this theme was more intense
in this analysis than it had been in his previous, more traditional analysis.
In particular, the patient was preoccupied with his body as flawed. Turning
to dream 1, the patient expresses shame at being seen naked, at exhibiting
himself publicly. In his associations to the dream, the patient spoke of his
frustrated wish to have a light on in the bedroom the night before while
having intercourse with his wife, both to see her, and also, principally, to
watch her as she watched him. During the analysis of the dream, the inhibition
of these wishes led to resistances to the emergence of underlying, deeper
drive wishes.

In dream 2, what is evident is the patient's defense of turning passive
into active; that is, from the one who is being looked at on the podium, in
an expression of his uncomfortable exhibitionistic desires, he becomes one
who turns a powerful, voyeuristic eye on the stunned, indeed overwhelmed,
audience. In a prior session, the patient had reported an experience in law
school when, in an examination situation, he was able, through a clever
artifice, to surprise, stun, and embarrass his evaluators, and thereby avoid
their criticism of him. Thus the defense of turning passive into active was
demonstrated as characteriological for this patient, particularly in dealing
with exhibitionistic and voyeuristic impulses, manifested both within and
without the analysis.

The third theme identified by Kohut deals with defensive resistances
emanating from childhood experiences that traditional analysis relates to
anal-retentive erotism. This theme was almost entirely absent in the patient's
analysis with Kohut, but figured prominently in his previous analysis. Here
Kohut makes an important point that will be returned to later, in a different
context:

> the patient reminisced, not infrequently, and especially during the first year
> of analysis, about . . . [the] topic [of anality] as it had been discussed by the
> previous analyst. In this connection, he tended to repeat with what seemed to
> me genuine fondness certain phrases that the analyst had used in his (transference)
> interpretations, such as "first you are shutting yourself off tight and then,
> suddenly, you are making a big production." It seemed that what little mourning
> about the loss of the previous analyst this patient could experience was expressed
> via these memories of the former analyst's interpretations. . . . (p. 196)

Although, as stated above, anality played no significant role in his
analysis, Kohut nevertheless included material from the patient's early life
relevant to anality as a source of resistance in treatment. As he says,

> I do so in the context of my attempt to provide as complete a picture as possible
> of the traditional outlook on defense-resistances, and especially in view of the

fact that the patient's previous analyst had clearly put great stock in this dynamic-genetic connection. (p. 196)

The patient's mother gave him enemas throughout childhood until he was 10 or 11 years old, seeing it as a remedy for "irritability." Furthermore, she felt that bowel movements should be early in the morning, rather than later in the day, as was the patient's spontaneous tendency. Kohut remarks that this information about the patient's early life would seem to be in tune with the outlook of the former analyst; namely, the patient resisted the analytic process just as he had resisted parting with the cherished feces. Furthermore, it ostensibly fits with this interpretation that only pressure could force the patient to comply with the basic rule, resulting in a sudden outpouring of material after a protracted dearth, just as his childhood constipation had given way to the sudden "big production" as a result of the enema.

Finally, the fourth theme identified by Kohut deals with defensive resistances emanating from childhood experiences that traditional analysis relates to an incomplete resolution of the Oedipus complex. In discussing the possibility of oedipal pathology in his patient, Kohut speculates that all of the preceding defense-resistances could be secondary to an overall defensive retreat from oedipal conflicts to preoedipal conflicts. Furthermore, Kohut says, one might speculate that the patient's competitiveness with his younger brother was a regressive version of the more nuclear competitiveness with his father, that his voyeuristic-exhibitionistic features and fear of passivity derived from frightening primal scene observations, and that the anal theme was *in toto* a defense against castration anxiety. However, to quote Kohut,

despite my own openness to discern the Oedipus complex in this patient's analysis and thus come face to face with the resistances that constitute clinical manifestations of the defenses against castration anxiety, I was unable to discover this classically pivotal configuration, at least not in its role as the nucleus of psychopathology. . . . not in the three dreams I examined, and also not in the material that preceded [or followed] them. . . . (p. 199)

In this way, Kohut demonstrates his familiarity and skill with what he terms "drive- and ego-psychological etiology," which he feels can be used to explain the symptoms and character traits of any patient. "But," he adds, "as analysts we must have the capacity to postpone closures and to apply closures tentatively, observing the analysand's reactions to our tentative interpretations, and to consider as many explanations as possible." To quote him further, "Progress in science, I like to say, is impeded more by our commitment to old knowledge than by our incapacity to acquire new knowledge" (p. 199).

With this, Kohut completes his drive- and ego-psychological approach to the specific defense-resistances of his patient. He now turns to the self psychological approach to defense and resistance, but rather than focus on the individual defenses and resistances of the patient as he did in his discussion of drive and ego psychology, he instead focuses on the patient's total personality, and only secondarily turns to the specific defense-resistances of this individual. Such an approach to the material is

> an intrinsic constituent of the overall stance of the self psychologist . . . to construct first an hypothesis concerning the structure and central program of the patient's nuclear self and only subsequently to assess such details as psychic mechanisms against the background of this tentative overview of the personality. (pp. 200–201)

Kohut goes on to explain that without knowledge of the vicissitudes of the patient's self, we cannot appreciate the significance of his defenses and resistances.

Turning first to the patient's childhood, it is apparent that the emotional milieu was determined by his silent, powerful, and disapproving mother. She imposed a "quasimilitary, machinelike outlook" and a "cold and joyless" atmosphere on the entire family. An event in the patient's childhood, termed "the interrupted basement game," serves as a significant emblem for the difficulties in the family. The father had once played hide-and-go-seek with his two sons in the basement of their house. They were all having a good time, laughing and shrieking with delight, when the mother suddenly appeared and looked at them. She did not utter a single word but her wordless disapproval was unmistakable. "All the joy seemed to leave the three of them, and after listlessly playing on for awhile, they stopped, the boys going to their rooms and the father as usual going to his club" (p. 204).

Other illustrations of the atmosphere include the mother's taking the patient to a skyscraper immediately following his fearful dream of falling off some high building to prove to him that there was nothing to be frightened of, as well as her aforementioned attitudes toward bowel control and regularity. To summarize, the mother seemed to lack warmth, was duty oriented, lacked a natural understanding of people and especially children, and was moralistic. She also was quite pessimistic about her family's health and about their future careers.

The father appeared to be a more potentially joyful person than the mother, though he was overshadowed by her in the patient's mind for a long period of time. He was successful in his career and had been a college athlete, but he maintained a distance from home and was mainly silent about his work and his achievements.

In discussing this patient's personality, Kohut notes the similarity of the emotional constellation of the family to other patients he has described, namely, Mr. X (1977), Mr. M (1977), and Mr. Z (1979). Exposed to development-thwarting influences from the side of his mother, who possessed a near paranoid rigidity, and was insecure and hypochondriacal, and a father who withdrew physically and emotionally, this patient attempted to heal the self via the creation of compensatory structures by turning to the potentially development-enhancing reactivation of the selfobject father. But the question remains, how did the patient manage to stay as relatively healthy as he did, to become a reasonably well-functioning and clearly nonpsychotic adult? Kohut asserts that as a child

> he had managed to keep a significant remnant of his nuclear self alive, remaining at least potentially capable of responding with renewed structure building to new opportunities for further growth. Expressed in technical terms, he remained potentially analyzable. Expressed in everyday, human terms, he never quite gave up hope. (p. 208)

Kohut asks further why the patient was able to preserve his nuclear self. How did he preserve this core structure? He speculates, first, on congenital capacities promoting health and development taking the form of an innately present vigor of the nuclear self, increasing resistance of the nuclear self to disintegration, and enhancing the capacity to fight noxious influences. Such congenital vigor of the nuclear self promoted in the patient an innate capacity to form *compensatory* structures, that is, the capacity to hope for a satisfactory selfobject that would in the future enable him to consolidate the structures he had already formed in childhood. As with Mr. X, Mr. M, and Mr. Z, he more or less relinquished the mirroring selfobject and attached himself to a potentially idealizable one.

Still referring to innate capacities, Kohut then distinguishes the patient's capacity to form *defensive* structures, "structures used to maintain the remnants of the self—i.e., to maintain the status quo, however unsatisfactory it may be" (p. 210). One such defensive structure retained in its original form is that of turning passive into active, illustrated in dream 2, where the patient counterattacks the audience by unexpectedly snapping a picture of them at the very moment when he had received at least a moderate amount of the mirroring he needed. Another defensive structure identified in this patient was that of withdrawal from others to an isolated preoccupation with his own thinking and reasoning powers. This defensive structure, unlike turning passive into active, was developed further and became quite useful to the patient.

Having identified those *innate* qualities of his patient that allowed him to become a reasonably well-functioning and clearly nonpsychotic adult, Kohut turns to the self-enhancing aspects of his *environment* that supported the preservation of a self, and the hope for an adequate selfobject that would strengthen and consolidate it. To begin with, the patient's father, though more vigorous, joyful, and less disturbed than the mother, probably did not contribute, to any significant extent, to the patient's remaining marginal vigor. At best, he did not interfere with the patient's development, at least in early life. Later he actively sided with the mother to discourage the patient from pursuing a career.

The maternal grandfather was a more invigorating figure for the patient's self. First, he was an unsurpassed male figure in the life of the patient's mother, for whom her husband remained second rate and could therefore never become an idealizable figure for her son. A positive aspect of the mother's idealization of her father, however, was that her son could see that there was at least *one* male capable of being idealized by her. Second, he was a constituent of the life-affirming atmosphere in the grandparents' home, where the patient had spent three happy summers during which he was more outgoing than usual; and, third, he was an available object satisfying certain of the patient's idealizing needs. The grandfather had risen from comparative poverty to great wealth, led an adventurous life, and was much admired by the grandmother.

In terms of the patient's mother, while her overall influence was deleterious, she did provide areas of support, particularly during the summer vacations at her parents' home where she seemed to benefit, along with her children, from the invigorating atmosphere provided by the grandparents' presence. Also she read aloud to him nightly, leading to the patient's genuine gratification from reading later in life. Nevertheless, life-sustaining forces cannot be attributed to the mother. On the whole, in life and in selfobject transferences within his analysis, the patient moved gradually from the mother and toward paternal symbols of grandfather and father.

Having outlined the dominant influences in the patient's childhood that thwarted or enhanced the firm establishment of his self, Kohut returns to a discussion of the defenses and resistances of his patient, in order of increasing psychological depth and significance: namely, resistances related to sibling rivalry, exhibitionism and voyeurism, anality, and homosexual and competitive aggressive impulses related to the father. In each case, Kohut demonstrates the operative principle regarding the function of resistances and defenses: the principle of the primacy of self-preservation. In terms of sibling rivalry, there is no doubt that his younger brother played an emotionally important role in the patient's life, being better endowed physically and loved more by his mother, which the patient handled by a defensive attitude of chronic superior withdrawal. This attitude also played a significant role during the analysis; whenever the patient felt understood, he would invariably withdraw. While others, representing his brother, might wish to be understood and be responded to, he did not; he was indifferent to his analyst's ability in this regard. I will quote Kohut in relation to his patient's second dream at some length, because what he says here is central to his thesis:

> Thus, after proudly reporting to me that he had behaved maturely toward his wife and, in his dream, receiving recognition from me (albeit shared with a brother) of his progress, he suddenly turned the situation topsy-turvy and,

raising the camera and exposing me to the painful limelight, denied having asked for a self-confirming mirroring response from the mother-analyst. . . . Clearly, what is involved here is not a struggle for object love but a need for self-enhancing reflection. . . . [the] so-called "defense-resistances" are neither defenses nor resistances. Rather, they constitute valuable moves to safeguard the self, however weak and defensive it may be, against destruction and invasion. It is only when we recognize that the patient has no healthier attitude at his disposal than the one he is in fact taking that we can evaluate the significance of "defenses" and "resistances" appropriately. The patient protects the defective self so that it will be ready to grow again in the future, to continue to develop from the point in time at which its development had been interrupted. And it is empathic recognition of this fact by the analyst who essentially sees the world through his patient's eyes while he analyzes him that best prepares the soil for the developmental move forward that the stunted self of the analysand actively craves. Such recognition serves the patient better than anything else the analyst can offer. . . . (pp. 222–223)

Kohut adds that traditional analysts do acknowledge the protective aspect of resistance, but they nevertheless continue to have difficulty with this concept for two reasons: one is the analyst's own vulnerability to the narcissistic wound of seeing his help rejected; the other and more important one is the scientific model of truth facing, of making the unconscious conscious; anything that opposes this morally tinged goal is considered resistance. Though self psychologists find this model useful in specific circumstances (such as in dream analysis), they choose to subordinate it to their overriding theory of thwarted and remobilized self development.

Specifically, with reference to his patient's dream of stunning the audience by taking its picture, Kohut reasons that just as the patient had safeguarded himself against the intrusions of a partly crazy mother, so he chose in his dream to safeguard himself against the intrusions of a partly crazy analyst. The analyst, like the mother, had seemed to this patient more concerned with proving his own theories than with respecting the patient's individuality. It was in this context that patient and analyst came to understand the patient's stance of superior isolation vis-à-vis his brother (and others) not as contempt, but as protection against the damaging, oppressive demands and expectations of his mother. In fact, the patient's brother, as her conforming favorite, had been damaged by his mother, whereas the patient was able to preserve his self by his withdrawal.

Concerning the second theme, that of exhibitionism-voyeurism, Kohut explains that whenever the patient's need for self-enhancement through mirroring increased, he felt intensely painful shame and embarrassment owing to basic deficiencies in both maternal and paternal selfobject relationships. He preserved the integrity of his self by mobilizing his aggression, that is, by turning passive into active, becoming a sadistic voyeur and making the selfobject ashamed and embarrassed instead of himself. The move from being naked in public as in dream 1 to stunning the analyst-audience by taking its picture demonstrates the move from passive embarrassment to active sadism.

In order to discuss the third theme, that of anality, which had been credited by his former analyst with a truly causal role in his pathology, Kohut offers an effective anecdote that should be read in its entirety in order to be fully appreciated. The essence is that the patient's first analyst had seen the holding back and evacuation of the enemas administered by his mother as an enjoyable and forbidden anal orgasm, an interpretation that the patient was very fond of repeating to Kohut. Kohut, on the other hand, did not find anality to be much a part of the patient's character. Why, then, did the patient so love the interpretation? Kohut discovered that it was not the content of the analyst's remarks, but his tone of voice at such times, which communicated so much to the patient—vitality, deep emotionality, and enjoyment of life, attitudes so lacking in the joyless atmosphere in which the patient had grown up.

Finally, in terms of the fourth theme, the defense resistances against the male child's oedipal competitiveness with his father, and his partly reactive passive homosexuality, Kohut offers a self psychological reinterpretation of this psychic constellation. In his analysis with this patient, the father theme was a central theme relatively late in the analysis and emerged with intense "resistance" only after the brother conflict and the preoedipal mother attachment had been analyzed.

> What emerged [in regard to the oedipal constellation] was . . . not a death wish against the father and a defense against it, but a yearning for a strong vital idealizable father-analyst. . . . In . . . dream [3] . . . the revival of the father-analyst who had a heart attack seemingly invited interpretation in terms of a death wish and reaction formation against it. In reality, however, the act of resuscitation expressed the patient's wish to transform the analyst from an old, sick, dying man into a living, vital, and responsive ideal. (p. 230)

It developed that not only had the mother prevented the son from idealizing a strong and vigorous father, but she also had obstructed him from idealizing his grandfather. Her own view of the grandfather as she presented it to her son was to see him as physically weak and close to death. But this view of the grandfather's frailty was happily contradicted by the boy's own experience with him in a most propitious way, and, in fact, in the transference, the patient's decisive rise in self-esteem was associated with a similiar availability of an idealizable selfobject.

Kohut concludes that his patient's development had resulted in the permanent establishment of compensatory structures to which he had turned after the decisive failure in obtaining the selfobject responses needed to consolidate the primary structures.

Let me close this abstract of Kohut's chapter on defense and resistance by quoting from the last few pages, which summarize his manuscript.

Even with regard to the father theme the self psychologist and the ego psychologist remain far apart. Not only are their interpretations of the basic dynamic constellations widely divergent (sexual drive-wishes for the mother motivating oedipal rivalry with the father, versus the need for a strong idealizable father in order to strengthen the self), but, even disregarding these differences in content, the self psychologist cannot agree that he is dealing in this instance primarily with a "resistance" of this analysand. . . . We cannot . . . accept the dictum that we are primarily engaged in a battle to increase knowledge and that everything that impedes progress toward "becoming conscious" . . . is to be considered a "resistance." Just as was the case with the "resistances" vis-à-vis sibling rivalry, exhibitionism, and anality, so also with regard to the paternal selfobject. All these so-called resistances serve the basic ends of the self; they never have to be "overcome" . . . rather, they are healthy psychic activities, in all their ramifications, because they safeguard the analysand's self for future growth. (pp. 233–235)

REFERENCE

Kohut, H. (1984). *How Does Analysis Cure?* A. Goldberg, ed., with P. Stepansky. Chicago & London: University of Chicago Press.

7

Discussion

Self Psychology's Additions to Mainstream Concepts of Defense and Resistance

MORTON SHANE

In discussing this chapter, I will limit myself to a few points and resist the temptation to address the larger issues of competing paradigms. I prefer, where I can, to integrate new views within the ever-widening mainstream of psychoanalytic theory and technique. The chapter under discussion serves as a case in point. Kohut brings to the subject of defense and resistance his particular frame of reference and thereby contributes to my understanding of this important sector of psychoanalysis. For example, although we all shun the surgical metaphor that did, in part, inform Freud's early thinking, Kohut reminds us effectively that we as analysts are particularly vulnerable to falling into this way of thinking when dealing with ideas of resistance and defense. Thus, while it is now commonplace in all psychoanalytic teaching that one respects the defenses of the patient and not run roughshod over them, or, to retain the surgical metaphor, not penetrate the patient's defenses in hot pursuit of the content that is defended against, Kohut reminds us of the reason for this caution: there is a motive for all defenses. In self psychological terms, that motive is the principle of self-preservation.

It is this, I think, that constitutes Kohut's main point in this chapter, that defense and resistance must be considered in relation to the purpose they serve in maintaining the integrity of the self, and only secondarily in terms of what they defend against. Of course, when we speak of what is defended against and the person's specific motives for setting up defenses, we are in the realm, whether we like it or not, of ego psychology and conflict. Ego psychology holds that dysphoric affects such as anxiety, guilt, shame, or depression, which would be aroused by the awareness of unacceptable desires, ideas, or states, motivate the ego to initiate defenses against such awareness, leading to compromise formations that express all sectors of the personality. Such compromise formations may interfere with healthy functioning of the person and are therefore an appropriate focus for therapeutic attention. Self psychology, on the other hand, in its primary focus on the status of the self, minimizes the role of conflict, stressing instead developmental arrests and deficiencies. Defenses and resistances are not conceptualized principally as impediments to a knowledge of what is hidden; instead, they are seen as necessary bulwarks against a further weakening of the self. It stands to reason, then, that Kohut can more temperately forego his patient's relinquishment of defenses and resistances unless and until something better comes along to strengthen self structure. His emphasis is upon development of the self in the self–selfobject matrix, which is not invariably dependent upon such relinquishment of defenses. In fact, a healthy development of the self may even require the retention of defensive structures. Moreover, self psychology regards with favor the existence of compensatory structures, as with the patient in the example, who turned from the disappointment with the selfobject mother to more satisfying, father-like, idealized selfobjects. Kohut makes clear that such compensatory structures might well be seen by traditional analysts as defensive rather than preservative.

The traditional analyst, if any good, also waits for something better to come along before working interpretively on a resistance or a defense. The theory holds that through the therapeutic process and the reassuring presence of the analyst, the patient's ego has been strengthened, possibly by a diminution of the disruptive effects of dysphoric affects, or a more reasonable superego response to hitherto forbidden desires has been reinstated, and so forth. Nevertheless, and regardless of one's guiding theory, self psychology brings this important reminder: the total functioning of the individual must always be kept in mind over and above our interest in getting to the truth, the patient's hidden motives. I am not saying that there are not important differences between the two theories in terms of technical emphasis: my understanding of this chapter leads me to believe that a self psychologist is less likely to interpret and to work analytically on defensive constellations, and is more likely to let them be, while empathically acknowledging the reasons for their existence. My own predilection is to respect the patient's defenses and resistances, but I don't believe it is helpful for respect of the defenses to extend so far as to allow them to endure without investigating the patient's motives for maintaining them, with an optimistic expectation that through interpretation, the patient will be able to develop and move beyond them to more maturity, including more mature defenses and resistances. For example, Kohut's patient who must always turn passive to active, will, it is hoped, at some point be fully able to understand why he does so, so that he will have other options when faced with his strong mirroring needs. What Kohut adds to our understanding of technique is that, despite all of this, and, I would add, regardless of his or her guiding theory, an analyst does need to know when enough is enough. He or she should not feel defeated, or make the patient feel defeated, when the patient demonstrates a structural need to retain, and even to retain unexamined and uninterpreted, certain defensive constellations.

As a corollary to this central thesis, Kohut reminds us that, as analysts, we should always be aware of our own narcissistic vulnerabilities, our need to do a "perfect" job, and to be regarded by our patients as effective and useful. Though Kohut sees this latter as a secondary point compared with his more fondly held proposition that truth seeking is a fallacy of western man, and therefore the basis for our tendency to overinterpret defenses, I am more persuaded by Kohut's masterful understanding of our narcissistic vulnerabilities. That is, I believe that it is the injured narcissism of the analyst as an individual, rather than the biases of the culture concerning truth, that renders the analyst so susceptible to overinterpretation and emotional attack on his resistant patient. Kohut's message in this chapter, combined with his previous writings, is a necessary corrective to zealous overanalyzing. He has said in the past that if a patient wishes to terminate an analysis, the analyst should take that wish very seriously and not superimpose unnecessarily on a patient the analyst's grand scheme for perfection. Kohut's statement on defenses and resistances seems to be a natural extension of this position. In effect, Kohut warns against being so vigorous in our analytic attempts that we lose touch with our patient's need to maintain what may be termed defenses and resistances. We can fall in love with the pseudo-precision of defense mechanisms, and our need to analyze them and too vigorously uncover what they hide, and lose, thereby, the empathic human contact with our patients.

As a final point, I am still not persuaded that self psychology can provide a superordinate framework for all of analysis. I was therefore gratified to read in this chapter that traditional analysis has not been and cannot be swept aside completely. Kohut's statement that the beginning psychoanalyst needs to learn about conflict, conflict resolution, and compromise formation as seen in slips, dreams, symptoms, and the transference neurosis, and his contention that the beginning analyst will benefit from using a traditional model with his early cases, seems to support my own fondly held conviction that self psychology, as valuable as it is, is *additive* to the body psychoanalytic.

8

Discussion

The Primacy of the Preservation of Self

PAUL H. TOLPIN

There are so many complex details that make up and support the overall argument of Kohut's chapter that I have decided to discuss it in relation to some experiences with a patient of my own, which I shall link to Kohut's discussion of his lawyer-patient.

I once had a patient whose childhood was, for the most part, as lacking in health-promoting experiences and as injurious to her as were the childhood experiences of Kohut's lawyer-patient whose dreams are used to illustrate his ideas on defense and resistance. Without going into the details of her history, I shall relate a brief exchange—a question I asked her one day and her answer to that question—that focuses on Kohut's concerns in this chapter.

After the patient, Mrs. A, had been in psychotherapy for several weeks, I gradually began to realize how massively unavailable her parents had been for her throughout her childhood, and consequently how much more terrible the unannounced, sudden desertion at age 3 by her beloved nurse was for her. One day when the full horror of the abandonment and isolation of her childhood became clear to me, I asked in amazement: "But what saved you?!" She thought for a moment and then replied, "I was intelligent and I was beautiful." I was taken aback by her answer. What she said was certainly objectively true, but I hadn't expected that kind of response and although I didn't know what to make of it at the time, I felt that she was on to something. Only later in the course of a 5-year analysis did I come to understand and believe, despite the necessary oversimplification of such a brief reply, that what she said so ingenuously was essentially correct. Her intelligence *had* enabled her both to escape from her emotional deprivation and to grow through the use of, among other talents, precocious reading abilities that transfused her with a kind of life and excitement, and a world of ideas to which she had little access otherwise. In part her reading substituted for experiences of her own. In addition, when she developed into a strikingly beautiful woman, she came to realize that she could always depend on a response from men. In a way she would never, except by choice, have to be alone again. She was half aware that she could not ever let herself be without a responsive, admiring, and admired man. However, she also had kept her distance from prolonged intense involvement all of her adult life. More could be said about her alternating need for closeness and for emotional distance, but I shall explain. Guided by ideas Kohut describes in the chapter, I came to understand what this alternating need meant and how the patient had indeed saved herself.

Among other ways, my patient was able to save herself, that is, to prevent or to minimize the disintegration of the coherence of her self, by taking advantage and making the most of inherent qualities that were, at least in part, called upon to stabilize and enhance her sense of vitality and self-worth. She used her cognitive and intellectual gifts to fill the emptiness of her life and to organize herself. She read stories about exciting people and events and she created a relationship with ideas and images that was enormously satisfying. She connected with them, and they filled some of the empty spaces in her self. She learned to love thinking. Her intelligence was also used to effect her self-absorbed, protective withdrawal. In other words, a form of intellectualization, coupled with other emotional attitudes, was used characterologically as a life-protecting defense. As far as her looks were concerned, from her early years, she used her physical attractiveness to enhance her sense of desirability. It partially offset her pervasive feeling of having been abandoned to an utterly indifferent world. She used a variety of complex and subtle measures —not always successful—to safeguard herself from attacks of the awareness of the danger of abandonment and the accompanying feeling of chaos. In a more general way she developed a "hysterical personality," which made available to her the eager response of boys and men, and of women too, in a different way. For both men and women her overall attractiveness came not just from her looks, but from her sense of how to please others. People responded positively to this and, those responses were life saving. Building on certain narrow but positive childhood baseline experiences, including those with the devoted and beloved nurse, with her *not-at-all motherly* but good-in-a-crunch mother, and with her unusually self-absorbed, silent, though sometimes delightful (and in her mind magically endowed) father, she developed quasi-sexual and later strongly erotic, restitutional relationships with men. These relationships supplied her, at times, with adult versions of the childhood selfobjects she needed to confirm her, to look up to, and join with to strengthen herself.

In analysis her fear of exposing her feelings of emptiness to herself as well as to me and, more primary, the urgency of her need to fill in and to stabilize her endangered self by allowing a transference attachment to deepen were at war with each other. Her urgent need for an active positive response and her fear of my indifference or rebuff gave rise to a variety of clearly recognizable defensive techniques and symptom formations. Among them were some of the specific defenses and symptom formations described by

Freud and Anna Freud, but more important than use of these defenses in the usual drive and object-related sense, was the way Mrs. A defended herself, that is, the organization of her self, from collapse. She used everything available to maintain a hard-won emotional equilibrium. Without that equilibrium she was in danger of attacks of massive anxiety-depletion experiences and disintegrating or disintegrated panic.

In treatment I explicitly focused on the *foundational* injuries that had led to the manifest circumscribed defenses and symptoms. What was disavowed, denied, repressed, and what had led to symptomatic acts, behavioral disturbances, and to her "hysterical" personality were understood as secondary defensive formations. They were also understood as useful and positive responses developed to help avoid the disintegration panic, and/or the sense of depletion and despair that occurred whenever her dreadful sense of aloneness and abandonment began to flash back into the radar screen of her consciousness.

The crucial issue for this woman was to maintain the coherent intactness of her self and to acquire from those she made contact with in her adult life whatever psychological supplies they would give her or she could extract from them. These were present-day versions of the developmental supplies that had been unavailable in her childhood and that she had been unable to make a reliable part of herself. Again, her primary unconscious concern was to maintain the integrity of her self and as much of a sense of fullness as she could muster within herself and from her actions and interactions with others. Her intelligence and her beauty were two resources employed for that purpose.

Now I want to relate this material more directly to Kohut's patient and his discussion of defense and resistance. In the chapter on defense and resistance, Kohut presents a brief history of his lawyer-patient's development, of the personalities of his parents and others of importance in his life, and of a small part of the analytic work in the 4th year of treatment. After he demonstrates how the patient's material might be understood along traditional lines, Kohut moves on to a self psychological point of view. He describes how by various means his lawyer-patient also had to avoid the recognition of *his* particular needs and wishes in relation to selfobjects. Specifically, the patient had to avoid the awareness of his childhood deprivations, his wish for a vigorous joyful response from his mother and for a lively engaging father whom he could idealize.

The patient wanted to be responded to not by way of enemas, hypochondriacal concerns, and baleful looks, but as a "healthy child," as the school doctor once called him. That diagnosis sounded wonderful to him because it declared unequivocally that he was admirable—that he was somebody really worthwhile. It condensed into one short phrase everything that was meaningful to him at that time. It held the essence of what he wanted and what he defended himself against as illustrated in three dreams

Kohut sketches in the chapter. In these dreams the patient wants his body to be admired, he wants his mind and his skills to be admired, he wants to be alone with the analyst with no rivals, and he wants the analyst to be a healthy, vigorous, admirable man he can idealize.

The patient defends himself against the impact of those wishes in various ways that are part of his repertoire of countermeasures. In contrast to the characterological defenses and symptom formations I described in my patient, in his patient Kohut focuses largely and in detail on characteristic, at-the-moment defenses such as turning passive into active (for example, turning the tables on the audience by taking their picture when *he* is being bestowed with honors and admiration, which is too much for him). But the ultimate purpose is the same for both patients: to maintain the achieved organization of the self as much as possible, and to prevent its deterioration by experiences or affects that would be overwhelming. In treatment the patient's aim is to protect himself from the repetition in the transference of the nonresponse or distorted response injuries that over childhood forced his core self wishes into hiding. Because of past injuries he is afraid to allow those wishes to be recognized by himself or by the analyst in the transference—who would repeat those injuries unless he understood what they were and could convey that to the patient.

In the opening paragraphs of the chapter, Kohut asks whether contemporary psychoanalysis and self psychology, in particular, consider the analysis of defenses, that is, "resistance analysis" to be as indispensable an element in clinical analysis as Freud considered it. He ends the chapter with a complexly qualified "no." It is not, he says in effect, *unless* one sees the terminology, for the most part, in a new light.

The new light is the basic shift to an orientation in which the development and the organization of the self from birth on is the central axis and in which self-selfobject experiences play a dominant role in an orientation to the patient's pathology. That reorientation changes the way one understands the patient. The defenses are still there—Kohut describes them in the various dreams of the lawyer-patient in this chapter—but they are understood in a different framework and with a different priority. Most importantly, they are also responded to by the analyst with a *different reactive tone*. The tone is set by the analyst's primary concerns. Consequently it is where he focuses his understanding and interpretations. Ultimately the analyst addresses himself mainly to the primary injury of the core self, and to the recognition of that injury. He also addresses himself to the healthy core that has developed and that remains waiting to be recognized for what it is so that it can, if at all possible, be encouraged to enlarge its domain within the self. Of course there are oedipal wishes, diadic experiences, and individuation. There is rage, hatred, sadism and there is love and affection and there is sexuality and lust, and they range from healthy feelings to serious pathological reactions. They revolve around and are given a particular shape by the central organizing experience of the developing or the developed self—whether it is optimally functioning or whether it is in danger of falling apart. The more endangered it is, the more secondary and tertiary defensive systems develop, the more narcissistic rage and erotization begin to take over, and the more chronic self-preservative but pathological characterological attitudes develop and become fixed—even if they are emotional dead ends that may prevent the patient from getting what he wants most. But they are also buttresses built to keep his psychological tower from falling down.

I have tried to show with my patient what Kohut in a far more intricate way was trying to show with his, that the organization or disorganization, the fullness or the emptiness of the self is central to the understanding of defense and resistance. This is why Kohut answers no to the question whether the analysis of defenses is as indispensable an element in clinical analysis as Freud considered it to be. It is not the defenses, but the recognition of the necessity to preserve the self and the enhancement of the self that is central. Defense analysis still has a place if one understands the focus on defenses in the larger context of the self attempting by any and all means to remain as cohesive, as solid, and as far away from disintegration-depletion experiences as possible. Kohut subsumes all this under the principle of the primacy of the preservation of the self. Within this principle the *pathological* manifestations of sexuality and aggression are understood to be reactive to disintegration-depletion experiences, or less massive threats to the self. Some of the subtleties and complexities of these threats and the defenses against them are described by Kohut in the chapter. Beyond those that he presents are the innumerable varieties of pathology that we see in our clinical practice. There are as many variables of these as there are patients. The details of those and how one works with them must be passed over here. For that we must leave the more experience-distant realms of theory and with a shifted orientation and enlarged possibilities return to clinical practice for confirmation and further revision.

9

Discussion

Resistance and Defense: An Intersubjective View

BERNARD BRANDCHAFT

I

It is impressive to observe the development of Kohut's thinking as it is spelled out in his chapter on defense and resistance. In providing new insights to the concepts of defense and resistance from the perspective of the experiencing self it stands out as a substantial contribution to the development of self psychology and psychoanalysis as a whole.

It is exciting to remember that this significant reconsideration of the concepts of defense and resistance could be said to have begun in 1957 with the paper on "Introspection, Empathy and Psychoanalysis." From that point forward, neither Heinz Kohut nor the psychoanalysis to which he was professionally wed could ever again be the same. It was there that he made the observation that "the observational method defines the contents and the limits of the observed field," and these in turn, with what data are available for observation, "determine the theories of an empirical science" (Kohut, 1957, p. 212). How simple, how unassailable, how elegant!

The subsequent development of Kohut's theory shows the progressive results of the application of this principle, and the reexamination of old and rarely questioned assumptions with the use of this added tool. It is an inspired and dedicated lifework that culminates in the unequivocal statement that

> it is the self and the survival of its nuclear program that is the basic force in the personality and that, in the last resort and on the deepest level, the analyst will necessarily find himself face-to-face with these basic motivating forces in the patient. (Kohut, 1983, p. 233)

Kohut begins this chapter by recalling that the theoretical model that shaped Freud's earliest therapeutic efforts was hypnosis. Freud had come to recognize that he needed new data in order to extend his therapeutic limits and he undertook yet another step in the direction that had launched him on his career. In another paper (Brandchaft & Stolorow, 1984), we have referred to successive steps in Freud's early career in which his use of a different stain in his study of amnesia, and a different perspective from Charcot in his study of hysteria, enabled him to set the stage for the development of the new and revolutionary science of psychoanalysis. The decisive step that Kohut recalls is the third in the series. The change from a demand that the patient get rid of his symptoms, to an attempt, via introspection and empathy, to understand the free associations of his patients and the underlying patterns from which they emerged, the use of a different method of observation, led to a new understanding of psychopathology and the establishment of psychoanalysis as a depth psychology. It was inevitable to further development that an analogous change take place—from an implicit or overt demand that the patient get rid of or give up his "resistances" to a more concerted attempt to understand them within the framework of the contextual unit in which they appear in psychoanalysis, and from which they arose in childhood.

Kohut's outlook for psychoanalysis, contained in the legacy of his last work, is optimistic. It delineates what he considers a revolutionary advance and it anticipates advances yet to come in a science still in its infancy. It spells out that vitality in a science consists of opening the door to new methods of checking and questioning existing theories just as closing the door leads to rigidity and ossification. It is interesting to reflect upon the contrast between this outlook and that of Freud, as contained in his own corresponding summation, "Analysis, Terminable and Interminable." At the end of a long career marked by a genius that is not likely to be equalled again in our science in his unceasing attempts to extend the limits of psychoanalytic treatment, Freud's outlook was decidedly pessimistic. Strachey (1937) observes in his introduction to that work, "at the very beginning of his practice, Freud was worried by very much the same problems as these, which may thus be said to have extended over the entire length of his analytic studies" (p. 215).

In this paper, Freud recognized that more understanding was essential. But the founder of our science fell back not upon extensions into depth psychology but into the field of biology, as Basch (1984) has pointed out, to account for the limitations and failures of psychoanalysis that continued to worry him. Successively he enumerated as decisive factors the biological base that underlay each psychological component of the structural theory that was his final theoretical legacy: from the instincts, their relative constitutional strength; from the ego ("[it] continues to defend itself against dangers which no longer exist in reality; indeed it finds itself compelled to seek out those situations in reality which can serve as an approximate substitute for the original danger, so as to be able to justify . . . its maintaining its habitual modes of reaction"; Freud, 1937, p. 239), a final statement that the pleasure principle is primary in the organization of experience and is *biologically* inimical to the introduction of the reality principle. Holding fast to the conviction that the road to recovery was the bringing to consciousness the unconscious impulses being defended against, Freud said that "the ego treats recovery as dangerous" (p. 238). Subsequently, when the analyst continues to interpret in this way, the patient withdraws, ceases to support the therapeutic efforts, and disobeys the fundamental rule. The patient's refusal to accept the analyst's perception of his (the patient's) reality was the motivational force behind what Freud considered the most tenacious of resistances, "the resistance against the uncovering of resistances." Psychoanalytic technique thus became tied to the belief that recovery depended not only upon making conscious the unconscious object instinctual contents of the id, but in persuading the patient, as an unquestioned acceptance of reality, that his "resistances" were directed against analysis as a whole, and thus that he was the enemy of his own recovery. Discounted was the patient's own perception of the reality of a fragile self and a tenuously maintained organization of self experience.

Yet more constitutional factors were added to the list "the adhesiveness of the libido," "depletion of plasticity," and "psychical inertia," and finally a "need to fail," a "need to suffer," emanating from the last of the tripartite structures, the superego, shaped by a biologically rooted death instinct— yet one more decisive influence of which the patient had known nothing, one more he could not directly verify in himself, and quite predictably an invitation to one more resistance!

Thus at every turn and with every disjunctive response from the patient to the analyst's perception of the essence of his unfolding personality, a new disorder in the patient was added to the growing catalog held accountable for his and the analyst's failure. A process of progressive pathologization of the patient has taken place. With each new discovery of another unseen hitherto unrecognized and unsuspected piece of pathology has come a new and fresh source of resistance, or an intensification of an old one.

This scenario has continued to be played out in countless analyses and with as endless a number of variants as ingenious minds can invent. Today groups of analysts are still identifying new configurations of "resistance" to pour into these old bottles, a multiplicity of affect units of self and object configurations arising from the operation of splitting, projective identification, pathological envy, internal object inconstancy, et cetera, et cetera. And what dispassionate observer could fail to understand the withdrawal of patients, or begrudge them their failure to follow the basic rule, or their lack of appreciation for the efforts of the analysts when an acceptance of these unappetizing characteristics is held to be the necessary and only path toward health. Surely a fresh look at the concepts of defense and resistance is overdue.

I have referred to pronouncements contained in Freud's summation, but they admittedly give only one side of the story. For Freud in this paper also advocated that analysts—not only some analysts—should return to analysis periodically. Certainly he recognized that the limits of analytic understanding could be extended not only by biological speculations or discoveries, but by extending introspection into the impact of the patients upon the analyst's state of mind and mental functioning, and upon the structures of subjectively organized self and object configurations that make up the personality of the analyst. Such efforts must, as a matter of course, also involve a continuous reexamination of the assumptions and their origin that underlie and determine his perspectives on himself and his objects, the theories he uses. Should anyone doubt that Freud retained this hope for progress, I would refer to a letter he wrote to Stephen Zweig: "I have assuredly not dug up more than a fragment of the truth," wrote Freud on November 17, 1937 (Jones, 1955, p. 215).

II

With these latter observations of Freud, classical psychoanalysis and analytic self psychology converge. Freud laid the basis for recognizing that psychoanalysis is a science that seeks to investigate events that occur within an interacting field. Kohut moved a decisive step forward in coming to understand that the reactions of patients could not be understood without reference to the specific impact of the theories by which he organizes his perception of his patients and all the cues, mannerisms, and intonations that constitute his style and by which he communicates verbally and non-verbally those perceptions. So Kohut was able to identify and describe a different type of object relatedness, the selfobject relation, a different kind of transference, the selfobject transference, and a different area of devel-opment—that of the self in continuous and reciprocal interaction with self-objects in a dialogue of mutual regulation.

It was the investigation of this interaction from within the subjective experience of the patient that forced Kohut to reexamine and then revise his views on the nature of defense and resistance. It is now unmistakable to anyone willing to repeat the same experiment, that resistances arise in analysis because patients subjectively experience a threat to the basic structure of the self or to nuclear elements that are necessary for the establishment of an independent center of perception, initiative and direction. That is the reality of the patient that analysts have further to explore. To quote Kohut,

> The patient protects the defective self so that it will be ready to grow again in the future, to continue to develop from that point in time at which it is interrupted. And it is the empathic recognition of this fact by the analyst, who essentially sees the world through his patient's eyes while he analyzes him, that best prepares the soil for the developmental move forward that analyzand actively craves. Such recognition serves the patient better than anything else the analyst can offer. (p. 233)

It is this flood of new perspectives upon familiar configurations, this brace of fresh discoveries, and the renewed appreciation of the still unlimited potential of psychoanalysis for deeper knowledge and increased therapeutic effectiveness that I believe accounts for Kohut's optimism and distinguishes it from Freud's final outlook.

Inasmuch as the interaction that occurs between patient and analyst involves the structures of the differently organized subjective universes, this principle has been referred to as intersubjectivity in analysis, and it is operant in development, and indeed in all human relationships (Stolorow, Brandchaft, & Atwood, 1983). The aim in stressing the principle of intersubjectivity is twofold: (1) to distinguish sharply this concept from that of analysis as an investigation of the purely intrapsychic and/or the interpersonal. It holds that all intrapsychic phenomena are codetermined, as, for example, the nature of infantile fantasy and the type and course of defenses; and (2) to extend our understanding in depth of the complex factors in the interacting structures of the analyst that limit or facilitate the analytic process.

Reflective investigation into the organization of the specific structures of the analyst's own subjectivity, the governing principles of that organization, and the epigenesis of their formation cannot but yield new insights upon the field in which pathogenicity occurs or continues. To emphasize this objective is far from an enterprise in blaming the analyst. Such an outcome, when it occurs in an analyst, is an unfortunate consequence of a specific guiding principle. If one discovers something about himself in his interaction with patients that he could not have discovered before, he may feel culpable for not having had prior knowledge. Wherever such a principle shapes the analyst's attitudes, it leads to defensive needs and unyielding countertransferences. There is nothing of greater utility to an analyst in his work than to recognize and surmount the activity of this organizing principle.

Kohut describes some of the structures of the analyst's own subjectivity that are most commonly activated and engaged—his own archaic selfobject needs. It is the analyst's narcissistic vulnerability, says Kohut, "his frustration at seeing his help rejected . . . and being narcissistically wounded, we tend to become enraged and then to rationalize our counterattack in scientific, moral, or, most frequently, morally tinged scientific terms." Underneath this reaction one can hear the whisperings of the analyst's own deepest and most ancient yearnings, still active, or powerfully revived, for unconditional acceptance of the importance of what he sees and what he says, of his competence and of the benevolent ideals that motivate and guide him in the "thankless task" of an analyst. The yearnings to which I refer are not primarily those of love and hate, and no reanalysis, every 5 years or sooner, that confines its focus to them, will be of real assistance to him.

The particular model that analysts use has been arrived at through some amalgam of the analyst's particular structuring of his life and professional experiences and the outcome of the deployment of his own mirroring and idealizing needs in his analysis and in his training. Once established, this ideal and the perspective it encompasses subsequently govern how he organizes the data of his analytic engagement. It provides him with the sense of continuity, the continuing link to important selfobjects in his past, present, and future, as he is able consciously and unconsciously to experience that link and threats posed to it.

One criterion generally prevails over all others in the determination of whether an analytic candidate is ready for acceptance into the ranks of approved and accredited analysts. Has he been able to analyze successfully the resistances against aggression, to confront the patient with the evidence of unconscious hostility in its transference form and uncover its genetic roots in the infantile neurosis of conflict-laden preoedipal and oedipal relations? This criterion becomes deeply embedded as an essential ingredient of his professional subjectivity. And he comes to believe that his patient should join him in this goal, should measure himself in the analytic relationship, as the analyst has come to measure his own self, by how well he lives up to that expectation. The therapeutic alliance is supposed to be based on some inviolable contract of this kind, though patients can be found to have their own ideas of what constitutes a therapeutic alliance.

In analysis, patients attempt to proceed toward their own goals. These goals, as Kohut observes, are related to strengthening the basic structure of the self and its regulatory capabilities and to mounting an effort to resume interrupted and thwarted self development. In this, as in the original process, they need the help of understanding their yearnings, aspirations, and interferences from within their own subjective framework. When the analyst in such circumstances interposes his own expectations upon the patient and the patient collides with these expectations, what the analyst calls resistance regularly occurs. Subsequently, the analyst attempts to do what he has been trained to do, and the "resistance to resistances" makes it appearance. Not to worry, he is likely to reassure himself, everything is going according to plan! It is familiar territory, charted out by the great masters and his own teachers; all else is unfamiliar, perilous, and antianalytic!

How unfortunate that psychoanalysis has taken over a term for these presumed pathological reactions that in everyday language is used to describe the sometime courageous measures taken by heroes in pursuit of the right to determine their own fate! How constricting that fresh generations of psychoanalysts continue to subscribe to the principle of "intentionality"— if they are frustrated and defeated that that is the intention of the patient and the motive for resistance. When a patient feels frustrated and believes that that is the analyst's intention, it is clearly recognizable that the patient has failed, in that experience, to attain the level of development at which he could recognize the analyst as an independent center of initiative, that *post hoc propter hoc non est!*

All that reveals itself to a prudent observer of the field of these interactions is that there is a human tendency to "recycle" subjective experiences around persistent conscious and unconscious preestablished organizing principles. What is here being played out is not a conflict of instincts but of aims and personalities, and of the interactive consequences of incompatible aims (Brandchaft, 1983, p. 352). For the patient it poses the alternatives of preserving his archaic hopes through aggressivity or through disengagement on the one hand or compliance on the other. Often compliance is the road of choice. The dictum of childhood holds fast in analysis: "When the psychological organization of the parent cannot sufficiently accommodate to the phase-specific needs of the developing child, then the more malleable and vulnerable psychological structure of the child will accommodate to what is available" (Stolorow, Brandchaft, & Atwood, 1984, p. 69). For the analyst the alternatives are a recommitment to the concrete goals he has set for himself and around which he has become organized, or an attempt, through renewed introspection and enforced empathic immersion, to recognize and rise above the existing structures of his subjectivity, and thereby assimilate another's reality into his own. Too often the analyst chooses the first route— digs in his heels, because the second seems to him to involve compliance, "giving in to the patient," a surrender of principles and ideals and a breach in the walls that have come to protect and sustain him.

III

A comment is in order on a neglected aspect of the clinical approach to self-protective measures instituted by the patient in response to or in expectation of damaging or invasive experiences that pose a threat to his functioning and/or to the continuation of his own nuclear program. Each new shift in psychological state that a patient undergoes brings into existence a shift in the intersubjective field, creates a new intersubjective context. A patient, for example, will protect himself by distancing devices—by staying away from a session or, by delaying the payment of a bill, against being drawn into a nexus of subservience to the expectation of a needed other. When this happens, the experiences in which caretakers have responded to their childrens' withdrawal or assertiveness and rage—as indications of truculence, negativism, defiance, "oversensitivity" and the like, from the parents' own experience of narcissistic vulnerability—are condensed and reinvoked. Thus in this situation the patient automatically and repetitively comes to feel and expect that he displeases and isolates himself from the analyst. Aware of this intersubjective aspect of the complex state that has occurred, the analyst can recognize contextually not only that these are in their essence appropriate protective measures, but also the patient's fear that his determination of the measures to use and the course to take will threaten or offend the analyst and thus weaken the tie. This recognition and consistent interpretation, perhaps more than any other measure, enables analytic contact to be maintained and strengthened.

Each withdrawal or critical assertion from the patient only shifts the need for an understanding selfobject to whatever is at that moment the subjective experience of the patient—it does not obliterate that need. Indeed, it is inconceivable that any withdrawal should be so complete or that any human activity should be so solitary that it does not at the same time keep alive the wish to maintain a tie to selfobjects under the conditions that the patient can safely maintain at that time. The loss of all ties to selfobjects is incompatable with psychological life. The analyst's acceptance and subsequent investigation of the reality of the patient's experience that leads to "resistance" facilitates a broadening of the therapeutic tie over time.

IV

This curious situation, in which an individual must attempt to preserve his ties to selfobjects that are needed if he is to sustain himself and retain the hope of resuming interrupted growth, and, at one and the same time, protect himself against threats to his nuclear structure and nuclear program, constitutes the major source of conflict—external, intersubjective, and intrapsychic. This "allocation of libido," as others before it, has necessarily been hidden from view because psychoanalytic researchers took neurotic symptoms (and conflicts) as their starting point, to paraphrase Freud (1914, p. 76), and too often as their final destination.

I believe that the principle of maintaining a tie to a needed selfobject is coequal in primacy to the principle of self-preservation. The consequences of the continuous intersection of these two basic needs seem to underlie the conflicts of ambivalent instinctuality that have been the focus of psychoanalysis in the past.

Thus self psychology serves classical analysis by returning it to its base in empirically testable and observable psychological data, and, taking up where the development of psychoanalysis itself began, opens the path toward a purer and deeper understanding of the psychology of conflict and its resolution.

REFERENCES

Basch, M. (1984). Selfobjects and selfobject transference: Theoretical implications. In A. Goldberg & P. Stepansky, eds., *Kohut's Legacy: Contributions to Self Psychology* (pp. 21–41). Hillsdale, NJ: Analytic Press.

Brandchaft, B. (1983). The negativism of the negative therapeutic reaction and the psychology of the self. In A. Goldberg, ed., *The Future of Psychoanalysis* (pp. 327–359). New York: International Universities Press.

Brandchaft, B., & Stolorow, R. (1984). A current perspective on difficult patients. In A. Goldberg & P. Stepansky, eds., *Kohut's Legacy: Contributions to Self Psychology.* Hillsdale, NJ: Analytic Press.

Freud, S. (1914). On narcissism. *Standard Edition*, 14: 75–76.

Freud, S. (1937). Analysis, terminable and interminable. *Standard Edition*, 23:211–253.

Jones, E. (1955). *The Life of Sigmund Freud* (Vol. II). New York: Basic Books.

Kohut, H. (1957). Introspection, empathy, and psychoanalysis: An examination of the relationship between mode of observation and theory. In P. Ornstein, ed., *The Search for the Self* (pp. 205–232). New York: International Universities Press, 1978.

Kohut, H. (1983). *How Analysis Works.* New York: International Universities Press.

Stolorow, R., Brandchaft, B., & Atwood, G. (1983). Intersubjectivity in psychoanalytic treatment, with special reference to archaic states. *Bulletin of the Menninger Clinic*, 47(2):117–128.

Stolorow, R., Brandchaft, B., & Atwood, G. (1984). Development and pathogenesis: An intersubjective viewpoint. In G. Atwood & R. Stolorow, eds., *Structures of Subjectivity* (pp. 65–85). Hillsdale, NJ: Analytic Press.

Strachey, J. (1937). Introduction to "Analysis, terminable and interminable." *Standard Edition*, 23.

10

Discussion

Kohut's Reformulations of Defense and Resistance as Applied in Therapeutic Psychoanalysis

JEROME D. OREMLAND

Kohut's chapter "The Self Psychological Approach to Defense and Resistance" is of particular interest in that it bridges theory of development and function and theory of technique. In this chapter Kohut, as is his proclivity, gives us a clear clinical presentation so that we can fully understand what it is that he would like us to consider. He asks us to reevaluate one of the shibboleths of therapeutic psychoanalysis, "resistance."

The concept, "resistance," like its related concept "energy," has an appeal to those of us who grew up in the 20th century with its lexicon of ohms, watts, volts, and the like. "Resistance," "energy," and similar metaphors are convincing and at the same time spurious. Kohut in this chapter helps us look beyond the language to see the essentials in the concept, resistance.

Kohut accurately notes that "resistance" is a concept inextricable from therapy; "defense" is a concept of development and functioning. In short resistances are constellations of defenses that are brought forth in characteristic ways as the analytic process develops. In this chapter, Kohut views resistance as responses to various kinds of threat to "self." This is a valuable switch in emphasis from resistance seen as a mitigating response to threatening emergence of drive, although this new view may be *but* a subtype within a more generic concept of resistance as a response to mitigate full awareness of an idea and its implications in transferential context. To me, resistance is inseparable from transference. It is an interpersonal process involving analyst and patient, of course, not analyst as is, although that contributes, but analyst as construed to be. At times, it seems that, as in an example offered of the reanalysis of a colleague, Kohut demonstrates his great ability to analyze transference missed or incorrectly interpreted by a predecessor rather than illustrating a shift in understanding from the traditional to the "self-informed" point of view. It is more a call for accuracy rather than a change in basic orientation. Let us review that incident. Kohut writes:

A colleague whom I had analyzed for a number of years told me, as he reflected
on what he had achieved during the treatment that . . . it was in the analysis
with me and not in his training analysis with an analyst who repeatedly and
insistently confronted him with the evidence of his hostility (especially in the
transference) that he had for the first time experienced an intense wish to kill.
And he told me, in retrospect, of an analytic session long ago (I believe it was
about a year or two into his analysis) when he experienced this wish for the
first time—at least for the first time with unmistakable intensity. It occurred
in the aftermath of the analysis of a dream . . . on which we had been working
for several sessions. The dream in question had taken place in a city block not
far from my office. The patient observed a frail man walking along the block
that led to a broad boulevard where a statue of a husky, muscular, proud warrior
on horseback was to be found. As the patient watched the man walking along
slowly, unsteadily, and weakly, he noticed that the man was not real but some
kind of straw doll. Overcome with anger, the patient plunged a knife several
times into the straw doll man. To his amazement—there was no evidence of
guilt or horror about the deed in the dream—thick red blood flowed out between
the straw.

The patient remembered that he had had analogous dreams during his
previous analysis and that the analyst had always, after listening to his associations, interpreted oedipal hostility against the father (i.e., the wish to belittle
him and kill him) and encouraged the patient to get in touch with these emotions,
especially in the transference. And the patient also remembered how frustrating
it had all been: the evidence seemed clear-cut and incontrovertible but his
insight was only intellectual. In particular, he had been unable to experience
a genuine wish to kill the analyst—only moderate conscious anger at the
analyst for not being able to help him—and how, in treatment with me, did
he proceed for the first time to get in touch with such a wish? The reason, as
he saw it, was the following: I had never referred to his anger, never confronted
him with the murderous intent depicted in the dream, and never talked about
defenses against emotions that would have to be experienced in order to make
the insight psychologically valid, genuine, and meaningful, as his former analyst
had done. Instead, against all his expectations that my response to the dream
would parallel the response of the former analyst, I had on the whole listened
quietly for several sessions to the material that emerged after the dream, partly
via direct associations to the dream elements and partly in seeming independence
of the dream. And when I finally responded, I focused neither on the dream
in isolation nor on the specific aggressive act depicted in the dream nor on the
specific murderous wish he supposedly harbored and against which he defended
himself by splitting off his emotions. What I concentrated on in my interpretation,
according to his memory, was his disappointment in having a weak father,
both in his childhood and now in the transference—(It was my physical frailty
that the straw doll exhibited.) It was in response to my interpretation that in
the analysis he was still trying to get to a strong father (the statue of the man
on horseback) and that he was disappointed and frustrated because I was not
such a father, that he began to talk not only about the small event in the hour
preceding the dream that triggered the dream but also about his early life.

These recollections — that he had been the last-born child of by then aging and overburdened parents; that he grew up in an atmosphere of retrenchment, depression, and withdrawal; that his father was chronically ill, dying when the patient was eleven—fleshed out my skeletal interpretation and ultimately led to his full awareness of the intensity of the rage associated with his wish to get rid of the sick and depressed father. (pp. 138–139)

My first level of criticism of Kohut's recommendations regarding therapy, illustrated by this example, is that although this is beautiful work, it illustrates the power not of self psychology but of accurate interpretation of transference.

Toward that point, I feel that Kohut's review of the history of analytic therapy is misleadingly incomplete. As he notes, "Freud's earliest therapeutic efforts were, and for a time remained, hypnosis. . . . The preanalytic hypnotist ordered the hypnotized patient to get rid of his symptoms; the analytic hypnotist ordered the patient to produce an account . . . to illuminate the endopsychic causes of his symptoms" (p. 112). Kohut asserts that subsequent developments in psychoanalytic theory including ego psychology has resulted in "few" changes of what he calls the "penetration-to-the-unconscious-via-the-overcoming-of-resistances" therapy model.

I agree that the preanalytic hypnotist ordered the patient to get rid of his symptoms and that the early hypnotist-analysts ordered their patients to produce an account of their dynamic and genetic background, a paradigmatic change of vast significance. Yet, I feel that there have been important subsequent paradigmatic changes as the early analysts learned *to interpret* symptoms and *to interpret the mode* of historical accounting. This led to a technical shift of even greater significance as the early analysts learned to interpret *in transferential context* the difficulty the analysand has in producing an account of the dynamic and genetic background, resistance in technical shorthand, based on the recognition that what is transpiring between analyst and analysand is essentially a re-enactment of the account that the analysand is having difficulty producing. This resulted in the birth of still yet a new breed of analyst. Furthermore, as part of this advanced paradigm—that stems from incorporation of aspects of object relationship theory, a contribution curiously underestimated in Kohut's historical account—the analyst knows that the very experience he, the analyst, is having in this dialectical interchange with the patient is itself revealing that very resistance. And is the most reliable guide he has to his as yet unverbalized interpretation that will release both from the compelling feelings and will provide pathways for the patient's productions further to confirm and bring historical perspective on the nature of the interchange. Although these new therapeutic paradigms are curiously underplayed by Kohut, they seem to me to be but living experience, in the most sophisticated and compelling way, of one of Freud's greatest discoveries, the return of the repressed.

With this introduction, I would now like to evaluate what I read as the important therapeutic shift that Kohut clearly advocates in this chapter and throughout the book. My view will be a critical one because I think, unlike his theoretical innovations that are expansive, his therapeutic shift is limiting. Yet, I don't want to hold strongly to this position because I've come to recognize that when one deals with the work of genius one wants always to be cautious before critically discarding any ideas.

As a basis for evaluating the implications of Kohut's shift in emphasis regarding psychotherapy, I'd like to note the important tripartite division of the therapeutic enterprise developed by Philip Rieff (1968) in *The Triumph of the Therapeutic*, that I feel has extraordinary significance to psychoanalysis. Rieff, in his study of the therapeutic enterprise, essentially uses Jung, Wilhelm Reich, and Freud as allegorical figures. In brief, he sees three predominant modes in therapy personified by these men: (1) identification with a greater purpose and the cosmic good, a religious mode, Jung; (2) surrender of oneself to a social–political purpose, a movement, Reich; and (3) steadfast rational pursuit of knowledge, Freud. Rieff knows that all therapy is a composite of all three, that in every completed analysis there is new insight, a sense of joining a movement, and a feeling of joining the enlightened with a greater purpose. Yet, when we evaluate therapy, I think we must look to the predominant intentions of the therapy, *not* to the results of the therapy.

My view is that Kohut, as clearly described in this chapter, and in my reading of his other works, is moving therapeutic analysis away from rationalism and insight, Freud, toward mystical purpose, Jung. Kohut's very emphasis on the *self*, particularly his emphasis on the self as a superordinate, coordinating, developing agent; his emphasis on the central role of psychic integration in "growth and healing," metaphors I don't like; and his emphasis on transmuting internalizations, which Jung (1966) unfortunately calls "alchemy," are closely similar, if not identical with the *best* of Jung. This is not my area of criticism, although I'm not sure a superordinate "self" is a better concept than "personality" with all the limitation of that word. I hesitate to invoke parallels to Jung because I know that Kohut's detractors will quickly seize any similarity to Jung to affirm their view of Kohut's limitations, failing to appreciate important considerations that Jung's observations raise regarding psychoanalytic theory. Putting personality theory aside, I would like to show that within this chapter is evidence to support criticism that Kohut, unfortunately, moves in *therapeutic application* toward a mystical-religious position, parallel to but not identical with Jung's.

Let us look carefully at the case of a lawyer that Kohut presents. As Kohut skillfully gives us various models to understand the patient's characteristic modes of behavior, he writes regarding one hour:

[the patient] gratefully added that he believed his new-found ability related to me, that it has been brought about *not* only by what he had learned from me about himself, but what he had learned from the way in which I would speak to him . . . from the way I would make reconstructions from his past and review situations . . . giving him explanations of his behavior. Indeed [the patient] added, that at certain times when he performed more humanly, more securely, more assertively than ever before, it fleetingly crossed his mind that I would be pleased with him and, barely noticed by him but still acknowledged in passing, that he spoke with a little bit of my voice with my choice of words with my general human attitude. (p. 122)

Kohut continues, "since his communication came at the end of the session I said nothing about it beyond remarking that I too was glad that he was now freer that things were better and that I was glad about it" (p. 122).

I would like now to contrast that intervention with the next intervention Kohut describes in the analysis. In the next session the patient had become quite hostile toward Kohut saying things like "analysts were dogmatic— they force their opinions on the patients—some analysts are sicker than their patients—an analyst about whom he'd read in the newspaper had been psychotic, involved with the law and ultimately put into prison where he died." Kohut writes, "after listening quietly to this tirade for a while, I remarked that this broadside against analysis was in striking contrast to the spirit in which the previous session had been tendered, and I wondered whether there was not some meaningful connection between these two empathic attitudes." Kohut continues: "Specifically, I commented that his attack on me must in some way be connected with the grateful admission that, by identification with me and in anticipating of the pleasure that I would experience from learning about his progress, he had been acting in an increasingly relaxed and mature way."

I offer that by contrasting these two interventions we can see a significant, though not unfamiliar, shift that Kohut is proposing. In response to the positive transference material—the first hour—there is acceptance and acknowledgment of the gratifications to the analyst. In response to the negative transference material—the second hour—Kohut analyses it. I believe that one can develop criticism around this dyad for the nature of the therapeutic transaction Kohut is proposing. I do not see this as a corrective emotional experience, Alexander's influence, and I do not see it as analysis. My second level of criticism is that I see this work as a fostering of positive transference and the analyzing of negative transference toward therapeutic goals. It is essentially a psychotherapy, from my view an interactive analytic psychotherapy, closely tied to Kohut's emphasis, and I feel overemphasis, on the necessity for idealizable imagos. Yet, even this is not my strongest criticism, for I respect, though don't endorse, such interactive analytic therapy.

For my major criticism, let us turn from the specificity of these inter-actions to Kohut's discussion of the nature of therapy itself. As Kohut accurately describes,

> the so-called "defense resistances" are neither defenses nor resistances. Rather they constitute valuable moves to safeguard the self; however weak and defensive it may be against destruction and invasion. It is only when we recognize that the patient has no healthier attitude at his disposal than the one he is in fact taking that we can evaluate the significance of defenses and resistance. (p. 141)

In this, with a slightly different (and I feel improved) emphasis, Kohut epitomizes Freud's extraordinarily important discovery that all symptoms are integrative restitutions. But Kohut continues, "the patient protects the defective self so that *it* will be ready *to grow* again in the future to continue to develop from the point in time at which *his* development had been in-terrupted." Further regarding therapy, Kohut states that the analyst through his empathy recognizes this and "best prepares the soil for the developmental move forward that the stunted *self* of the analysand *actively craves* and such recognition serves the patient better than *anything else* that the analyst can offer" (italics added) (p. 141).

I think in these beautiful phrases one can hear some of the best of Jung's view of the mind's central integrating proclivities, a view of extreme importance, somewhat underplayed in traditional psychoanalysis. Unfor-tunately, Kohut *with* Jung, but fortunately not as far as Jung, goes beyond emphasizing the integrating tendencies to imply a teleological view that the self is moving toward preordained self-integrations, self-validations, and self-realizations of a higher order and inferred higher purpose. I hold that this "vitalism" is closely related to the religious concepts of Divine Plan and Divine Will. It reflects a kind of mystical thought that individual man and mankind, as microcosm of and in concert with the cosmos, is moving toward a higher, preordained order. Jung was to take this concept of self to its ultimate, and, for him, the self was to become *the cosmos*. (I mention this as a reminder that when Jung talks about a superordinant self, he really means superordinant.)

It is my view that a similiar teleological emphasis informs Kohut's thinking revealed in his belief in "the developmental move forward that the *stunted self actively craves*." Further, his statement that this movement is facilitated by the analyst's empathetic attitude, "*better than anything else the analyst can offer*," moves psychoanalysis from a rational-insight orientation to an orientation emphasizing the importance of acceptance by other. Acceptance by other in religious terms is *grace*. Though using a different lexicon, Kohut is saying that through *grace*, the best in man comes to the fore.

Further in these important pages, Kohut sharpens the focus in a masterful way of the difference in orientation that he intends to foster. He talks about the traditional analyst's "attack on resistance." He offers two explanations for this. One is lesser, providing a new, important, and beautifully reasoned explanation, couched in countertransference terms. To quote Kohut,

> the analyst's narcissistic vulnerability, his frustration at seeing his help rejected . . . results in the analyst being narcissistically wounded . . . and enraged which results in our rationalizing our counter-attack in scientific moral or, more strictly, morally tinged scientific terms. (p. 141)

The greater reason, Kohut suggests, is that "we are steeped in a morality tinged theory about the therapeutic centrality of truth-facing." I think in this statement we see most boldly the thrust of his therapeutic endeavor, but I hope not of his theoretical explorations, as he contrasts the difficulties that we encounter because of our "morally tinged scientific model about the need to make the unconscious conscious."

Here I think we are at the apogee of Kohut's departure. I agree with Kohut that there is an overriding value system in psychoanalysis, and that the value system of psychoanalysis amounts to a morality. Yet, I believe the value system of psychoanalysis is a direct extension of, in fact, the consummate result of 18th-century rationalism, and not early 20th-century objectifying scientism as Kohut asserts. The edict "to make the unconscious conscious" or in Kohut's earlier language, to integrate that which theretofore was horizontally and vertically split off, is, I believe, the slogan of this morality. To me it is a direct attack on prerationalistic mystical thought proclaiming that we will attempt to *know* the unknowable. To me psychoanalysis epitomizes the value that it is better to know regardless of the consequences—the essence of rationalism.

Freud parallels Copernicus. Copernicus held a steadfast dedication to man's knowing more about his universe. Copernicus held to the principle that regardless of what it does to man, it is better for him to know that he is but a biological accident on a curiously insignificant satellite, of a minor although auspicious star, in an insignificant galaxy that is an infinitesimal part of an unsizable universe. Copernicus knew that to gain solace by not knowing, to keep the illusion that man was at the center of the universe was, and here we see the commonly disacknowledged crossover between science and morality, morally wrong. Freud, also, held steadfast to the dedication to man's knowing more about himself regardless of the consequences. His aim, like Copernicus's, was not ameliorative. Freud does not attempt to alleviate pain. "The Better is the enemy of the Good," he cautioned. Freud offered knowledge, not cure, even less so, salvation. I feel Jung inadvertently and definitely unintentionally, paid the ultimate compliment to Freud when in his stinging 1933 paper, "Sigmund Freud in His Historical

Setting," states "Freud's theory does not stand for a new way of life." I think we all know unfortunate examples of what happens when psychoanalytic theory, or worse yet, the psychoanalytic process becomes a way of life.

Freud following in the tradition of the great 19th-century pioneers in the social sciences, August Compte in sociology and Wilhelm Wundt in psychology, had the *hubris* to attempt to apply the principles of rationalism to the study of irrationality, itself. *The Interpretation of Dreams*, as an attempt to rationally understand irrationality, in some ways is the consummate monument to rationalism, even though Freud also at times failed to maintain the Spartan rigor demanded by this orientation. In a footnote in Chapter II of *The Interpretation of Dreams*, although in vigorous pursuit of rational understanding of that most ephemeral of mental products, the dream, he falters. Freud writes, "I had a feeling that the interpretation of this part of the dream was not carried far enough to make it possible to follow the whole of its concealed meaning. . . . There is at least one spot in every dream at which it is unplumbable—a navel, as it were, that is its point of contact with the unknown" (p. 111).

Rieff, I feel, accurately prophesied that the tendency of therapeutic endeavors is always toward the ameliorative. There will always be, in Rieff's terms, "a triumph of the therapeutic," the tendency of blissful wish fulfilling experiencing to triumph over painful realization. In Freud's terms, the patient—and I would add the therapist in unwitting collusion—is always tempted to treat himself with transferences. I think Kohut in his therapeutic posture unfortunately succumbs as Reiff predicts. He attempts to move psychoanalysis from a science of knowing to a practice of alleviation, as revealed in the title of his book, *How Does Analysis Cure? Cure*, I hold, is not a psychoanalytic concept. I think we can see this tendency in another of Kohut's beautiful phrasings, "in the self psychological outlook on the psychoanalytic process, the model . . . of resistance to becoming conscious although retained and clearly useful in explaining certain aspects of the psychic process . . . becomes subordinated to the theory of thwarted and remobilized self development responding to the self development-thwarting and self development-enhancing selfobjects" (pp. 141–142). To my mind, Kohut would be truer to psychoanalysis and himself if he were to say, the model . . . of resistance to becoming conscious is an inevitable and yet crucial part of the process of fully *understanding* one's self-development as being thwarted and being remobilized in response to the self-development thwarting and the self-development enhancing self-objects.

The criticism I am lodging is a formidable one: one that essentially says that, in practice, Kohut advocates a kind of psychotherapy rather than a kind of psychoanalysis—a psychotherapy based on acceptance with the implication that through acceptance comes self-fulfillment. I fully realize the importance of the charge and want to reiterate my major view. As yet,

I am not convinced that there is a coordinate relationship between the theoretical ideas that Kohut presents with regard to mental functioning and the way he suggests applying them in therapy. I am not sure, and time will have to tell, whether the therapeutic thrust advocated was idiosyncratic to Kohut's proclivities, particularly as he fully sensed the approaching termination of his physical life, *or* the inevitable therapeutic outcome of the important theoretical changes that he is proposing with regard to the fundaments of mental functioning. We must bear in mind that as great ones approach the end of their lives we frequently see the kind of change in view of mankind that Kohut is proposing. Such a change in view may be a manifestation of the wisdom that comes with the relinquishment of various narcissistic positions as the true finiteness of life is realized. Yet, such views may also be a part of the mourning of the loss of the self.

As I have stated, although Kohut's therapeutic position seems antithetical to what I hold, I'm not inclined to discard it because it comes from a panoptic mind. In fact we may eventually have to acknowledge that, as Kohut implies, the essential power of psychoanalysis is in the experiencing of idealizable imagos as they are endowed with meanings and become a complex manifestation of that important endopsychic stabilizer, neutralizer, protector, and director, the selfobject. I think, however, careful scrutiny will reveal that this describes God, only in a different lexicon. I hold that when the analyst allows himself to be reacted to as an experience as an end, rather than attempting to understand the connotations of such reacting in terms of developmental necessity, such use of the transference is alleviation through faith. I feel we can offer a great deal more.

I am pleased to have been asked to provide a commentary on this chapter. There is much in it that is new, much in it that helps us better understand what we do, and much in it that is controversial. In short, it is the work of a brilliant mind.

I knew Kohut only somewhat, but well enough to be sure that he would have valued these criticisms because he would have sensed that they arise out of a genuine, though struggling, attempt to understand his ideas.

REFERENCES

Freud, S. (1900). The interpretation of dreams. *Standard Edition*, 4:1–338.
Jung, C. G. (1966). *Collected Works of C. G. Jung* (Vol. 15). Princeton: Princeton University Press.
Rieff, P. (1968). *The Triumph of the Therapeutic*. New York: Harper & Row.

CLINICAL PAPERS

11

Idealizing Transference: Disruptions and Repairs

JOHN M. HALL

PLAN

My overall strategy in this chapter is to give a brief history of Ms. A, then summarize certain phases of the analysis to set the stage for exploring a number of detailed vignettes, hour by hour, that will demonstrate the "disruptions and repairs of the idealizing transference." I've chosen vignettes from the early, middle, and termination phases of analysis. Tracking these vignettes, these way stations, over the course of the analysis will, I believe, demonstrate the patient's increasing tolerance for disruptions in the transference as well as her growing capacity to explore such disruptions. Concomitant with this analytic growth, the gradual transmuting internalization of selfobject functions can be seen leading to structure building and, ultimately, to a successful termination phase of the analysis.

OVERVIEW OF ANALYSIS

Ms. A's analysis lasted about 2 years and 9 months and entailed 430 analytic hours. Despite the relative briefness of time, I believe the analysis was completed—at least in terms of what was essential for the patient. That is, I believe a pathognomonic regression was reached with this patient and to a large extent worked through. Specifically, an idealized selfobject transference emerged, and the major aspects in this childhood constellation entered into the analysis. To a lesser extent, transference reactions (mirroring) reflective of earlier stages of development as well as those involving multiple maternal caretakers including the patient's deeply disturbed paternal grandmother also emerged but, unlike the idealized selfobject transference, were not as consistently or systematically worked through. What follows is an elaboration of this brief summary statement.

DESCRIPTION OF MS. A

Ms. A is an attractive woman—tall, slender, blonde, with large haunting eyes and a model's features. She was 26 years old when she started analysis. She appeared extremely bright and articulate. She was in law school at the time and already on the staff of the Law Review. As an undergraduate she had excelled in mathematics. As a graduate student she had excelled in philosophy. Ms. A seemed to be one of those rare individuals who could have done well in almost any intellectual pursuit. She idealized the "true" scientist and the "truly" rational man. In this regard Hartmann's (1956, p. 257) dualistic thinking about reality comes to mind. He felt that "socialized reality" is validated by "intersubjective acceptance," and "objective reality" (whatever that is) is validated by the normal criteria of science and logic. It was as if, given the patient's early childhood experiences (which we will get to soon), she had a hypertrophied, compensatory need for this kind of reality—defined by scientific principles. She saw her husband as a brilliant rational, logical man though not only that. She saw her lover as a brilliant scientist though not only that. A number of her early repetitive questions and comments regarding psychoanalysis come to mind such as: "At least can I interest you as a scientist?" "Can you prove psychoanalysis is scientifically valid?" Or "Why did you go into this field of medicine? Because you are not a scientist?" Or "If it weren't for how my dreams fall into place, I would see nothing scientific about analysis. Without the dreams there would not be a smathering of logic to this insane process." Perhaps it was "fortuitous" that Ms. A was a prolific dreamer.

For a long time she almost always wore black or dark clothes—clothes that also seemed out of fashion in some ill-defined way. Gradually, almost imperceptibly, this changed.

There was an uninhibited, un-self-conscious childlike quality about her posturing on the couch. If she were angry, she would punch the couch. If she were happy or joyous, she would clap her hands together and bounce on the couch. During the early hours she often looked back. Occasionally she would get up in the middle of an hour and make a dash to the restroom because of diarrhea or the urge to vomit.

There were seldom long silences. She worked very hard in analysis, and for a long time I felt I had little margin of error in terms of my interventions. I was either on target or disruptively off the mark.

SUMMARY OF THE CASE

Ms. A presented with chronic feelings of worthlessness. She also described a persistent sense of not feeling safe most all of her life; to her the world was a dangerous place. She had always excelled academically, but that had never relieved these all pervasive feelings. She approached each examination, each presentation, and each class (particularly those law school classes in which being called on was infamous) with tremendous fear. Failure would be a devastating blow. Getting A's was a life and death situation. In so many ways, Ms. A essentially said: "I have no other way to feel good about myself." Yet after any success (and there were many) she would experience a quick letdown with little sense of accomplishment or sustained good feelings.

Since the age of 3, the patient had had periodic bouts of nausea and vomiting. In early childhood, these symptoms were sufficiently severe to necessitate hospitalization on one or two occasions. Since adolescence she had had bouts of diarrhea (occasionally bloody) and "night sweats" during stressful times. Ms. A also described vague somatic theories to account for her symptomatology and had a strong belief in the use of self-hypnosis to ease stress and prevent and cure illness.

At the time of the initial interviews, Ms. A was deeply disturbed by her relationship with her husband. When first married she saw him as a good, kind genius of a man—a young lawyer full of brilliance and drive who was yet humble. Now she felt he had changed into an arrogant, controlling, suspicious man still brilliant but ineffectual, unable to complete tasks. She was often enraged with him and yet also felt overwhelmingly responsible for his downfall. "I convinced him he was a genius, and that destroyed him." For a year prior to the start of her analysis Ms. A had had no sexual involvement or interest in her husband. She also described him as intensely and chronically jealous. By her description, he seemed to be quite paranoid.

Ms. A had also been involved in an affair with a former professor, Guy, for the past 2 years. She described a frequent, tremendous longing for the great sense of security and soothing she felt when near him. "I always feel alive and confident in his presence and maybe for the first time in my life." The sexual involvement in this relationship was somewhat satisfactory to the patient (she was usually orgasmic) but clearly of secondary importance. During the initial interviews and subsequently, she never expressed the need to see him because of sexual desire or wanting mutual love. Her longing for him seemed to be based on a frantic need to feel safe and alive.

When the patient was 1 year old, her mother returned to her career, and as a consequence Ms. A spent a great deal of time with her maternal grandmother. Early memories about her maternal grandparents are warm and pleasant. When the patient was three, her parents moved to another neighboring town, and Ms. A spent her days with her father's mother whom she described as aloof, cold, scary, and odd. The time spent with this woman was bleak and depriving. Most likely Ms. A's grandmother was covertly psychotic. During an early hour, I was detained by an emergency in a nearby hospital, Ms. A could not get into the waiting room. The door was locked. It was a Saturday morning, and the corridors were deserted. She experienced a tremendous relief when she finally saw me coming. That night she remembers with vividness something she had forgotten for years. This grandmother once locked her in a closet because she didn't want to take her shopping in the rain; Ms. A had felt alone, trapped, and terrified. Ms. A added, "I couldn't wait to start school to get away from her. No school phobias for me!"

Ms. A has always felt she had a warm, extremely close relationship with her father until she was 5 years old. They were "pals," and they sang together and played lots of games. She greatly preferred being with him to being with her mother. If she got sick at night, which was frequent, he would hold her and comfort her for hours. Ms. A felt her mother was distant. "It was as if she didn't know what to do; being a mother overwhelmed her, frightened her." When Ms. A was in emotional turmoil, she experienced her mother as prone to panic. She also felt her mother did not like to hold her. Because of her bouts of nausea and vomiting in early childhood Ms. A saw quite a number of physicians. In their presence she would feel safe and protected. "They were like gods to me." However, during her early 20s she went through a whole "slew" of doctors because of her gastrointestinal symptoms and came to see "all the mistakes doctors make" and began to distrust them. "Doctors are as mortal as anyone else, only more so."

A few months before the birth of her brother, when Ms. A was 6, her father became psychotic. He was delusionally convinced a woman acquaintance in a nearby town was in love with him. He was subsequently hospitalized and given a diagnosis of paranoid schizophrenia. During her father's decline prior to his hospitalization, Ms. A recalled going with him to meet his "girlfriend." She was not to tell her mother but inadvertently did so. He raved at her, accused her of betraying him, and stormed out of the house; the patient was shattered. On the day her father was hospitalized Ms. A sat on his lap screaming: "You're not sick! You're not sick!" He said little, held her tight, and wept.

Ms. A feels the man who returned to her from the hospital was totally different from her "old father" and never to be the same. He had a number of exacerbations of his illness and a number of further hospitalizations throughout the patient's childhood.

Also throughout the rest of Ms. A's childhood, he spent many hours watching TV. He developed a chronic delusion that as he watched TV, he was on TV, the star of some local show. This went on for years. At times the patient felt that only she saw how sick her father was; everyone else minimized it. At other times Ms. A blamed the world for being intentionally cruel and causing her father's pain. He was often frightening and unpredictable. All during her childhood she had hopes he'd be restored to her. These hopes blended with her own wishes to rescue him and her own sense of omnipotent responsibility for what happened in the family. The patient's mother worked hard, and the patient shouldered many responsibilities for raising her brother. Gradually her relationship with her mother improved.

Excelling in school became extremely important to Ms. A. She idealized her grade school teachers and formed intense positive relationships with them. Yet she always felt uncomfortable with peers as if she were an outcast. Often she had wondered if she every really had any authentic friends. She spent long hours alone playing school. She would teach herself, give herself assignments, and then do them. She repeated this sequence over and over again. During his more stable times, the patient's father would encourage her to learn, become successful, and not make the same mistakes he did. According to family legend he could have become a successful business man before the onslaught of his psychosis if only he would have joined a new company that had offered him a unique opportunity, but he would not. The patient, in the telling, added: "That's crazy, I would have gone ahead and taken a chance like that for advancement."

One of the high points of Ms. A's adolescence was becoming a cheer-leader. She also felt somewhat more popular and at ease with friends during high school and college. Ms. A recalled one incident in which she was just talking to some boys, enjoying herself for once. Then she turned around, and her father was staring at her. Later he gave her the "third degree." She went on to say: "To him to try and look pretty was a sin and he often—no, always!—assumed the worse."

Ms. A felt she adjusted well to college despite a long siege of home-sickness. Yet she continued to have episodes of vomiting and diarrhea, and she often took her exams while she was a patient in the infirmary. Never-theless, she graduated summa cum laude and went on to graduate school. She soon met Fred, her husband to be, and after a "whirlwind" courtship of a few months they were married. After receiving her master's degree and with Fred's encouragement, Ms. A entered law school. In retrospect Ms. A felt she married him because he was brilliant, seemed to offer security and safeness, and accepted her despite all her hidden flaws. The marriage was troubled almost from the beginning.

In summary, Ms. A presented for treatment with four major areas of concern: (1) a sense of worthlessness all her life coupled with a persistent sense of not feeling safe, (2) bouts of nausea and vomiting since childhood, bouts of diarrhea since adolescence (she related these somatic symptoms not only to times of stress but also—and I have not stressed this side of it—to times of success and "happy" times, such as holidays), (3) a troubled relationship with her husband, and (4) a wonderful, but conflicted affair with a former professor. She described feeling soothed, secure, and alive only when she was with him. She wanted to end the relationship, yet at the same time saw herself as so deprived so much of her life that she felt entitled, indeed desperate, for any comfort she could get.

Of Ms. A's four areas of concern, the last two were probably the most pressing. That is, her current experience of these two central figures in her life—her husband and Guy—were her main motivation for treatment. Initially in her treatment she greatly denied her husband's profound psychopathology and psychotic deterioration, which was the proverbial repetition of her childhood experience of her father. On the other hand, Ms. A's involvement with Guy, her idealization of him, and her sense of unique safety in his presence contributed to her awareness on some level that there was something missing within herself, some deficit, some function she could not provide for herself. I believe she also had some awareness that the relationship with this older married man was doomed. In a way the constellation of feelings involving these two figures can also be seen, retrospectively, as the harbingers of the two sides of the transference—"the dread to repeat and the hope for a new beginning" (Ornstein, 1974, p. 231) that would eventually be systematically mobilized in depth and worked through in her analysis.

EARLY HOURS

Heralded by two terrifying dreams about her father the analysis began. In the first dream she is in a movie theater, sitting with children on either side of her. She sees her father three rows ahead of her, staring at her; she is terrified. The scene changes, she's walking in front of the old medical school (my office is in the "new" medical school). Her husband asks her what has happened. She replies, "I saw my father and am upset." In the second dream, Ms. A is in the house she grew up in. Her father has returned home. He had been drinking. He comes in through the front door (usually he used the back door). Ms. A is with her mother in the kitchen. Her father is looking for an argument. He has a knife (which looks like one Ms. A currently has in her own kitchen). Ms. A turns to her mother and says, "We'd better leave." Again, she felt terrified.

These dreams quite clearly reflected the patient's anxiety about starting her analysis—the fear of repetition, the fear of regression. Less obviously (and really only in retrospect) there are also hints in these dreams indicating the patient's concern about her husband's psychotic deterioration (her running into him in the first dream, the kitchen knife from their current apartment in the second), or maybe I'm reading too much into these dreams. Be that as it may, at the time the analysis began I was not fully aware of the extent of Ms. A's husband's psychopathology.

At the time, the early analytic hours with this patient seemed stormy. Looking back they seem less so. The reason for this shift in my view is probably related to the simple fact that in looking back now I know where we were heading then. Nevertheless I'll try to resurrect the flavor of these early hours along with my early approaches to interventions before we delve into the first vignette. In doing this, I would again like to stress Ms. A's uninhibited, un-self-conscious posture on the couch, which from early on in the analysis I took as a positive sign of trust despite her rage and her suspiciousness of me. Also from the beginning I was struck by Ms. A's childlike enthusiasm that fired her creative intellectual pursuits and ultimately her analysis.

As the patient related these first dreams (particularly the one in which her father had been staring at her), she looked back at me. This "looking back" behavior continued for a number of sessions. She tended to look back: (1) when she was frightened by a strong feeling or memory, (2) when talking directly or indirectly about her father's psychosis (*his* "paranoid" staring at her), and (3) when I spoke, with an apparent need to have visual cues at such times. Often she would jokingly say, "Just checking to see if you're still there."

A propos of the intense anxiety of her first dreams and of her childhood memory (in which she was both teacher and student, giving herself assignments and then doing them), it wasn't long (fifth session) before the patient brought a notebook to the sessions and began a "do-it-yourself" analysis (the notebook contained a year-by-year recollection of her childhood that she had just begun to write). In this way she titrated her regression. Needless to say the previous session had been a difficult one, which I'll briefly summarize. Ms. A had begun that session by saying, "Already the therapy is affecting me. I was depressed, and I vomited all weekend." She couldn't seem to find a comfortable position on the couch and restlessly tossed and turned. At one point she exclaimed, "You're on the periphery; I'm doing this myself." At another point (after a brief silence, but a long one for Ms. A) she said, "Please just say something. Aren't you allowed to? Are you still back there?" She looked back frequently. She began prefacing what she said by the comments, "Do you remember my telling you this before?" She tearfully recalled playing "mumbo-jumbo man" with her father (their special hide-and-seek game). After his return from the hospital (his treatment included ECT), he didn't even remember it. She added, "All my life I've wanted a new dad." I connected the recollection of playing "mumbo-jumbo man" with her wondering about my remembering things she had told me, and I "tactfully" explored her looking back at me. Both interventions were of limited value and did not fully address her overwhelming anxiety and the spill over of feelings between sessions. Thus, in my looking back, it is no surprise that she brought in her notebook the very next session with the comment, "There will be no more silences now!" She added, "Analysis is voodoo [mumbo jumbo?] and not scientific anyway."

As the hours continued, so did Ms. A's fear of regression. Irrational thoughts (free association or magical kinds of thinking) brought up an intense worry on the patient's part that she might become schizophrenic. I now think this concern, as troubling as it was for the patient, was the more superficial layer of a deeper dread. That is, beneath this manifest concern was the primordial, unnameable fear of faulty mirroring of infantile grandiose-exhibitionistic urges. She also, in various ways, expressed somewhat analogous concerns about my stability. On overhearing a "joking" comment I made to a colleague, the patient began a tirade about all the "crazy" psychiatrists she knew, how they were unpredictable and unreliable. Also, Ms. A would become bothered if it seemed I had a cold or looked "depressed." Essentially her concern was I'd go "crazy" or "crumble" like her father. At other times, as an attempt to cover up her sense of helplessness, she saw herself as a powerful seducer of men and feared her own powers of destructiveness with a vivid conviction. She had destroyed her husband. Maybe she had had an effect on her father. All men sooner or later, with the exception of Guy, fell off the pedestals she had put them on. The implications were clear and so was the resistance to the transference.

As an analysand Ms. A was an excellent teacher. That is, if she felt one of my interventions was off the mark she made no bones about it. If an intervention was on target, often a piece of resistance was cleared away, temporarily, and the analytic material deepened. We both worked hard. It was hard to keep up with her vacillating feeling states. Often, early on, I tended to respond too quickly to her angry challenges and likewise interrupt the flow of her positive feeling. Nor did I, at the time, fully appreciate the extent of her fear of being empathized with and her, in fact, attacking the very thing she longed for so much (Schafer, 1979). It seemed that if her yearnings and resistance to such yearnings were truly understood, the dam would burst, and we'd both be swept away by her needs. Nevertheless, despite my feeling at times that we were on an analytic roller coaster, she experienced me as calm, as trying to understand her at least, and, with some analytic stamina, the analytic work proceeded.

Her dreams about her father continued. In one dream, Ms. A is at a party having a friendly talk with a psychiatrist she knows. She lies down on a couch and he covers her up. Her father walks in. To her surprise he and the psychiatrist exchange warm greetings. She is terrified about being discovered. In essence, I think this dream reflects the patient's need to cover up her warm, positive feelings being mobilized in the transference lest she again be traumatized as she was with her father. In another dream, she is having sex with a man. At first she thought it was her husband, then her lover Guy, then she realized it was her father and woke up in panic and in disgust. Her associations led to the previous session when she had said emphatically, "I'm not going to fall in love with you like I'm supposed to. I'm sorry if that messes up your project." Again without going into further detail, I believe this dream reflects, in a blatantly sexualized way, the patient's dread of repetition. That is, if she brings her yearnings into the analytic situation she could once again reexperience the chaos surrounding her father and his psychotic deterioration.

Nevertheless, gradually, almost imperceptibly, the idealizing transference intensified. In one session Ms. A, commented, "My husband has
to be a hero again before I can ever have sex with him." In the next session
she joked, "You know if you could be a star like Robert Redford I could
fall in love with you like I'm supposed to." I need only say that for Ms.
A, given her self-experience of the world around her, heroes have a precarious
existence; they topple. Likewise for herself the stardoms of everyday life
(the A's on tests, the successful presentations, and so forth) were never
sustained and often brought with them vomiting and diarrhea.

An extraanalytic event occurred that seemed to accentuate the mobilization of the transference. Ms. A's father wanted to see her. She had not
seen him in years. The patient feared she would say something that would
cause him to commit suicide or else he was maybe thinking of killing her
on of all days, Father's Day. She was very frightened. She also felt I had
understood the particular depths of her feelings. After her visit with her
father, she felt great, "30 thousand pounds lighter." She had suddenly taken
up painting as a "hobby" and brought in her work for me to see. One was
a figure in black (as I mentioned earlier the patient often wore black) with
the sun bursting down upon it. Another was an explosion of colors that
appeared to jump off the canvas. She commented, "All my life I've tried
to make art look real, but these paintings are more carefree, expressive,
spontaneous!" At the end of the session she added, "I told my father the
truth, and he didn't destroy himself. Of course I'd still be afraid if I opened
this door, and he was there." This last comment of the patient's indicates
both her hope and dread as well as some significant analytic movement. At
least her father was in the waiting room! Furthermore I believe Ms. A
started painting at this critical time in an attempt to contain her overwhelming,
hopeful excitement.

Over the next few sessions, Ms. A's curiosity about me increased. "I'd
like to observe you without you knowing it." She described "little" feelings
she had that I was different, unlike other psychiatrists she had briefly seen.
In some ways I was like a "Rock of Gibraltar." It became harder for her
to leave at the end of the sessions, and she would give me long, lingering
looks as she left. At one point she sighed, "Lying here is like confessing
to God, like He's looking down on me, and I'm lying here in heaven with
clouds all around. I'll be sentenced to heaven or hell. I want you to understand
me, feel how I feel. Sometimes I wonder if you're maybe laughing at me.
It's like I'm a rat in a maze. You could help—take away some of the maze
blockers but you don't. You want me to do it. You wait knowing somehow
I'll get through it at the end—playing the maze. . . . Oh! I just remembered
a dream. I was on the lawn playing Monopoly by myself, and a man comes
up behind me. He points a gun at me and says, 'Give me your Monopoly
game.' I say to him, 'Can't you wait a little while?' And then I say, 'Let's
play the game together!' "

Given her association to the maze and her early use of her notebook in a "do-it-yourself" analysis, the implications to this dream seemed clear. I commented, "What if I'm the man in the dream?" She got enthusiastic: "That fits. I'm scared, but I do want your help. We'll do the maze together!"

Perhaps I've lingered too long over this early phase of the analysis. My goals in doing so were twofold: (1) to muster sufficient, convincing evidence for the kind of transference that was developing and (2) to demonstrate the resistance to this transference. That is, the idealizing transference was what was being resisted and the idealization itself was not a resistance.

VIGNETTE 1

There had been a blank wall at the foot of the couch, and I finally got around to putting a picture there (a tree with the sun behind it). The first time Ms. A saw the picture she formed a remarkable attachment to it (she loved it), and during the next 30 hours or so she made frequent references to it.

In that first session in the *presence* of the picture (and it had that quality) she began by saying Guy was going on vacation. She started to cry; she wondered if he would come back. In his presence, she felt good and loved him. Not in his presence, she felt bad and didn't even feel her love for him. "Seeing him is like getting a new battery; I feel energized— for a little while anyway." She added, "Nothing is going to change. Maybe I drive him away. He says, kind of joking and kind of not, that I will be the first woman Supreme Court Justice, that I'm a star. [Obviously, Ms. A's analysis took place some time before the appointment of Sandra Day O'Connor to the Supreme Court.] When I'm around him, I feel like one. My father wanted to be a star. To be a star will be doom. To even think of being one gives me a shuddering feeling." The patient became more tearful and added, "Sometimes when I cry at home, I wish you could be there. A long, long, time ago, before my father got sick, he could comfort me."

There was silence, and I commented: "And there must have been so many times you wanted that old comfort, and he wasn't there for you anymore and you felt alone, helpless with your feelings, bewildered by all the changes in your father." Ms. A burst into tears and then shook her head, "I don't perceive being helpless, I don't; I have an effect on others, an impact." She became silent again. Then suddenly she wanted me to repeat everything I had just said. I asked her what her thoughts were about that. She said my voice was so soothing, especially when I was talking about her, really talking about her. In the silence she had had the image of leaning against her father, crying on his shoulder, right before he went into the hospital. She saw his shirt vividly; it had a black, red, green, and yellow pattern. She added, "I did feel helpless; I do feel helpless. Your voice being soothing allowed me to experience all these feelings." As she left, she added, "I don't want to leave today. The painting is beautiful; I wish I could paint like that."

In the next session, Ms. A began by ostensibly talking about a new friend; she wanted to give up her isolation—she was tired of being alone. She went on, "With the picture here I feel less alien. I feel I'm accomplishing something here. I want to come and cry here. Sometimes I imagine there is a dark badness in the tree there, and it leeches out to all the branches. That's me. We've got to get the badness out." Later she talked about the fantasy of coming back as a bird in her next life, having a nest—maybe in a tree like that (pointing to the picture), and being taken care of—always— by someone who loves birds like she does. I wondered if she didn't have a "safe nest" feeling here sometimes and yet that thought could be frightening. She responded, "Yes, I feel safe from the world here but not from you. You're interested in my form, what follows what. I'm interested in content. I don't want you to like me as a person. I want to trust you, depend on you—yet I'm afraid. Once I trust people and like them, I start acting different. It's scary. I distort things. I want you to appreciate me." I then said, "Earlier you talked about accomplishing something here. You want very much for me to understand those feelings." She replied that that was exactly right. She added: "You know occasionally I feel special in a good way. The picture frees me up. I say to myself 'Oh boy, I can go and look at that picture.' I could look at it for hours. I feel attached to this room."

In the following session, Ms. A came in distraught. She and her husband had had a terrible fight about analysis and money. The patient described telling him about her enthusiasm for analysis. He tore analysis apart in a scientific, logical way and ranted and raved about her "attachment" to me. The patient added, "I can't survive such abuse. I just want to die. I told Fred if I don't get away from him I'm going to kill him." Her rage quickly accelerated and spread. "I have more thoughts but what's the use of saying them. I want no more pain if I have to withdraw from *all* people!" She turned to the picture, imagined the sun was a retina and the tree limbs were vessels, stared at it, and desperately attempted to go into a self-hypnotic trance on the spot. She stopped and said, "I'm in pain." I commented on the intensity of her feelings and how she turned to the picture because she felt I was not providing the soothing she needed. She agreed. It was the end of the hour. She gave me a long look and left.

In the next session, and the last one of this vignette, she began by saying, "How can I put my life in your hands? I was very disappointed last time. I'm stressing myself for nothing. I needed something from you last time. I feel bad. I have trouble seeing this analysis does any good. I need evidence to show my husband." I commented that she saw me as not being here for her last time. She laughed, "That's it. I try to keep an open mind. Freud was a great scientist, but I believe analysis has been bastardized. Analysis is like being thrown in a cell to feel worse. If all this is to make me be dependent on you, I'll choose to go stark raving mad first. You're like all the rest [other psychiatrists the patient had briefly seen]. I'm tired of making excuses for you. You're like Richard Nixon. You don't defend yourself—the accusations are right. You should give me straight, honest answers or scientific proof. Are you an analyst because you're not good at anything else? Are you in it for money? I tell you things I've never told anyone, and yesterday you couldn't think of anything to say to help me. Jesus! I'd feel better talking to the snowflakes. [It had been snowing a lot lately.] I'm hurting. I want support, the magic of words. I want you to be a. . . . " The patient stopped and I asked what she was going to say. She continued, "I want you to be a star. I didn't want to say it. Yesterday you weren't being your creative self. I can't take that. I want so hard to think you're good."

At this point not wanting to repeat yesterday's performance, I intervened, "Earlier in the week your feelings about the analysis and me were quite different. Yesterday you felt I failed you miserably. That was devastating. I struck out. So many times you've felt the stars you need to have hope in, crumble. Now, right here it feels like it's happening all over again." She remained quiet for a while and added, "There's something else too. I was bothered all right by you not saying enough yesterday. I *was* hurting. But I was bothered, I was bothered. How important are you to me that your failing could wreak such havoc?"

The patient's rage settled even more quickly than it had come.

VIGNETTE 2

This sequence of hours occurred about a month later. Throughout this time the new picture in the office had continued to be very important for Ms. A. In the first session of this vignette, she began by saying it was fun to see me in the elevator. In the few prior extraanalytic encounters she had felt uncomfortable. This time she described it as getting a few extra minutes. She then switched to describing an interaction with Guy. She needed to be cuddled but it wasn't allowed. Guy was busy. She went on, "I felt desperate when I left here last time." I responded, "Perhaps you wanted to stay longer, you were feeling safe here." She nodded her head yes and started crying: "I love that picture. I feel better—warm and safe when I'm near it. I wish I could take it with me. I'm painting one just like it."

In the next session, the patient began by saying she woke up sick in the morning with diarrhea and vomiting. She induced a self-hypnotic trance to make the pain go away. While doing this, she recalled a dream. She hesitated, "It's hard to tell you this. You were in the dream, standing straight. You called my name and told me something important. You were against a cream colored wall like this [she pounds the wall]. There was nothing else. You wore a beige suit—maybe the one you had on yesterday." She described feeling hopeless and having pain because of the diarrhea. Yet she appeared very peaceful, calm. She turned on her side and cuddled up on the couch. There was a hint of a smile on her face. She went on to say that the analysis was making her feel worse. She wondered if she were regressing. "After all, I've started to enjoy 'Sesame Street' on television." She added, "I'm depressed after I leave here, like I don't want to live but the feeling doesn't last. I get up from the couch and feel dizzy. You said something a while back that has made me feel my father's illness was not my fault. . . . You know, the color of your suit was a lot like that picture." At that point I did not wait any longer and commented, "In the dream, I'm against the wall like that picture is . . . I wonder if your good feelings toward the picture aren't a reflection of your feelings about me, about being here with me." She, very quietly, said yes and then drifted off to other topics—her hopes of being rescued by Guy—or if she broke up with Guy would there be someone else?

In the next session, the patient was very excited. Sne described badly burning her hands while cooking. She went in vivid details. She described how she healed herself with self-hypnosis by focusing all her mental forces on the wounds. She added, "The mind is very powerful; I have no burn marks at all. It's amazing." It was very clear she wanted some response from me. I think I said something like: "It's important to you—the idea of the mind being powerful." The content of what I said was certainly mediocre, but what upset her more, I believe, was the perfunctory tone to my voice. My initial reaction to this material, and I can still recall it, was irritation. It seemed childish, magical and especially so in a gifted law student with an unusually sophisticated background in logic and science. Maybe she had called analysis voodoo too many times, or I had not tended to my analytic toilet enough—to use Glover's (1955) words. At any rate, I did not appreciate her enthusiasm or the extent of her regression at the time or her immediate need to feel powerful, in control. And we were off to the races.

She responded: "Just when I start trusting you, you lapse into dogma. You didn't even want to look at my hands. I thought I could get some response from you or at least appeal to some vestige of scientific curiosity in you—if you still have any. Maybe lousy physicians become psychiatrists, and lousy psychiatrists become analysts with dogma." She looked back showing her hands to me. She had also brought in a newspaper article about the effects of self-hypnosis. She repeated, "Every time I start to trust you, you disappoint me." I responded, "It seems when you feel that trust, that feeling I'm understanding who you are—then you're able to reveal your dreams, your hopes, your sadness, but then to feel that trust disappear right when you're in such a process is devastating—like the rug being pulled out from under you." The clouds of rage quickly settled. The patient said two things: (1) "That's exactly right," and (2) "The picture is sometimes safer than you are, you know."

As a postscript to this vignette, the patient brought to the very next session her painting, her rendition of the new picture in the office. I don't think she really painted much after that. Her talents lie in other directions. Anyway, her references to the picture became less and less frequent and finally stopped. In terms of her analysis the picture's significance just passed, and I don't think either one of us noted its passing. Somewhat analogous to Winnicott's (1953) description of the transitional object, the picture had filled its function for awhile and was no longer needed. I'll briefly add one other thing: during these hours in which the picture was such a focus, Ms. A did make reference to her actual transitional object on a number of occasions. It was a one of those "old-fashioned" Teddy Bears. She called it "Teddy Pops."

A few sessions after this last vignette, Ms. A had still another dream about her father. She described it as her "rat dream," her "Irma dream," and one of the most important central dreams of her life. The night before this dream, Ms. A had been sorting through some papers. She came across an old research project involving rats and mazes that she had assisted on as an undergraduate. Musing on this and other "projects," she contemplated all the possible career directions she could have taken, all the roads she could have traveled. That night she dreamed she was back in the house where she grew up. She was the age she was now but her mother, father, and brother were all younger. The way they would have been back then. A storm was brewing. She was in the basement. Suddenly a gust of wind blew her law papers around. She saw cracks in the foundation and worried about the house not holding up in the storm. The rat cages from her old research project were there but empty. Her mother had accidentally, thoughtlessly, let them out of their cages. Suddenly she saw the rats. They were all mixed up with each other, and then they got mixed up with wild rats. The rats were everywhere. There was no way she could ever sort them back into their right cages. Her "Nobel prize" experiment was ruined. She raged at her absent mother. Then her father came along and soothed her. He understood how the rats were part of her "Nobel prize" experiment and how important all that was to her. After telling the dream, Ms. A exclaimed: "That's the first dream—*ever*—that I wasn't afraid of him!"

There are two aspects of the dream I'd like to address at this time. First, I feel it is very representative of this patient's self-state dreams. The vermin, the rats in the dream, and the cracks in the foundation are an attempt to give circumscribed content to the unnameable dread of the crumbling of the self (Kohut, 1977, p. 105). In retrospect, I feel the dream reflects both Ms. A's experience of her mother's failing as a mirroring selfobject as well as a turning to her idealized father for soothing. With his psychotic deterioration she experienced him as failing as well. What follows then in Ms. A's analysis can be conceptualized as a returning vis-à-vis then transference to the selfobject/analyst—a recreation in the sense Loewald (1971) uses the term. Secondly, I bring this dream up now as a parenthesis (certainly not the last one) to her first couch dreams in which she was so terrified of her father. It's purely arbitrary on my part, but I've always seen this particular dream in this case as the end of the beginning.

ANALYSIS OF A *FOLIE À DEUX*

At this point I'd like to discuss the title of this chapter. It is odd to do this right in the middle of things; but I have been holding back reservations about the title. Disruption and repairs of an idealizing transference are really "old hat." Such a process is inherent in Kohut's (1971, 1977) conceptualizations of the various selfobject transferences. That is, *the very key* to the working through of these transferences lies in their inadvertent disruptions. When the disruptions and repairs entail optimal frustration, there is an opportunity for transmuting internalizations of selfobject functions to take place. Indeed, if there were no disruptions of the transference (an inconceivability!), there would be no transformation of the early claims for merging and mirroring into more mature forms of narcissism. In the case of Ms. A, the disruption manifested in the first vignette was beyond optimal; there was a significant fragmentation. Perhaps the second vignette is more reflective of optimal frustration. That is a hard call to make. My main point, however, is that this process of disruption and repair is ubiquitous, happening over and over again in any analysis; and, as I said, it is "old hat." So with that in mind, I offer an alternative title for this part of the presentation: "The Analysis of a *Folie à Deux*." It is still "old hat," but it is, I believe, an old hat trying on a new feather.

As an aside, Gralnick (1942) felt that in the model of a *folie à deux* lies the clue to mental illness. I don't know about that, but I do think it would be interesting to explore a *folie à deux* that develops *de novo* in an analysis and then is resolved. In particular, Ms. A developed a *folie à deux* with her psychotic husband that waxed and waned in tandem to the transference through a number of months of her analysis. That is, when there was a disruption in the transference, the *folie à deux* appeared. When the transference was reestablished, the *folie à deux* dropped out of the material. Needless to say, when this development occurred in the analysis, I had my moments of doubt.

To return to the case, as the mobilization of the idealizing transference continued, Ms. A began using Guy, more and more, as a "safety valve." (This was her term.) Often after analytic sessions she would go to his office to be cuddled, soothed, comforted, to feel safe. Her idealization of him intensified. The analysis, itself, was progressing. It seemed that there was a tremendous fear on the patient's part that she would be retraumatized if she brought into the analysis all the longings and narcissistic needs that were emerging. Thus a certain equilibrium was more or less reached. With Ms. A rapidly shifting these feelings back and forth from myself to Guy, as an auxiliary transference figure, and occasionally back to her husband, Fred. Indeed, it was hard not to look at this phase of the analysis as an analytic shell game.

Almost simultaneously (9 months into the analysis) two events occurred, however, that, along with Ms. A's deepening regression, changed this "transference equilibrium": Guy left town to take a new position and, more or less, broke off the affair and Ms. A's husband became increasingly psychotic. After being fired from two prestigious law firms, he had become convinced there was a conspiracy against him, in general, because of his innovative ideas and, in particular, because of what he knew about an important legal case that was pending. The conspirators were either going to kill him or else discredit him by making him look crazy. Furthermore, he felt I, being his wife's analyst, was probably one of them and her continuing in treatment meant information about him was being leaked to the conspirators. She, in effect, was betraying him.

As I have mentioned before, Ms. A's husband had probably been psychotic for a year or two, and this was the most recent exacerbation of his illness. The patient had been denying her husband's illness and would continue to do so for quite awhile longer. However, it was becoming more and more evident that one of the patient's main motivations for treatment was the psychotic deterioration of her husband that in effect was the repetition of her childhood experience of her father. After Guy's departure, Ms. A saw her husband once more as the idealized genius she felt so lucky to marry. Again he became the most brilliant person she knew or would ever know. Ms. A, with varying intensities, believed his delusions and at times elaborated on them. On occasion she would become suspicious of Guy and connect his departure from town with the conspiracy. Of course, her suspicions fell on me as well. At the very best I was being duped by the conspirators. At the very worst I was a malicious participant. Despite this inner turmoil, Ms. A continued to function well at school and with friends. Also, and most importantly, the *folie à deux* was only apparent when there were disruptions in the transference.

VIGNETTE 3

The week Guy ended their relationship Ms. A presented the following dream: "I was by an empty concrete reservoir and set some important books and law papers down on the edge. I went into a house and came back. All this water suddenly rushed into the reservoir, and my books were swept away. I tried to get them but fell into the water. I almost drowned but finally retrieved my books. People took me into the house to get warm. George, who is kind of a friend, put his arm around me and asked if I were feeling better. I said I was, and then he started to kiss me. But I told him not to. I was still recovering." Associations clearly linked George to me. Ms. A became tearful and lamented that there was no substitute for Guy. She always assumed people didn't like her anyway so she never could ask for what she wants. She went on: "I feel as empty as that reservoir was. I can't contain my sadness." I commented, "You seem to feel that without being close to some special important person, you can barely continue with what's important to you." Ms. A agreed, "I am vulnerable, and there are no sub-stitutes for him. There was such a joy in seeing him and sharing my work with him. I am terrified of turning to someone else." Though I was aware, at the time, of the clear transference aspect of the dream, I did not address it. That is, I thought the dream reflected her intense longing to turn to me and her intense fear of doing just that. My not directly intervening with that understanding only intensified her fear that I would desert her, crumble, and the rest. In short, given her father's psychotic downfall, my avoiding the transference interpretation reinforced her dread of repetition. I, too, was in the process of readjusting to the departure of Guy and his function as an auxiliary transference figure.

Ms. A was angry and desperate in the next two analytic hours. She presented "convincing" evidence that there was a conspiracy and demanded an alternate hypothesis from me. She was pretty sure someone was trying to kill her husband because of his important ideas and all that he knew; he was definitely convinced of that. Ms. A wondered how many people were involved in this plot. Perhaps Guy was even responsible. As a last resort she and her husband would go to the State Law Board or else call in Mike Wallace from "60 Minutes" to investigate. At this point, I had a fleeting, uncomfortable recall of Ms. A's father's TV delusion, and I felt bewildered and concerned about the patient. Ms. A went on to say that she fears for her own life. They would have to kill her too because she knows what her husband knows. She hesitated and then said, "Please make it feel better." I responded by saying that I could certainly understand her wanting an alternative hypothesis to help settle these painful worries. Ever so slightly, Ms. A calmed down and associated to her father's psychosis. "Maybe he was right that the world was cruel, so cruel to him." The patient went on in this vein for awhile. Eventually, partially in desperation, I commented that Ms. A's current experience with her husband is, in so many ways, a reliving of earlier experiences with her father. The patient agreed and then said, "That doesn't help me. It's nice for psychoanalytic theory, but it doesn't help me." She became tearful; "I think you may appreciate the pain I'm feeling, but your appreciation is not enough."

The next session began with a harsh silence. Ms. A was enraged with me. She screamed: "You're driving me crazy! You dig deeper instead of helping! I should have jumped off the building when I left here yesterday. I fell apart. You don't care about me! What's happening around me. What if Guy is involved in this plot to kill my husband? That tears me apart. There's something sick about this whole thing. We could go to the governor or a senator—but who can we really trust? It's spreading."

I intervened, "Like a brush fire going in all directions—a feeling of blackness, distrust in the world. Everything is crumbling. And inside I think *you're* terrified of crumbling. Losing Guy is like losing a part of yourself." Ms. A became tearful. She talked further about losing Guy and how she now feared she was about to lose her husband. Every system, every power structure around her was failing. The rage returned in a tidal wave. She exclaimed, "I need data, information, alternative hypotheses. I can even begin to wonder if you're involved." She wondered if my office wasn't "bugged." She demanded a signed statement from me confirming the confidentiality of the analysis. She would then have better grounds to sue me if a "leak" were subsequently discovered. She wondered if anyone had access to my notes. Do I lock them up? Maybe she should take a break from analysis till all this is cleared up. Maybe someone is even paying me off.

I intervened again, "It's terrifying that everything around you is collapsing; trust is evaporating. I can understand your desperation to stop all this chaos around you." Ms. A calmed down and talked about her badmouthing her husband at times. She added, "I created distrust of him in others. He's not crazy. They are. He's brilliant. He's a genius!" Eventually the patient touched on the loss of her father. Now she was going to lose Fred, too, because of the conspirators. She had to rescue him. I responded, "You feel a tremendous burden to save Fred like you wanted to save your father so he could be there for you." Ms. A tearfully responded she had to rescue him. She then actually smiled and said, "I don't feel any better, but here is the only place I can let out my anger." And I indeed felt I had been put through a wringer.

Between the previous session and the next, there were 2 days, and Ms. A had what she called a "fish" dream on each of these nights. Her mood had changed, and she felt quite positive about me, saying, "Really, for the most part, I trust you." In the first dream an angel fish jumps out of the aquarium, and her husband puts it back. The patient's fear in the dream is that this will keep repeating unless something is done to the tank. In the second dream, George (the same George as in the "reservoir" dream) is working on the aquarium, putting structures and foundations in the bottom of the tank; Ms. A is helping. Fortunately, in psychoanalysis, opportunity usually knocks at least twice, and I did not hesitate this time. The patient herself had commented that George resembled me. I, in turn, responded that she had some hope to build a foundation here with me. I then connected this dream with the earlier "reservoir" dream and her fears about turning to me with her needs when she felt so desperate. Ms. A agreed and responded how often she felt there was nothing of intrinsic value in her so who would really be there for her. She added that she feared I, too, would also see no worth in her. "There's nothing special in me. If I were special, maybe I could have saved my father, and he could have helped me. I would try so hard to reach him, and I couldn't." With the reestablishment of the selfobject transference, as manifested in the second fish dream, the *folie à deux* dropped out of subsequent analytic material until, that is, the next disruption in the transference.

Discussion of Vignette 3

I'd like to briefly review this segment of the analysis from a more theoretical point of view. At this particular point in the analysis there had been a significant mobilization of an idealizing selfobject transference, much of it displaced onto Guy, "the safety valve." With the loss of auxiliary selfobject figure and the omission of a transference interpretation, there was a massive disturbance of the patient's narcissistic equilibrium and a concomitant profound regression. This episode of fragmentation was resolved when the selfobject transference was reestablished with the aid of the appropriate, and belated, transference interpretation. Attempted empathic clarifications and "reliving" interpretations were of little value in "reversing" the fragmentation.

How can this "psychotic-like" transference be understood? Kohut (1971) suggests that the psychotic counterpart of the idealized omnipotent, omniscient parental imago is the delusion of an all-powerful persecutor or "influencing machine." Ms. A's fleeting delusion that her analyst is a conspirator could perhaps be seen in that light. Following this line of reasoning further, one could hypothesize that there was a temporary abandonment of a cohesive narcissistic configuration organized around the selfobject transference. Then, in order to escape the intolerable state of a total fragmentation of the self, Ms. A developed a restitutive delusion, a psychotic transference. This is, at best, only a partial, and probably misleading, explanation for two reasons. First, it indicates a potentially more ominous course for the analysis than was actually the case. Secondly, the restitutive delusion *was not hers*; Ms. A identified with her husband's restitutive delusion, which, in turn, was a latter-day version of her identification with her father's psychosis. Ultimately, the identification is then in the service of desperately maintaining contact with her psychotic husband. Fred again became the good, kind genius she married, now persecuted by the world, and, likewise, there were similar, poignant associations about her father. This defensive formation is in contrast to the complete abandonment of a cohesive narcissistic configuration that could eventually lead to a more permanent psychotic regression. Thus, the patient's *folie à deux* is a stopgap measure stemming the tide of further fragmentation and is not itself a bona fide restitutive delusion arising out of a complete state of fragmentation. In this light, Ms. A's intensified identification with her schizophrenic father can be seen both as a florid indicator of the disruption of the selfobject transference and also as a "resting point" that limits regression and salvages some vital sense of self-cohesion.

It is beyond the scope of this presentation to apply this line of reasoning to the concept of *folies à deux* in general. But I would like to make one tentative point in this regard. The passive partner adopts the active partner's restitutive delusion in a desperate attempt to preserve the remnants of self–selfobject tie. With these kind of stakes, the cost of reality testing is a small price to pay because by this very identification process a more massive regression, with a subsequently more pathological organization of the psyche, is being prevented. In effect, a total self-fragmentation is "short-circuited."

At this juncture, I think it would also be useful to explore some of my reactions during the waxing and waning of Ms. A's *folie à deux* experiences. At times, I felt that the only way of not losing Ms. A, of maintaining some contact with her, was to join her in the *folie à deux*. For example, I found myself playing with fantasies of my office being "bugged" and also being very curious about what Ms. A's husband's brilliant ideas were, what did he know. I believe these particular reactions I experienced paralleled Ms. A's attempts to maintain contact with her psychotic husband—the repetition of early desperate attempts to hold onto her psychotic father. That is, through my "muted" fantasies, I was attempting to maintain contact with the patient, join her in a *folie à deux*. In turn, and through these complementary countertransference fantasies, I came to better understand Ms. A's identification with her psychotic husband for the emergency measure that it was and for the vital function that it served.

The two "fish" dreams in the last session in this vignette are representative of many "fish" dreams the patient had during this phase of the analysis. In fact she had 15 to 20 of them. Often, but not always, they were anxiety dreams—the manifest content being her frantic effort to keep the fish alive and in safe environments as they endlessly jumped out of their fish bowls or flew away. Important others, like her mother, her father, or her husband, stood around and did nothing to help. At times she would awaken from these dreams and find her bedclothes soaked with perspiration. Less frequently in the "fish" dreams, she is helped or soothed. In one dream she was on a swing. She looked down and saw all these frightening, strange fish on the ground; they didn't need water. Dr. *Kinder*, a professor of hers, came by, explained all about the fish, and she felt soothed. As the "fish" dreams continued on, Ms. A had ones in which the fish were amazing—they could talk, they survived when she thought there was no way they could. They were beautiful with brilliant colors, they performed unbelievable feats. In one particularly vivid dream, her father squeezed a fish. Ms. A thought surely the fish would die. It didn't. Through its clear, pale flesh she saw its heart pumping.

At the time the "fish" dreams started, Ms. A had given her husband a fish tank and some fish. She had done this about two weeks before the start of the vignette just discussed. Some of the fish had already died.

Later in the analysis, Ms. A recalled having her very first aquarium at the time of her father's psychosis. Many of the fish in this aquarium also died. Once her mother changed the water, and it was too hot. Thus, in general, the "fish" dreams are self-state dreams expressing the disintegration of the self–selfobject matrix of her childhood and its current repetition, given her husband's psychotic decline. Certainly, the first dream in the vignette represented that repetition. The patient was desperately turning to her psychotic husband for help in maintaining her narcissistic equilibrium. In the second "fish" dream, she is turning to the analyst with some hope of change, with some hope she can experience soothing and structure building. Ms. A eventually commented, "I only have these frantic dreams about flying fish when I feel disconnected from you. When I feel connected, I guess we're building a better fish tank."

VIGNETTE 4

The following sequence of hours took place about 2 to 3 months later. During this time there had been many disruptions of the transference with a concomitant increase in Ms. A's suspiciousness and belief in her husband's delusions. However, the working through process had begun. At times, Ms. A would be reflective about her own suspiciousness and would wonder, herself, about what had triggered these feelings. What follows, however, was not one of those times. In this particular hour, Ms. A talked with enthusiasm and excitement about her Law Review work and about an up-coming out-of-town presentation she was to make. Toward the end of the session she mentioned that she received a phone call from her father. Her stomach had tightened as she had listened to him. The conversation had given her the "creeps." She added, "I'm sorry I don't love him; I can't change him or cure him. My life is full of potential. His is dull, but there is nothing I can do. For me he is dead, a shell of a person. We live in different worlds. I explain things, good things that are happening to me, and he doesn't understand." Ms. A then had a poignant image of some old railroad tracks that hadn't been used for a long time. The ties were crumbling, rotting. Weeds were growing everywhere. The tracks themselves were cruddy and rusty. She reflected: "Those old railroad tracks are my relationship with my father, my needs for him to be there and to help me. There are so many years of being ashamed of him. He'd talk to the voices, and I'd want to scream at him." I suggested that perhaps she felt something that was started with her father had never been completed and that old wish for him to understand and appreciate her successes—perhaps like the ones she talked about today—lingers on in limbo. Ms. A sighed and said that was so right. On leaving she lingered at the door and gave me a wide-eyed, childlike look.

In the first session after her trip the patient exclaimed, "I made it back!" She gave a detailed and enthusiastic account of the trip and her successful presentation. She added, "And I didn't throw up!" She also talked about having written Guy about her trip. Yet, she hadn't mailed the letter because he probably wouldn't be interested. She stopped: "I don't know why I'm thinking about this, but I did worry on the trip about my brakes not working, and one of my tires was way overinflated." I failed to address Ms. A's concerns of overstimulation as well as her longings for affirmation of her success.

Ms. A began the next session by saying she fell off a chair yesterday and that she probably did so because trips always make her tired. She also had thrown away the letter she wrote to Guy. She commented that the office was cold today and went on to talk about being a failure; the empty feeling had returned. She became suspicious and started elaborating concerns about the conspirators: "I wish it would stop—all these things being done to my husband. The worst part is there is nothing I can do for him." The escalation continued. "His old firm is covering something up, doing something vengeful. Because of them, I risk starvation, and sometimes I feel you are the only one who can help me. Then again I get to thinking you're part of the conspiracy. It's all so crazy—it's like I feel you are helping me on one hand and destroying me on the other. This all gets too confusing. I don't trust you. It really seems that there are leaks from this office." At this point I stepped in and reviewed the rapid mood change over these two sessions and wondered if the patient hadn't felt deeply disappointed that her enthusiasm and excitement about the trip had not been acknowledged. I reminded her she had begun this hour by saying she had taken a fall. Ms. A's mood rapidly changed. "You're right. I looked forward so much to telling you. If I thought you had appreciated what I had accomplished I would have derived strength from it." The patient then went on with some enthusiasm talking about her deep enjoyment of her work. As an "aside" she mentioned one of her old students (she had taught in graduate school) recently contacted her. He is planning to go to medical school and asked her for a recommendation. She was pleased. "He'll make an excellent physician; he has lots of compassion and kindness." As Ms. A talked, I recalled to myself her image of those unused railroad tracks that she likened to her old connection to her prepsychotic father. Once more I felt we were back on track.

Discussion of Vignette 4

Again, there was a disruption in the selfobject transference when Ms. A's longings for me to appreciate her accomplishments and to buffer her exhibitionistic tensions (fear of no brakes and the overinflated tire) were not interpreted. She took a "fall" and felt cold and empty. Again, to stem any further fragmentation she identified with her husband's delusion, which is the repetition of her childhood attempt to maintain contact with her father. The unused railroad tracks thus represent the sudden loss of her father that precluded the internalization of the functions of the idealized parental imago. Being back on track is then the latter-day renewal of this developmental task vis-à-vis the working through of the selfobject transference.

As the working through of the idealizing transference continued in the analysis, Ms. A eventually reached a point when she could tolerate disruptions in the selfobject transference without the stopgap defensive identification with her father's (spouse's) psychosis. Ms. A in effect was eventually able to "hold" the tension of longing for the temporarily absent idealized selfobject, and, as a consequence, the massive regressive shift to the *folie à deux* configuration with her psychotic husband markedly lessened and was eventually worked through. One aspect of this process was that Ms. A, with human concern but without frantic disorganization, eventually divorced her deeply disturbed husband.

GENERAL REFLECTIONS

These last two vignettes stand for many. In the course of this phase of Ms. A's analysis (the analysis of the *folie à deux*), as the disruptions and reestablishments of the selfobject transference were constantly repeated, there was also the constantly repeating opportunity to observe the many complex facets of the defensive identification process with her schizophrenic father. In effect, this very identification process became a marker, a sensitive barometer for measuring the stability and mobilization of the selfobject transference, sharpening the strategic focus on the working through of the transference itself. To oversimplify it, often the state of the transference seemed to be inversely related to the state of the pathological identification. With the gradual working through of the transference, the acquisition of new psychological structures proceeded. Any direct interpretation of the defensive identifications was a tactical consideration or part and parcel of subsequent reconstructive summaries.

At the same time, more and more relevant memories and feeling states emerged that were indicative of the profound narcissistic vulnerabilities stemming from the impact of the trauma of her father's psychosis. Thus, the identification with her psychotic father was not so much undone but, more accurately, became an unnecessary vestigial defense because of the working through of the selfobject transference and because of the reactivation of transmuting internalization processes that working through implies — the return to those long unused railroad tracks that Ms. A likened to her early, positive, special relationship to her father. All this is the reverse of her childhood situation in which transmuting internalization could not take place due to repeated disruptions in the self–selfobject union triggered by Ms. A's experience of the vicissitudes of her father's schizophrenia. With such disruptions, the patient prematurely and traumatically experienced her separateness from the idealized parental imago and in the throes of this dilemma, her childhood solution was to identify with her psychotic father as she later identified with her psychotic husband. Such an identification, I believe, limited potentially overwhelming self-fragmentation experiences and preserved fantasized relationships with the object that was feared to be irretrievably lost.

Earlier, I expressed concern about the title of this presentation. I said disruptions and repairs of the transference are ubiquitous and "old hat." To reiterate once more, I think the new twist or new feather in this "old hat" is the particular emergence in Ms. A's analysis of the pathological identification with her schizophrenic father and how this identification process was in tandem with the disruptions and repairs of the transference. Certainly the *folie à deux* was readily apparent and indeed hard to miss. It seems, however, that in other situations, in analyses in general, there might be similar but more subtle kinds of defensive identifications (which at first glance might appear to be enfeeblements of the self or empty depressions) that would not be so apparent, and yet, these identifications would also wax and wane in the changing tides of transference. Their recognition in such tides would contribute to a deepening understanding of the analytic process and also further clarify the nature—the various natures—of identifications. In the psychoanalytic literature, identifications are seen as both defenses and building blocks of psychic structure. It seems that further clarification on this dual nature could be done by looking for, by exploring, the relationship between the vicissitudes of transference reactions and the vicissitudes of identification processes. Perhaps all too often identifications are conceptualized as more or less stable psychic structure. Identification is also very much a dynamic process (Schafer, 1968).

VIGNETTE 5

I'd like to introduce one more vignette—not so much to demonstrate a disruption and repair of the idealizing transference, though that is there— but to demonstrate a change in tone in the analytic material, to contrast this vignette (75 hours before termination) with the earlier ones.

Toward the end of an hour, Ms. A began talking about her work in an outlying public defenders' office. (This was a unique, elective outreach program her law school had developed.) She had initially been terrified of this position, but with the encouragement of two of her professors Ms. A had gone ahead with the elective anyway. She grew to love it and often spoke of her work there with great enthusiasm and excitement. On this occasion, as she continued talking about her experiences in the public defenders' office, a particular client kept coming to mind—Tim. He had developed a crush on her, idealized her, and she compared the way Tim seemed to come alive around her to the way she used to be with Guy. She wondered if she could ever really have an impact on Tim, change the way he thinks, help him get on the right track. She went on to talk about all life's twists and turns. She reflected on the exciting interviews she had recently been on. Would she stay in town? Would she take the ideal clerkship out of town? She was also wondering about how best to leave her husband. I said: "There sure are a lot of forks in the road coming up." My comment was more akin to saying a thought out loud than to any "intended" intervention, or so I thought. I did wonder a little bit about my comment after it had slipped out. Ms. A's only response was, "Yes, I've been talking to B. D. [a favorite law professor] about my fear of leaving." We had reached the end of the hour.

Following this hour, the patient had a difficult weekend. She developed nausea, diarrhea, insomnia, and terrible menstrual cramps. She had even called her gynecologist. Also, she felt there must be something in her eye because her contact lens felt miserable. She was tense, and her suspiciousness had returned in full bloom. She felt one of her professors wasn't being fair about a joint paper they were doing and wanted her to leave town. Ms. A's suspicions quickly generalized again to the last firm that fired her husband and then to me. She added, "I don't want to stay in town anymore." After a brief silence, I asked, "I wonder if some other issues aren't intensifying these feelings?" Ms. A replied, "I wondered too. I searched myself a bit to see. Yet most of my life is going very well now."

She then talked about reference letters that haven't arrived where they should—at the out-of-town places where she was interviewing. She again returned to her suspicions: "They've finished off my husband, but they still haven't got me. Well, I don't believe all the stuff he believes anymore, anyway. Well, only a little."

She talked further about wanting to leave town. I contrasted her recent wishes. Yesterday and last week she wanted so much to stay and today she is desperate to leave.

She went on: "Well, everyone around here is a schmuck . . . well, not everyone. . . . To think of who you are is just too stressful." She reviewed her past suspicions. "Now my solution is to block out all thoughts about your character. I've been burned so many times, and besides it's mean to suspect you." I commented, "Even so, I wonder if you didn't feel I was being a bit of a schmuck for bringing up last time all the life decisions you have ahead of you. . . . " She laughed, "Yes, you were and right at the end of the hour. I know they're there, but you saying it then was a jolt, like pulling the rug out from under me." She turned on her side, curled up, and went on, "You know, sometimes I hope I'm no one—to stand out means to be knocked down. It's safer to blend into the crowd. Leaving, staying are very intense feelings. Yes, do I want to grow or be safe instead?"

Ms. A wondered as she left the office how I keep my plants alive, by magic? She said: "I couldn't keep my plants alive without light." (At the time, I had an office without windows, but that's another story.)

Ms. A was in a jubilant mood the next day. She excitedly talked about the paper she was finishing. She then began talking about the crossroads she was on. Should she stay with her husband? Leave him? What job position should she take? "My husband fosters my paranoia. Yet I would hurt him if I left." She became tearful. "He's so self-centered. He needs me like I've needed Guy. But now I see I can sustain my clients like Tim. Almost can say I can sustain myself."

She went on: "I don't know what to do. Yesterday I even considered going to medical school. I want to be a student the rest of my life. The real world frightens me. I thought about something you said about the analysis. Maybe coming her keeps me going. I don't believe that but what if it's more than I think it is. My paranoid feeling is I couldn't survive without it. What if I'm all regressed when I leave here and won't be able to see daddy four times a week. You know, I feel like I've failed you. I didn't fall madly in love with you."

I said, "So you felt it was my expectation that you do that and then we'd proceed down a certain course?" Ms. A replied: "Yes. Fred says analysis is an addiction, and I'll freak out when I leave here."

The patient then talked about a prestigious clerkship for a federal judge that she might have a shot at. She was daring to be hopeful about it.

She went on: "I can't have both safeness and excitement; they seem like incompatible wishes. It's such a good day—why am I crying? It still bothers me that I didn't fall madly in love with you. Yet I know now it's my analysis."

The patient sighed and started gently sobbing. She recounted her struggle to feel safe in here, her slow realization it was *her* analysis and not an exploitation. She added: "Sometimes the trust for you still goes away, but I can reflect on it now . . . I was saving this for the last day to say to you, but suddenly it now seems appropriate. I'm sorry how mean at times I've treated you—it felt like I had to—but you're right up there with Dr. Z [the one physician she felt stood by her during a traumatic time in her adolescence].

You have a kindness and honesty that I can't quite believe at times. . . . All these tears and on a good day too."

The patient overslept for the first time and missed the next appointment. She called to see if I had another time I could see her. I couldn't reschedule, and she came to her next regular appointment 2 days later.

The patient was upset that I hadn't been able to reschedule her. She stated: "The one time in 2 years I ask you to and you say no. It scared me to death that I totally forgot the appointment. I just wondered why I set the alarm so early and went back to bed. Then I wondered what you would say about my forgetting. You would say I didn't come because I expressed so much caring for you. It's hard for me to talk about you. That's what it's all about. I have trouble letting people know how I feel. . . . You know I've felt so often you don't like me. I have no evidence at all. I was pissed off I couldn't reach you by phone. I know that's crazy. I have no right to expect you to be right by the phone waiting for my call. It's just whenever I need someone they're not there. . . . I had a dream the night after the last session. It's as important as my 'Man in the Sky' dream. [In this previous dream, Ms. A is in a terrible storm and the face of a man shines down on her from the heavens, and she feels safe.] My brother and I are in a house. I'm rearranging furniture. I have a new, beautiful room with heavy, strong, sturdy furniture. There's beautiful wood paneling and plants. The bed is in front of the window. It's made of very heavy, solid wood—it's beautiful, shiny. The room is lush. But my favorite plant *F. exotica* is not there. My *F. mitida* is. I've had my *F. exotica* for years. I began looking for it but what I visualized in my mind—in the dream—is the *F. exotica* plant in B. D.'s office [the favorite professor]. I finally find it in my brother's room. His room is beautiful too. Once I find the plant I don't seem to mind that it's not in my room. The plants are all the same genus but different species. My room had such strength and character; it had a golden feeling. You know that room is me getting stronger."

Recalling some of her comments in recent sessions ("I'm almost sustaining myself," "How do you keep your plants alive without light?"), reflecting on the course of the last few hours, and recalling other dreams in which her brother appeared (often as a marker for her father's psychosis), I did not wait for associations but said, "I would just add that the room is also this room—your experiences here, your analysis. Your concern in the dream about something very special not being in your new room I think is related to your beginning to wonder about what it will be like when you leave here."

She agreed: "Wednesday, that's what I wanted to talk to you about. It would have been easier to have told you then when I was under stress but I *still* can tell you. . . . The trouble with you . . . the truth is . . . I've always liked you. I wanted a replacement for Guy in the beginning but at some point it really scared me. I was terrified the same thing would happen all over again, like with Guy. But somewhere along the line I changed again. A replacement for Guy would not have made it better. A replacement would only mean perseveration and stagnation, not growth. I also felt you hated me—no reason, just fear. But Wednesday it came to my mind that for a long time I couldn't have let myself develop any feelings for you. . . . I felt so strongly for you right then, and you weren't available. I needed you to be right by the phone for me, and I felt so childish, and I do get scared when I think of the possibility that some day soon I might be leaving this."

I responded: "With the depth of feeling you were experiencing, how could it have been otherwise?" As Ms. A left, she said, "Again, such a good day and I'm crying."

In the next session the patient presented one of her "central" dreams. I might add that when I think of Ms. A's analysis, I think of this dream. If I were summing up her analysis, what took place, what was accomplished, I would talk about this dream and say this is what happened:

> I wonder where I am at first. I seem to be in the public defenders' building. Then I'm walking in a hallway. Some kind of test is taking place. To my right I see an old teacher of mine. Her room is beautiful. There's a gigantic blackboard. There is also a cathedral ceiling with skylights; light is streaming in. I say to the teacher, "Oh, it's a transactional analysis class in a new room. You must love it." On the blackboard there were four or five groupings of parallel lines and also a drawing of two stick figures—a woman lying on her back and a man beside her, propped up by his elbow looking at her. The students are drawing these figures and filling them in with colored chalk. The figures on the board look like the outlines of murdered people, dead people like you see on TV shows—detective shows. Yet the students' drawings are something more; they have substance. The colors are green, yellow, and red. I was filled with wonderment.

That the analytic situation was superimposed on a teaching situation is especially significant for Ms. A given her long hours of childhood play in which she filled both roles—teacher and student. This play, I believe, had been a compensatory attempt by the patient to give herself what was lacking in her environment and to soothe herself. In a sense in this dream the analyst is now included in that solitary play of childhood.

The transforming of the stick figure outline drawings, the "analytic pair," to the students' colorful chalk drawings of substance appears to be a vivid image of the working through process, or perhaps more specifically, a concretization of the long wished for opportunity for renewed growth. The voids within the outlines of dead people are being filled in with color; the light is streaming in.

Ms. A's fund of knowledge never ceased to amaze me. To wit, she described the series of parallel lines in the dream as part of a molecular orbital theory model. She went on, "It's the theory that explains electrons move in jumps, not gradually. That's my feeling about analysis; it goes in spurts. The model itself represents more stable energy levels." Again this image seems to be a striking concretization of improving tension regulation and resilience.

I'll briefly address some other elements in the dream. The patient's spontaneous association to the specifc colors was that she had recently read that these three colors are childhood preferential colors, that is, the colors that a child 5 or 6 years old would pick as favorite colors. I would add that Ms. A was between 5 and 6 when her father had his first psychotic break. I would also add that the colors—red, green, and yellow—are the very colors of her father's shirt in that poignant memory she recovered early in the analysis—the memory of the day her "old" dad went to the hospital and never returned.

The reference to the public defenders' building refers to Ms. A's own position in a nearby town that was becoming increasingly important to her at the time of the dream. In short, a place where she did "analytic home-work," as she called it. Finally, references to TVs (her father's TV star delusion) have often been markers for her father's psychosis and her own tremendous concerns and fears about archaic grandiose-exhibitionistic tensions. Thus the manifest content in the dream, "The students are drawing these figures and filling them in with colored chalk. The figures on the board look like the outlines of murdered people, dead people like you see on TV shows . . . " translates into: "I want/am getting something in this situation that I wanted as a child but could not because of my experience of my father's psychosis and my resultant sense of deadness and emptiness." The belated developmental process is in progress in the dream. The workings and the working through of the idealizing transference are apparent. It is, after all, *both* figures that are being filled with color.

The patient commented, "This is my second beautiful room dream; something important is happening. I'm less afraid of becoming like my father. . . . In the dream the light is beautiful."

It is difficult to recapture the patient's deep sense of joy in her telling of this dream and others of similar ilk. The joyful emotion seemed to reflect the celebration of her awareness that she had achieved a decisive firming of her self. I agree with Kohut that joy is a different affect than pleasure and has its own developmental line. "Joy relates to experiences of the total self whereas pleasure (despite the frequent occurring participation of the total self, which then provides an admixture of joy) relates to experiences of parts and constituents of the self" (1977, p. 45).

A few days later Ms. A referred back to this dream as a "Hall of Fame" dream. She surprised herself with the pun on my name. This led to thoughts she had that I would write a book about her; I'd become famous; we'd both share in that fame. She went on to say that these kinds of thoughts about me scared her. "Always, the more I see you as a star, the more I fear you'll be a falling one."

TERMINATION

The termination phase began in earnest about 4 months before the last session and after much working through of the idealizing transference. Over a great number of sessions she presented her reasons both related to external circumstances and perceived changes within herself. She had been able to acquire an ideal clerkship in the East that would significantly advance her career. There were no similar opportunities in this city. She had come to recognize her husband's profound psychopathology and was ready to separate from him without undue guilt. She felt she had made enough gains within herself to be on her own though it would be scary. Her enjoyment of her work had deepened particularly in regard to working with clients. She had often feared that her interest in law was merely esoteric and theoretical. Now she felt that with her work with clients, everything had come "alive." She thought of Guy less often and with less intensity. She feared becoming addicted to the analysis. At one point she said: "You do not understand that I have more than I had." She likened herself to a vase that had cracks but was now solidly in one piece and functioning. At another point she added: "If we continued, it could be like the two of us going down into a great cave. You could get out. I never could." Implicit in these analogies was the patient's fear that a deepening regression in the analysis could lead to an irremedial disintegration of the self.

The patient expressed one remaining concern. Though her relationships with male professors and male students had improved and stabilized, she still had difficulties relating to men as peers or potential lovers. There had, however, been some brief, but significant, friendship interactions with men. Throughout termination she vacillated between hope for a new kind of relationship with a man or resigning herself to an isolated life. Finally she decided the verdict was not in. She would first learn to truly rely on herself and then see.

She also eventually brought up that she no longer feared going crazy like her father. She was her own person. The loneliness, emptiness, bitterness, and anger—all involving her father—had lessened. What was was.

There were those times in the termination phase, however, when the patient's improvement appeared to be a sham or a figment of my therapeutic optimism. At such times it seemed that her well-being depended on the continued presence of the selfobject. Her "unrelenting" yearning for Guy would return as well as her confusion about the "validity" of her husband's delusions and her suspicions about me. These episodes, though, were always very brief and allowed opportunities for further working through. Ms. A's increased self-awareness during these times indicated much had already been accomplished.

Ms. A's major concern during termination was how much of the analytic experience she could take with her. In one particularly vivid dream, the patient was in my office. She sits up. On the table beside her there's a small light that is a replica of the bigger light on my desk. In the dream I smile and say to her: "What is it about you patients that you always look at this light?" Essentially the patient was wondering how much "light" she would take with her. She repeatedly likened herself to a plant or flower needing light. Would she wither or continue to bloom when she left? In another dream she was singing a popular song, "You Light Up My Life." She added: "I was only off key a little bit."

About a month before termination the patient described a rare important moment. She suddenly felt the world was okay, less hostile than she used to imagine; she felt safe and good about herself for no particular reason, and that feeling was generated totally within herself. She was at peace. At the end of this special moment she smiled at a man who had been helping her in the library, and he smiled back. I believe this moment is an example of the patient's more or less successful attempt to extricate herself from her father's dangerous paranoid world and move with a sense of "aliveness" toward her own, freer view of the world.

The termination did not appear forced. It followed a natural course with a sense of consolidation. The return of symptoms gave one more opportunity for further working through. The major task, and to a large extent accomplished, was the internalization and integration by the patient of self-object functions vested in the idealizing transference. One of the last comments the patient made was the following: "I used to feel like I was in a boat in the middle of the ocean, helpless, with a disorganized feeling. There are still storms, but I recognize now I can guide the boat a little — enough." Guiding ideals, perchance?

REFLECTIONS ON TERMINATION AND CONCLUSION

One of Kohut's more general comments on termination is as follows: "In other words, the analysis of a case of narcissistic personality disorder has reached the phase of termination when the analysand's self has become firm, when it has ceased to react to the loss of selfobjects with fragmentation, serious enfeeblement, or uncontrolled rage" (1977, p. 138).

In the case of Ms. A, the very fact she could contemplate moving by herself to another city hundreds of miles away—away from her husband, Guy, and her analysis is, of and by itself, indicative of a significant consolidation of the self. I don't think it can be considered primarily as a defensive flight into health—such an act was not in the patient's psychological repertoire. Ms. A's move can be better understood as a *readiness* for taking a risk into health. In this regard, in a follow-up interview 10 months after termination, Ms. A described her experience of the move in this way: "It was as if I hatched from an egg there. It's all very hard to describe, and it was very hard to break through the shell, but I just did it. There were many times I felt I couldn't do it—that I needed to be back in analysis. But now I feel more alive than ever I did. I made it. My life is really pretty full. I called you when I got back in town [she was visiting her family] because coming to see you is a bit like coming home to the one part of this city that seems connected to my new life, to who I am and am becoming. There's always other reasons I suppose [she smiled], but I just wanted to show you how I was doing."

More specifically Kohut felt the phase of termination is reached when (1) "*the primary defect* in the self has been exposed and, via working through and transmuting internalization, sufficiently filled out so that the formerly defective structures of the self have now become functionally reliable" (1977, p. 4) or (2) after some significant preliminary working through " . . . *the compensatory structures* have become functionally reliable, independent of the area in which this success was achieved" (1977, p. 4). Further, Kohut states: "Most frequently a weakness in the area of exhibitions and ambitions, is compensated for by the self-esteem provided by the pursuit of ideals" (1977, p. 4). I think the case of Ms. A, more or less, follows this second course. That is, a pathognomonic regression was reached, an idealizing transference developed and was worked through—revitalizing that sector of the self and its compensatory structures.

Now one can always devise a "thought" exercise and wonder whether another analyst focusing his efforts on the manifestations of the mirror transference, resonating with that transference, and then understanding and interpreting it correctly might in this way have succeeded in allowing Ms. A to reach a pathognomonic regression to the *primary* defect in her self (her archaic grandiose self unresponded to by mother or responded to in a panic-prone way). Then, via the working through of the mirror transference, this primary defect could have been filled in. Belated development in this sector of the self could have occurred. How the results of this hypothetical analysis might compare with the actual analysis remains, of course, unknown. Yet, this "thought" exercise does stir up at least three questions.

The first question, in its simplist form but to the point, is where the mother is in this case material. The second question is how the nature of Ms. A's psychopathology contributed to the course the analysis took. The third question is how my functioning as an analyst contributed to the analytic endeavor.

In regard to the first question, perhaps one way to approach it is to say that indeed througout her analysis Ms. A did develop many transference configurations revolving around her early experiences of her mother and other maternal caretakers, but that given the theme of this chapter and the point I was trying to make, I chose to exclude such material. But the question remains. That is, though it would be easy to demonstrate such transference experiences, there would still be a sense of incomplete working through, a sense of the material dropping by the wayside. Perhaps, in this analysis as a whole, mother was surprisingly absent just because mother *was* absent in terms of the patient's earlier experiences. This deliberation brings to my mind still another of the patient's dreams—the last dream of this chapter.

Earlier, I pointed out another dream (the dream of the students filling in figure drawings with colored chalk, the "Hall of Fame" dream) as exemplifying what happened in Ms. A's analysis—the working through of the idealizing transference and the concomitant filling in of the defect in that sector of the self. The following dream I feel exemplifies the essential dilemma of Ms. A's childhood, indeed, of her life. Of and by itself the dream proves nothing of course, but it does reflect this point of view.

> I'm sitting in the waiting room and a woman is there. She has a baby that can amazingly talk. She does not want the baby. I end up holding it. The doctor across the hall talks to the baby. He is great with it. The baby talks back and laughs. I do the same. We are on TV as well. Then I am in a beautiful, colorful bathing suit. A person takes pictures of me. I'm surprised I don't look skinny and ugly in the pictures; I really don't look bad. Then I'm walking with Eddy [a friend with a recent onset of a severe emotional illness]. We're holding hands. I'm surprised his hand is so small. He asks me: "Am I ever going to be okay?"

The first part of the dream vividly portrays the patient's old wishes and yearning for mirroring, for maternal responsiveness, and joyous acceptance of her early grandiose-exhibitionistic urges, that is, the baby that *can* amazingly talk. Yet the baby was not wanted by its mother. Ms. A holds the baby—holds and "waits." Soon (at least in the dream) the baby responds to the idealized selfobject—the doctor who's "great" with the baby. I think the transference implications are clear here. This part of the dream reflects the mobilization of a reactivated nuclear self in the transference and the reexperiencing of the old childhood claims of this nuclear self vis-à-vis the current selfobject—the analyst. A belated working through process has begun. Transmuting internalizations of the idealized selfobject functions did not take place in childhood due to Ms. A's experience of the rapid psychotic decline of her father. Again, this old trauma, along with the ever present fear of its repetition in the analysis, comes through in the rest of the dream. Again, the reference to the TV reflects both the patient's grandiose-exhibitionistic tensions and her father's psychosis (his TV delusions). Eddy's small hand is a reversal. It is her hand holding on to her father, hoping against hope that her ever-needed idealized father would return to her, that they would finish their journey together. The question, "Am I ever going to be okay?" is one her father, throughout her childhood, had often asked her. It is also her own.

To return to the question of where the mother is in this case material, one could argue that Ms. A's *intense* early idealization of her father is, of and by itself, a reflection of her mother's unavailability in terms of both mirroring acceptance and early holding and carrying experiences that allow for calming mergers with the selfobject's idealized omnipotence. With this, however, I am coming dangerously close to begging the question. Thus, as a court of last resort let me appeal once more to a quote of Kohut's:

> Once more let me say: the earliest layers of the psychopathology will often recede from the self—a process that is in essence different from repression— after a modicum of work has been done with them, allowing the crucial work to proceed spontaneously. I am convinced that any interference with this unrolling analytic process from the side of an analyst who insists that the patient continue to deal with the archaic material is in error—however well meant and carefully buttressed by theories the analyst's actions might be. (1977, p. 219)

I do have one concern about the above quote but that concern leads back to the two other questions the "thought" exercise stirred up. I feel Kohut's comment, "allowing the crucial work to proceed spontaneously," carries the implication that all the analyst need do is stay out of the patient's way and the analytic process will unroll, unhindered, in a fashion preordained by the patient's psychopathology; the pathognomonic regression will spontaneously occur. Freud (1912) said essentially the same thing. Of course there is truth in all this, but there is also a problem. The analyst cannot keep out of the patient's way. Whatever theoretical framework is used, there are still two people in the room!

I would also add that it is extremely doubtful an analysis could take place if the analyst's primary goal was to keep out of his patient's way. With this in mind and taking the course of the analysis as a whole piece of cloth, I think the second and third questions are best combined: How did the patient and myself, in our work together, contribute to the analytic endeavor?

In a quest for an answer to this question I would like to go back to some clinical material we have touched on before—around the time in the analysis I arbitrarily called the end of the beginning. I think this material can stand for numerous other similar occurrences in the analysis.

To briefly review it, this is the time Ms. A wanted to show me what she had accomplished with self-hypnosis. She had burned herself and miraculously cured herself. I responded in a perfunctory manner, and she fragmented. Ms. A recovered when I clarified the immediate experience of her disappointment in me. Shortly after this, the patient brought in her "rat" dream, her "Irma" dream, in which her mother disrupts her "Nobel prize" experiment and her father soothes her.

As with any analytic material there are many ways to look at it. Let's try this way: this dream, as a whole, parallels the previous disruption and repair in the transference. That is, I, like her mother in the dream, do not mirror her grandiose, exhibitionistic strivings. In both situations, the patient becomes enraged, which is the byproduct of the disintegration of her unquestioning assertive, joyful grandiosity. I, like her father in the dream, offer a soothing response (the father's is in the form of direct comfort and holding and mine is in the form of a clarification). In both of these situations the patient experiences the omnipotent selfobject as providing certain psychic functions that allow the reestablishment of a sense of self. In this way the psychological disintegration product, the rage, disappears.

Therefore, in the dream as well as in the preceding analytical hours there seems to be a clear repetition of Ms. A's childhood dilemma. To put it in its simplest form: the patient experiences her mother as unavailable as a mirroring selfobject and turns to her father—the idealized selfobject.

In this clinical material (and there are many other examples of such a sequence) Ms. A experiences her very tentative mobilization of a *mirroring transference* coming to naught, being disrupted, and experiences the repair developing from the establishment and mobilization of an *idealized transference*. Given our present classification of selfobjects, it is as if the disruption takes place on one self–selfobject lifeline and the repair on another—the second lifeline holds. With this formulation I once again seem to be questioning the title of this chapter. Not really. There are, to be sure, many examples of disruption and repair of the idealizing transference in "pure" form throughout this case material taken as a whole. I am, however, questioning something else—our current classification of selfobject transferences. I am not questioning the concept of selfobject transferences. What I am saying is that it is far easier to grasp that a selfobject transference is emerging than to delineate clearly just what kind of selfobject transference it is. Certainly the classifications of "idealizing" and "mirroring" are useful for ordering arrested selfobject strivings. This in turn gives us a useful clinical tool for grasping the level and degree of impaired narcissistic development. Yet too strict an adherence to this current classification might prevent us from ordering selfobject transferences in other ways and in further seeing the complexities and interplays of the patient's selfobject needs and the flexibilities therein. To put it another way, I do not feel Ms. A's "rat" dream and the paralleling analytic hours are merely a microscopic version of the two chances for the development of a cohesive self Kohut (1977) describes (one chance via the mirroring selfobject and one chance via the idealized selfobject). There is more here. I think there is more potential and variability in the unfolding of selfobject transferences than our present theoretical constructs can as yet contain.

In the analytic experience, as the old claims for selfobject needs once more are mobilized, the patient sends out tentative feelers in the direction of the analyst. Fleeting transferences develop. Always the patient tests and risks. Eventually, tentatively, selfobject connections with the analyst are made. If there is a good enough fit with the analyst on a significant enough depth psychological level, a latter-day self–selfobject matrix can form that is new, more limited in scope and more promising in potential than the one of childhood and yet always, unavoidably, similar. With this step there is a chance that belated development can begin again. The emergence of such a therapeutic potential and the form it is limited to is dependent on a host of factors including the structure of the patient's psychopathology, the patient's dread of repetition (never to be underestimated), the amount of empathic failure that can be tolerated without massive fragmentations, the amount of empathy that can be tolerated, the ability to endure the continuous rise and fall of hope throughout analysis, and, perhaps most importantly, the way the patient experiences the analyst and the analyst's endeavors.

If we now shift our focus and look at the analyst's contribution to the formation of this latter-day self–selfobject matrix, we can safely say that the analyst's limitations (from idiosyncracies to countertransference propensities) are legion. It is simply not easy to make contact with the patient in the patient's universe. The reach is mammoth! Perhaps, on less safe ground to be sure, one could say the analyst's attributes are legion as well. Yet to focus on either the analyst's attributes or limitations, per se, is, I think, to fall short of understanding his contribution to the self–selfobject matrix. It is in essence the patient's self-experience of the analyst and his attributes and his limitations as the patient sees them (however the analyst himself or his most admiring colleague or his severest critic might define them) that counts. To a necessary degree, the patient, vis-à-vis the renewal of old claims on selfobjects and the yearning to continue once again on a developmental journey, unique to him and long ago aborted, attempts to form his analyst into the image of the selfobject he needs. And to a sufficient degree the analyst complies. He is always a different analyst with each analysand. We, like our patients, live in our own psychological universes, and as we empathically reach to understand a patient, we change and yet often are not really aware of that change. That is, there is a subtle flexibility to our analytic work that goes unnoted as long as it is continuous with and compatible to the core of our analytic "selves." By the very nature of our work, we strive to become the analyst we experience the patient needing. I am, of course, not talking about any contrived attempt at a "corrective emotional experience" but about something else, a more natural process that is seldom examined. It is the "um-hum" we say to a patient who in turn experiences it in sundry ways and in turn our awarenesses of the repertoire of self-experiences the patient derives from this simple utterance. It is the mutual and unique vocabulary and phrases that develop between analysand and analyst. It is the way the analysand comes to know—not the person of the analyst per se—but *his* analyst in *his* analysis in some ways better than the analyst, himself.

Therefore, whatever else it is, the analytic fit is mutual. The new edition of the self–selfobject matrix emerges and is shaped in depth and breadth by the renewed selfobject needs of the patient and their impact on the analyst and on his empathic reach.

Returning with these reflections at long last, to the case of Ms. A, I now no longer think that what I called the phase of analysis we began this discussion with—the end of the beginning—was arbitrary. Around this time the analytic die was more or less cast. That is, the idealizing transference came more and more to the fore, was established, and ultimately worked through. I do not think the structure of Ms. A's self pathology alone or my limits and attributes as an analyst alone preordained this ultimate course of our anaytic work together. I feel the course of the analytic work was preordained by her experience of the analytic fit, her awareness, on some level, of what she needed and what she felt she could get from the analytic experience. The analytic waters were tested and the crossing began. The analytic fit can, of course, change throughout the analysis, but however it changes the analytic data are always bound by the patient's experience of the analytic fit and the new edition of the self–selfobject matrix that such a fit allows.

Late in the analysis, Ms. A made two comments. She said, "You do not understand that I have more than I had" and "If we continued, it would be like the two of us going down into a great cave. You could get out. I never could." Of course, both comments could be considered resistance (I don't think they were), but I think they reflect more than the patient's healthy awareness of layers of her personality that cannot fully be dealt with without risking irreparable disintegration of the self. In each of these comments (there were also others of the same ilk) reference is made to me, to her experience of the analytic fit. That is, her assessment is bound not just by her self pathology but by her experience of her analysis. With certain self-evident reservations, Kohut advanced the tenet that "the analysand's capacity to assess his own psychological state is in certain situations potentially vastly more accurate than the analyst's" (1977, p. 19). I would add a corollary. Often toward the end of a more or less successful analysis, the analysand comes to know his analyst—or more accurately, the analyst that the analyst has become in striving to reach the patient—in certain ways far better than the analyst himself—and in particular he knows his own self-experience of his analyst's limits. For by the very nature of their work together these limits have come to parallel the depths of his psyche he dare not risk reaching.

Finally, all this speculation leads me to recall again a family story the patient once told about her father. The story also provides a way of summing up this presentation. According to the patient, her father had an opportunity to make it, to become a very successful businessman if only he had changed positions, that is, if he had dared to risk taking on a new job for a new energetic company. He could not. Ms. A remarked, "That's crazy. I would have changed positions. You have to be flexible. Make what you can of opportunities." Perhaps à propos of this story, Ms. A took her chance in analysis and was flexible enough to reach for me in my reaching to understand her. In that process we both contributed to what emerged in the analysis and what was worked through and what dropped away. The patient left her analysis with some sense of a central core to her personality. With some sense of meaning to her life, with vigorous ideals as a lawyer, with a sense of sustaining creativity and a share of joy. As I mentioned before, Kohut (1977) states a child has two chances to develop a cohesive self via the mirroring selfobject or via the idealized selfobject. For significant self pathology to occur both chances have to fail. For Ms. A, in the analytic setting with me, it seems the second chance was revived and worked through. Is that enough? I think so.

ACKNOWLEDGMENTS

I am grateful to Paul Ornstein, MD, Anna Ornstein, MD, and Robert Leider, MD, for their valuable reflections on this case material.

REFERENCES

Freud, S. (1912). On beginning the treatment. *Standard Edition*, 12:139.

Glover, E. (1955). *The Technique of Psychoanalysis*. New York: International Universities Press.

Gralnick, A. (1942). *Folie à deux*: The psychosis of association. *Psychiatric Quarterly*, 16:230–263.

Hartmann, H. (1956). Notes on the reality principle. In *Essays on Ego Psychology* (pp. 241–267). New York: International Universities Press, 1964.

Kohut, H. (1971). *Analysis of the Self*. New York: International Universities Press.

Kohut, H. (1977). *The Restoration of the Self*. New York: International Universities Press.

Loewald, H. W. (1971). Some considerations on repetition and repetition compulsion. In *Papers on Psychoanalysis* (pp. 87–101). New Haven: Yale University Press, 1980.

Ornstein, A. (1974). The dread to repeat and the new beginning: A contribution to the psychoanalysis of the narcissistic personality disorders. *The Annual of Psychoanalysis*, 2:231–248.

Schafer, R. (1968). *Aspects of Internalization*. New York: International Universities Press.

Schafer, R. (1979). Character, ego-syntonicity, and character change. *Journal of the American Psychoanalytic Association*, 30:867–891.

Winnicott, D. W. (1953). Transitional objects and transitional phenomena. In *Playing and Reality* (pp. 1–25). New York: Basic Books, 1971.

12

The Costs of Compliance: A Patient's Response to the Conditions of Psychotherapy

BONNIE WOLFE

Within the body of psychoanalytic literature, it is common for clinical reports to include a description of the patient's response to one or another aspect of the psychoanalytic situation, such as the disembodied voice of the analyst. It is relatively rare for clinical reports to focus on the organizing meaning to the patient of the overall conditions in which the analysis is conducted. Usually, practices that are accepted and familiar are overlooked. The following account of a psychotherapy case is presented in order to describe the relationship between certain accepted conditions and a particular set of responses by the patient, which had previously gone unnoticed.

Conventions regarding the form of interaction between patient and analyst are referred to as matters of "technique." Some technical considerations refer to concrete aspects of the setting and practical arrangements for therapy, others to the abstract principles that organize and guide the analyst's understanding of the process and conduct of the treatment. There is not a hard-and-fast distinction between the two, and there are many variations among individual practitioners in the understanding and application of these principles. Generally speaking, however, conventions regarding the more concrete arrangements for conducting analysis are maintained because they are believed to enable the essentially analytic process to occur.

For example, the posture of the patient relative to the analyst is believed to facilitate the emergence of the patient's free associations and the maintenance of the corresponding evenly hovering attention of the analyst (Kubie, 1950). Both of these attitudes—the patient's "compliance with the basic rule" and the analyst's "listening with the third ear"—are subsumed under a more general objective: that of illuminating the patient's unconscious mental contents. The "aseptic" demeanor of the analyst is one aspect of the attempt to provide the "neutral atmosphere" that is believed optimal for the emergence of unconscious structures of the patient's personality and psychopathology, and to avoid introducing contaminants coming from the analyst's personality (Menninger, 1958). Limiting of the analyst's responses to interpretations alone (Gill, 1954) is thought to reduce the likelihood of the inadvertent gratification of neurotic aims and thus provide the deprivation believed to be necessary in order to maintain the motivation for change. Overall, established forms have been seen as facilitating an "artificial, partial, and controlled regression for the purpose of a study of inner conflicts" (Waelder, 1960, p. 237). Technique is thus often thought of as a medium for highlighting preexisting structures, much as a stain and magnifying glass are used to illuminate a tissue segment.

The possibility that these procedures significantly alter the field under study and may have a deleterious effect on the outcome has not been systematically explored. Many writers from Freud onward have noted that an undue emphasis on one or another aspect of technique can serve to strengthen defense or resistance, and have recommended that the analyst be alert to this possibility. Some writers have noted that the selective emphasis on one or another technical objective may structure the course of the treatment. Brenner (1969), for example, noted that a special interest in dream analysis "determines one aspect of the course of the analysis," but he asserted that this "does *not*, in itself, distort in any way the basic content of the analytic *material*" (p. 344, author's italics). Elsewhere, he called attention to the importance of understanding the transference meaning of conventions such as the use of the couch, and he noted that these practical arrangements "have received less attention than their actual importance deserves" (Brenner, 1976, p. 189). But, whatever significance these arrangements might have, he believed that they were essential constituents of the analytic process, and that a patient's inability to comply with any "reasonable and conventional" arrangement recommended by the analyst was to be understood as a sign of psychopathology.

Other analysts have objected to the narrow interpretation and rigid application of technical precepts. Many of these commentaries have focused on the issue of the analyst's "neutrality." Loewald (1960), for example, maintained that "objectivity cannot mean the avoidance of being available to the patient as an object" (p. 18) and that "neither the self-scrutiny, nor the freer, healthier development of the psychic apparatus, whose resumption is contingent upon such scrutiny, take place in the vacuum of scientific laboratory conditions" (p. 19). Stone (1961) provided some specific examples of responsiveness (such as answering a patient's questions) and suggested that the withholding of "the reasonable human response which any person inevitably expects from another on whom he deeply depends" might serve the analyst's needs but impede the patient's growth. More recently, Wolf (1976) described an uncritical application of the rule of "analytic abstinence" as resulting in a "distortion of the normally unfolding analytic process" (p. 108), and Kohut (1977) described the classical analytic atmosphere of "muted responsiveness" as "grossly depriving." These differing attitudes about analytic "neutrality" are based on differing views of its impact—

whether it facilitates or obstructs the goals of analysis, whether any adverse impact on a patient's well-being is limited and necessary, or more extensive and unjustified.

Similar questions can be raised about other techniques, such as the use of the analytic couch. If a patient feels more vulnerable, rather than more relaxed, in a recumbent posture, the reactions that are evoked will be more fearful and guarded, rather than less "censored." While these reactions also reveal something about the patient, they represent a mode of response to a highly unusual circumstance, and thus reveal as much about the interpersonal situation as they do about the patient.

This issue has been addressed at its most general level by Schafer (1980), who described the impact of ideas and methods on the phenomena that are elicited and observed:

> What have been presented as the plain empirical data and techniques of psychoanalysis are inseparable from the investigator's precritical and interrelated assumptions concerning the origins, coherence, totality, and intelligibility of personal action. The data and techniques exist as such by virtue of two sets of practices that embody these assumptions: first, a set of *practices of naming and interrelating* that is systematic insofar as it conforms to the initial assumptions; and second, a set of *technical practices* that is systematic insofar as it elicits and shapes phenomena that can be ordered in terms of these assumptions. . . . [T]he data of psychoanalysis [must] be unfailingly regarded as constituted rather than simply encountered. The sharp split between subject and object must be systematically rejected. (p. 30)

Schafer's description, with its focus on the immediate interpersonal field as the substrate from which the clinical material emerges, is closely paralleled by the recent work on "intersubjectivity" in psychoanalysis (Stolorow, Brandchaft, & Atwood, 1983). Schwaber (1983) has noted that "the organization of the patient's immediate experience, whatever the intrapsychic stirrings within him or her, will be influenced, perhaps to a profound degree, by the patient's perception of the analyst and the surround, and by the meanings assigned to those perceptions" (p. 275). The "surround" would, of course, include the contributions made by various technical practices. Atwood and Stolorow (1984) have suggested that the "rules" regarding such practices be subordinated to the more general principle that the analyst's behavior be determined by an understanding of the "nature, origins, and functions of the configurations currently structuring the patient's subjective experiences" (p. 45).

In the clinical example that follows, some "classical" technical procedures were adapted for the purposes of psychotherapy, while others were modified by the introduction of educational and supportive measures. The prior therapist had requested that the patient lie on the couch, estimated the length of the treatment, advised him to inform his parents of his homosexuality, and apparently suggested that he report his dreams to her. Each of these decisions could be evaluated on its own merits. The account that follows is not intended to explore the rationale for such decisions, to demonstrate technical errors, or to illustrate preferred procedures. Rather, I would like to focus on describing the meanings these and other actions had to the patient, and the patterns into which these meanings were assimilated, as I came to understand them.

I came to believe that the cumulative impact of these and other actions was such as to convey a certain meaning to the patient—briefly stated, that the therapist knew best. She knew what was "wrong" with him and how it was to be "fixed" (including some specific nuts and bolts about how this would be accomplished and how long it would take). She knew what was best *for* him for the future and how he should conduct his personal affairs in the interim. And she knew how he should relate to her in order to accomplish these objectives.

CLINICAL EXAMPLE

The patient, a man in his early 20s, was referred to me by his prior therapist, a woman he had seen for approximately 2 years, who had moved out of the area on short notice. The patient lived at home with his parents and attended a nearby junior college. He had initially sought treatment because he experienced panic when he was separated from his parents—when they were away on trips or when he attempted a trip—and because he experienced a generalized anxiety whenever he was away from home. He felt retarded in his development in that he still lived at home with his parents, had no clear academic goals, and had held only unskilled, part-time jobs. He had recently, following the advice of his prior therapist, informed his parents of his homosexuality. In fact, he had close attachments to a number of young men in the same age group and similar circumstances, and to one man in particular, and he had homosexual fantasies, but he was not sexually active, another sign, in his eyes, of his retarded development.

He had been taken for psychiatric treatment by his parents during his childhood and adolescence (the specific reasons for this were unclear), and he had been hospitalized briefly late in his adolescence, apparently as a result of conflicts with his father. He described frequent conflicts with his father, an emotionally volatile, domineering man, and more harmonious relations with his mother.

Certain aspects of his demeanor were conspicuous at the time he began to see me. Most striking were a flamboyant style and a somewhat snobbish manner, coupled with his clearly superior intelligence. During the initial period of therapy, he expressed regret and curiosity about the circumstances of his prior therapist's leaving, and openly expressed the wish that she might remain in correspondence with him and might someday return. He fairly quickly took up again the pattern that had been suggested by her—coming for sessions two times a week, lying on the couch, and "freely associating." He had been told that he was approximately halfway through a projected 4-year treatment.

As I remained alert for other feelings about the abrupt termination, I gradually realized, with some surprise, that the patient assumed that my methods and attitudes were very similar to those of his prior therapist, if not identical, but I did not fully understand the meaning of this. I was uncomfortable with his perception of me, as if I were a new edition of an old book. I had an impulse to correct his "misperceptions" and point out what *my* ideas about therapy were—who *I* really was. But I sensed that he might also feel uncomfortable and unknown and not quite himself with a stranger looking at him. I now believe that his initial tendency to see us as quite similar may have helped him to sustain a sense of his own continuity in the face of the loss of someone who was quite important to him for just that purpose. I later came to understand how reassuring a sense of sameness could be for this man.

During this period, he related a number of anxious fantasies about separating from his parents—such as the fear that a great chasm would open up between Los Angeles and another city, should he or his parents leave, and that he would be unable to bridge the gap and reestablish contact with them. He dreaded separations from the one man with whom he had a close friendship, and did whatever he could to avoid them. These anxieties seemed likely to have been intensified by his therapist's departure, but clearly had older origins. The patient had no memories of traumatic separations from his parents. In fact, his fears were so constant and of such long standing that his mother rarely left him during his childhood—or at least this was his impression.

He also reported a number of nightmares and dreams that conveyed a fear of damage to some body parts. At times, his body was symbolized by a car whose radio had been ripped out or whose trunk had been exploded. At other times, he dreamed of older, masculine females, who had suffered some concealed damage to the lower part of their faces. He was sophisticated enough to recognize in these dreams castration symbolism, anal eroticism and retaliation, and an identification with his mother, who seemed more competent and reasonable (hence more masculine) than his "hysterical" father. But his speculations about the meaning of these dreams were quite intellectualized and generally unproductive.

At the same time that we were exploring this material, I was puzzled by his manner of relating to me. Sometimes he was supercilious and intellectualizing, and at other times he drifted into a semisomnolent state while lying on the couch, curling up in what appeared to be a regressed posture, and barely seeming aware of my presence. In both states, he seemed quite disconnected from me. I found it hard to concentrate on what he was saying, and began calling his attention back to the current, more wakeful reality. When he suggested that it might be better if he sat up for the sessions, I encouraged him to do so.

At this point, several developments occurred that helped me begin to get a better understanding of what the patient was experiencing. He reported a dream about a Dream-O-Matic machine, to which he would submit written accounts of his dreams, which would then be digested, analyzed, and responded to by a printed-out "interpretation." This was my first glimpse of the meaning the conditions of our relationship had to the patient, and of their adverse impact on him.

I was taken aback by the chilly portrait of me. But it was his painful experience, not the negative image of me, that stood out most clearly. I realized that I had taken up one practice that was familiar and comfortable for me, and one that kept my engagement at an intellectual level—the interpretation of dreams. How distant I must have seemed to him, how isolated he must have been feeling, and what a great price he had been willing to pay, if that was what was required in order to get my help.

In addition to the striking impersonality of my representation in the dream, I was struck by his attitude. He reported the dream in his usual way—somewhat supercilious and amused. The computer was efficient and clearly represented me, and he went on to discuss the various possible interpretations of the dream he had given the machine in the dream. It was his compliance—his willing, unquestioning acceptance of the procedure depicted in the dream—that made me aware that he had been assiduously reporting his dreams and dutifully exploring his associations to the dream material because he experienced this as a required part of getting treatment from me, and not because this was the direction his thoughts and feelings might spontaneously have taken. His "free associations" were far from free. They were dictated by his wish to do what would suit my needs.

After I expressed this thought, and indicated that I did not require him to follow a course I had in mind, but would be willing to lend myself to understanding his experiences, whatever direction that took and for however long that took, then he began to notice some of the numerous differences between my approach and that of his prior therapist.

I now think that some hope that I might respond to him in a different way may have been stimulated when I began to question him, over a period of time, as he lay curled up on the couch. "What are you experiencing?" "Where are your thoughts?" "You seem to be drifting away." It was after these more open expressions of my concern and of my not understanding his experience that he suggested sitting up, perhaps hoping that I had a more personal interest in him, that I might want to know how *he* saw things between us. Then, I would guess, my willingness to accept a change in his posture in relation to me further encouraged him to tell me his dream— what his experience of me and of my technique had been.

Certain developments in our relationship became possible after I commented on the patient's dream as I did, and I was able to learn more about some "silent" functions I had been serving for the patient without realizing it. The most striking development was his asking me a question about my personal life. I had announced my plan of taking a brief vacation, and he asked where I was planning to go. It was clear that this represented a departure from the sort of relationship he had with his prior therapist. The patient said that he would not have asked Dr. X such a question or, if he had, she certainly would not have responded. (He had also received quite a bit of therapy during his childhood and adolescence, so he was well-indoctrinated into "appropriate" behavior in therapy.)

Now here was a sticky problem. Should I encourage the patient to tell me his fantasies first and then give him an answer? Could I reverse the order? Should I actually never give him a direct answer? Or could I just answer the question, so long as I didn't mind answering, and then see what happened?

The idea behind not answering was that it would permit the patient to get a clearer view of his inner psychic contents, not distorted or stimulated or suppressed by information about the therapist, and thus more truly revealing of his wishes and fears (or drives and their deformations). But I had seen with other patients evidence of hurt and withdrawal when they were not responded to. Such reactions might go "underground." The longer lasting meaning and impact on the patient would then be unknown, such as an intensified feeling of being unimportant or intrusive. The patient might subsequently feel constrained about asking questions to which he really would like an answer, and certain feelings might then be excluded from consideration in the therapy, or retarded in their appearance.

On the other hand, when I answered the patient's question, certain reactions were precipitated, which I might otherwise not have seen for some time. I told him that I was going to Hawaii. To my surprise, his strongest reaction was not anxiety about the separation—the manifest symptom for which he had sought treatment—but contempt for my choice of vacation spots. Hawaii may have meant balmy breezes to me, but it meant one big Don Ho show to him, and he thought the less of me for it. This time, his snobbish reaction was turned against me.

The importance to *him* of feeling superior was not difficult to discern, although it was not until years later that I was able to understand more fully his vulnerability to intense feelings of inferiority. But I was surprised by his contempt for my choice of vacations, and I sensed that he felt betrayed. I had let him down by having such ordinary plans instead of being, as he had thought, a part of the cultural elite. I was then able to begin to understand how important it was to him that *I* be special and superior.

I now have a better understanding of the mirroring and idealizing needs he had turned toward me. I believe that his image of my superior intelligence and taste, and of his participating with me in a special intellectual project I was directing, were important to him in sustaining some hope of his having special worth at a time when he felt quite degraded. Unfortunately, at the time, my understanding was limited. When I failed to live up to his ideals, he was disappointed, and I was nonplussed. My inability to recognize and support the importance of his differentiating himself from me, under the circumstances, may have contributed to a subsequent weakening of the emotional connection he felt with me.[1]

After this period, the therapy lapsed into a doldrums. The patient continued to "bring in" material that superficially seemed important but left me with a nagging feeling that nothing was going on. I sought some consultation. I was informed that it was most unusual for a homosexual to consult a female therapist, and I received a diagnosis of the patient's "narcissism." These comments were thought-provoking to me, though possibly not in the direction intended.

I began to wonder why a homosexual patient might consult a female therapist and exactly what it meant to this patient to describe himself as a homosexual. Gradually, it became clear that this concept included a variety of unflattering views of himself that had begun to coalesce in the patient's mind at an early age, long before he knew the meaning of the term "homosexual." He had a hard time expressing this sense of himself, but it came out in worlds like "decadent," "weird," "lazy," and "deviant." It was then possible for the patient to recall how his early failures to do well in sports activities, his childhood interest in music, acting, and dressing up in costumes, and other means of displaying himself had seemed to stimulate his father's distaste and withdrawal. We began to understand some extremely valuable aspects of his efforts to develop homosexual relationships. He became infatuated with a heterosexual man, whose masculinity he admired, and who returned his affection. He then became aware of a great sense of relief he gained through these responses, an enhanced sense of his own bodily attractiveness, and a diminished feeling of being physically repugnant or loathsome. He revealed that in adolescence he had submitted to some humiliating surgery in an effort to "retailor" his somewhat overweight body along more "masculine" lines.

We could speculate from his current feelings that his early longing for his father's physical affection had been met with a disgusted and suspicious withdrawal, as if such wishes were a sign of some underlying deviance and perverse intention, rather than being a natural and healthy part of his development. At about this time, he began to lose weight, exercise at a gym, and pay more attention to his attire. A wish that I, too, might find him attractive emerged more openly.

1. I am grateful to Herbert Linden for clarifying this issue.

Concurrent with these developments, we began to understand more about his difficulty separating from his parents. One clue to the sources of his distress came from his worry after he had missed a therapy session. With some encouragement, he was able to express his fear that I would think he was a "flake" or irresponsible, that I might be unwilling to see him when he returned, or lose interest in him if I did see him. The latter fears were at first reflected in various dreams of visiting an aloof, inaccessible woman in a tall building. Gradually, he was able to articulate a more general, underlying concern—that I would feel offended if he decided that there was something temporarily more important to him than a session—and that I would react to feeling offended by withdrawing from him when he still needed my help, and by reminding him of his various inadequacies that would make it advisable for him to attend each and every session.

My policy was that he would pay for any missed sessions that were not cancelled or rescheduled in advance, regardless of the reasons for his absence, but I had no other condition or stipulation regarding his attendance. Later on, I had occasion time and again to notice that he seemed to feel that he "had" to be at the sessions —at particular sessions and "in therapy" in general—not that he wanted to be because of some aims he wished to accomplish or difficulties he wished to be rid of, but that it was something he "should" be doing because of what was "wrong" with him. "Of course," he said. What it was that was wrong with him he couldn't say. But surely I would know or discover this, if only he would continue to come in as he ought and cooperate as he should. There was no question in his mind about this.

At first, he was puzzled by my commenting on these attitudes, and by my stating repeatedly that I did not know what was wrong *with* him, other than by his telling me what was going wrong *for* him. His sense of being guided by external directives and of being constantly subject to external judgment persisted for a long time and only gradually receded as he became more able to recognize and express his own initiatives and priorities, which sometimes included being someplace else, and not at the session. He continued to experience considerable anxiety each time he missed a session. This diminished only as he learned from repeated experience that I did not criticize or condemn him on this account, but accepted at face value his explanation of the reasons for his absence, and that I did not find offensive or pathological the idea that he might find something more important, on a particular day, than delving deeper into his own therapy. Strange to say, it was his presence, not his absence from the sessions at such times, that might be described as a "resistance" (or an "acting-in").

Subsequently, it became clear that the patient's efforts to differentiate himself from his mother had probably been met with such response. When he began to make plans to move into his own apartment, he worried that he might run out of grocery supplies or in some other way discover that he could not manage a household as flawlessly as his mother did. Any such shortcoming, he felt, would be a proof that he was not yet ready to manage on his own. Worse yet, he clearly felt that, should he need to go back to his parents' home for temporary support, the door would be closed. He recalled feeling, as a child, that, if he were to attempt to do something on his own, he'd better be absolutely sure he could do it without slip-up before trying. Otherwise, someone would be quick to point out that he shouldn't have attempted it.

He reported that he often lapsed into passive, dream-like states at home—sleeping late in the morning, staying home from school, and not accomplishing any of the projects he had set for himself. In these states, he was relieved of the anxiety he experienced when he thought about moving out on his own, but he felt even worse about himself in the process—"lazy" and "decadent"—constituents of his debased self-concept.

We were then able to infer that his mother's self-esteem was based not only on her own competence, but also on feeling indispensable to others — able to fill in their deficiencies and direct the course they should follow. She needed to correct and complete her son's deficiencies in order to feel complete and important herself. Her needs had impeded the development in the patient of confidence in his own capacity to expand his skills and had resulted in a truncating of his ambition and an attenuation of his will. He had sensed and responded to her need without fully realizing it, and without realizing the impact this accommodation had on his own further development.[2]

In retrospect, it seems to me that his earlier posture and dream-like state on my couch were a reiteration of the role he experienced as necessary in relation to his mother, and that might be required by me—that of being a more helpless and less developed person than he was capable of being. I would also infer that the patient sensed and responded to his therapist's need to be "in charge"—to know more and know better than he did—in order to feel competent and assured herself.

The patient experienced his therapist's actions in this way and was ready to respond as he did partly because his childhood experiences had led him to expect this kind of relationship. The needs communicated by the therapist found fertile ground in the patient's psychological organization, as it had been shaped during his development.

More memories about early separations emerged during this time. The patient remembered his forlorn feelings and eventual tantrums when he was

2. For a more comprehensive theoretical discussion of the obstacles to a child's individuation that arise from the archaic narcissistic needs of parents, see Brandchaft (1985)—in particular, the idea that the child may comply with parental needs by the constriction of aspects of the developing self that threaten a parent's narcissistic vulnerability, and by the exaggerated development of behaviors that support or restore a parent's narcissistic equilibrium.

sent to sleepover camp or left at home while his parents were away on trips. The parents then quarreled. His father was usually angered by his behavior, while his mother rushed to his side and was then less inclined to leave him. Each parent's reactions left a legacy of difficulty for the patient.

His mother's protective concern—in the context of her other reactions to his individuating from her—deepened his sense that he was incapable of coping with strong distress by himself. His father's repudiating reaction conveyed to him the idea that such strong attachments to his parents and feelings of loss in their absence were quite abnormal.

His father apparently viewed the patient's reactions as a sign of a defect—not as an indication that he was temporarily having difficulty with an aspect of his development, but as a sign that he was "behind schedule," somehow faulty as compared with other children. He experienced his son's "weakness" as a "poor show"—one that reflected badly on him. The patient remembered his father's embarrassed and angry reactions to him during father–son Boy Scout outings and other such events. He felt that he had disappointed his father by failing to live up to his view of what a "real boy" should be like—a view that, on examination, seemed quite rigid and narrow.

His attitudes toward himself were shaped and distorted in this way. His awareness of having different interests and skills than his peers came to feel to him like a sign of some deviance in his very makeup. He developed enduring feelings of shame about a wide range of individual aspects of his own person. Such feelings, I believe, formed the core of the patient's inner conviction that he "was" a homosexual years before he "realized" this. I believe that he subsequently adopted a flamboyant "homosexual" demeanor as a negative means of asserting his worth—a defiant flaunting of the most degraded aspects of his father's view of him in order to retrieve some sense of choice and pride in his own identity. His father's homosexual fears may thus have made a homosexual of the son.

Eventually, we understood more of his father's contributions to his difficulty openly pursuing his own goals. He had experienced considerable inhibition in his academic worth, procrastinating until the last minute in writing papers, for example, and then dashing them off. He realized that his last-minute preparation of papers helped him blunt any anticipated criticism of them—after all, they didn't represent his best effort—and he could therefore keep intact his deeply cherished inner belief that he had some truly superior capacities. He revealed these thoughts to me in an embarrassed way, evidently fearing that I would think his belief in himself ridiculous or unrealistic. Then he was able to remember his father's constantly deprecating, critical responses to his displaying various efforts or products— such as a model he was constructing. His father found fault with its sloppiness and with his proceeding in a pell-mell fashion. He failed to recognize the importance of his son's enthusiasm for a newfound interest. The skill would surely catch up later if given a chance. Limited difficulties—an inevitable part of acquiring new skills—then felt to him instead like evidence of an underlying, permanent inadequacy. Numerous experiences of this sort, and fears of encountering such responses again and again, inhibited the patient's impulse to surge ahead and do his best.

It is important to note that the patient's mother had kept alive his sense of being special and even superior to others. If his father almost invariably found his differences from others to be a source of embarrassment, his mother sometimes found them to be a source of considerable pride. She liked to have him join in conversation with her adult friends. At times, when his father was away, she complained to her son about her husband's childish and unreasonable behavior. Her attitudes toward the patient helped stimulate his feeling of being a worthwhile, more grown-up person. He developed an unshakable confidence in his capacity to be articulate, witty, and sophisticated. He was thus able to sustain some conviction about his own worth, but it was based on a narrow range of his experience of himself.

Even this support for his feelings of worth was unreliable. When his father was upset and superciliously critical of his son, and especially when he burst out in an angry tirade, his mother's support of him seemed to dissipate. She focused all her efforts on placating her husband and restoring his emotional balance. Her husband's outbursts were apparently so upsetting to her that she felt they should be avoided at all costs. Others in the household, including the patient, were to conduct themselves accordingly. She thus conveyed to her husband the central importance of his psychological well-being. The patient may have sensed that his father felt threatened by the closeness between him and his mother. Some such circumstance, involving an open conflict between father and son, resulted in the patient's involuntary hospitalization as an adolescent. As a result, he was left with a fear of the "rug being pulled out from under him," of some sudden collapse in his sense of the value and importance of his accomplishments. He also experienced fears of envious attacks by others, should he have an outstanding success in one of the areas he dreamed about.

By this time, we had a fuller understanding of the psychological network within which the patient's self had been developing. He understood that his mother's happiness with him was enhanced by his displaying special talents, but that she felt disturbed if he did not sufficiently acknowledge her importance to him and recognize how indispensable she was. He also sensed that his tie to her depended on his conducting himself in such a way that his father's more severe narcissistic vulnerability would not be threatened. In moving away from his mother's guidance and tutelage, he experienced conscious anxiety about his own adequacy and less conscious anxiety about the collapse of her feeling appreciated and of her continuing support of him. In attempting to follow his own course even more fully, he ran counter to his father's need to be the center of the household—the one whose talent, temperament, and problems most needed to be catered to—and he then feared the collapse of his father's personality organization and of the psychological world on which he still relied. My accepting him as he was, without comparing him with others, without having some preestablished aims in mind for him, and without needing him to admire me or kow-tow to me, helped him gain a greater degree of self-acceptance and autonomy.

During the ensuing years in therapy, the patient made increasing steps toward autonomous living and developed a widening scope of ambitious strivings. He left the junior college and began to attend a major university where he eventually obtained a graduate degree. He left behind various menial and domestic jobs and found full-time employment related to his longstanding love of music. Each of these developments opened a path to long-term career opportunities that would permit him to display his unusual talents.

Each of these advances was accompanied—or preceded or followed—by some part of a complex of reactions we learned to recognize. One aspect of this was a resurgence of self-doubt and feelings of inadequacy. This he also felt whenever he requested changes in the course of therapy to suit his needs, not mine—for example, when he requested changes in the frequency of sessions or took vacations apart from mine. Each time, he worried that I would become withdrawn or shut him out. He often then had nostalgic longings for earlier, more formless stages of his life. He would, for example, visit old grammar school teachers and appear to find great comfort in their continuing friendliness toward him. In this, he was apparently able to revive memories of earlier experiences that made him feel more secure. He also experienced feelings of loneliness, coupled with some excited anticipation. The feelings of loneliness—an indication of his fear of being cut off from me and forever isolated from reaffirming contact with others—were gradually overshadowed by the excitement that accompanied the reawakening of expansive interests and the sense of new possibilities opening up before him.

These various discoveries helped the patient become more aware of the meaning of tensions in his relationship with his friend. He tended to accommodate himself extensively to his friend's schedule and interests—waiting by the telephone for calls and suspending his own activities. He became more aware of the worries he experienced when he pursued his own interests instead—worries that his friend would lose interest in him or would somehow feel "shown up." These fears had prolonged an extensive dependence on his friend's approval because they prevented him from developing independent sources of esteem through other associations and through the development of his own talents. He gradually became less paralyzed when his friend took trips out of town, and he began to take trips away from the city himself. He became more confident that he could cope with his distress and was increasingly able to do so without needing extra sessions and without seeking reassurance in other ways that he found humiliating. He was able to endure and counteract panicky worries about the loss of the relationship and persist in his own directions in spite of these fears. He began to pursue more actively a longstanding ambition of his own—one that required a public display of his efforts, necessarily exposed him to critical appraisal from others, and was in the same field in which his father had made a career.

At about the same time, he began to consider pursuing a graduate program in psychology at the university at which I had taught. His anxious scrutiny of my reactions once again revealed his concern that I would discourage his ambitions by disparaging his belief in his own potential. Eventually, he decided to pursue a doctoral program in his own academic field in a prestigious and distant university.

Financial problems precipitated the termination of therapy. He could see that there was more work that could be done. However, he decided that he no longer expected to be perfectly free from problems. This might be a good time to stop, since he was doing so much better and thinking of moving out of the city. As might be expected, he then experienced certain concerns. He hoped to be reassured that I would continue to be willing to see him, should he want to return for episodic or more regular visits. He worried that I might actually think that his stopping was ill-advised—that he still had significant problems that I could see, even if he could not. In other words, his assertion of his own perceptions, judgments, and direction was followed by some worried tendency to examine himself, instead, from my "superior" perspective, in the hope, I believe, of shoring up any sagging in my own self-esteem and of ensuring my continuing good opinion of him.

At this time, he related a dream of discovering a house he had never noticed before—near his parents' home but bigger and more splendid. As he began to explore the property, he discovered a large, beautiful garden with ponds—a romantic vista that stretched far into the distance. He was delighted and enchanted, but as he began to go farther, he found himself surrounded by water, worried about getting in "too deep," and turned back. The dream indicates the persistent presence of fears that inhibited the patient's further expansion of himself. In the context, however, the appearance of the beautiful vista, and his sense that he might return to it, seemed a more important theme. It signaled his sense of new possibilities opening to him, despite some residual problems, and his confidence in his own developing psychological momentum.

DISCUSSION

Many of the patient's attitudes toward me can be seen as indications of the mobilization of an idealizing transference. Certainly, there were signs of his admiring my superior intelligence and cultural refinement—qualities that were highly valued in the environment that had shaped his ideals. He enjoyed being able to look up to me, when he had reason to believe that my development along these lines had progressed farther than his own, and on the condition that he did not experience me as belittling him. Equally clear was his disappointment when he discovered cause to think less of me. From this, it seems reasonable to conclude that he was attempting to revive a circumstance in which he could derive inner strength from the support and approval of someone who was stronger or wiser than he was.

But what about the dreams in which I appeared as a computer or as an aloof woman in a tall building? Should these also be interpreted as evidence of a persisting need for an omnipotent selfobject with whom the patient could merge? In these images, my perfection has developed to such a degree that I am virtually inaccessible to human contact. It is difficult to see these as expressions of central aims of the patient. I believe they are, instead, representations of his experience of me and of the therapeutic situation— an indication not of his own needs but those of his selfobject environment.

To be sure, the patient understood and assimilated his perceptions of me along lines that were familiar to him. His compliance gave indications of what he had to do in order to maintain an emotional tie with those who were once, in fact, more knowledgeable and powerful than he. He had to constrict or alter certain aspects of himself in order not to upset or alienate them, and he had to force or exaggerate other aspects in order to please or calm them—a regularly occurring and regularly overlooked outcome of growing up in a family. The patient was thus able to stay in emotional contact with his parents, but only part of him was able to do so. Extensive other parts of his true self remained isolated from the context of an inter-personal relationship. A similar situation can occur in a therapeutic relationship.

I believe, as Schwaber (1983) has suggested, that the patient's computer-image of me "rather than being viewed as a distortion to be modified," should be seen as a "perception to be recognized and articulated," in order to better understand the patient's inner world (p. 274). As I learned more about the patient's sense that he "should" be in therapy so that I could discover what was "wrong" with him, I got a fuller understanding of his experience of me. He saw me not only as being knowledgeable about personality functioning and competent as a therapist, he saw me as being more knowledgeable and competent about *him* than he was—knowing more than he about what he was "really" like and knowing better than he what he "ought" to be like.

I was then able to begin to recognize aspects of my responses and communications to him which had stimulated this experience. Our repeated addressing of this issue enabled the patient to "work through" this obstacle to his development. We did not discover deep-seated and long-repressed wishes. We uncovered instead certain unspoken expectations about the requirements of others in relation to him, and a wordless readiness to respond in ways that might be described as aspects of his personality. What had been unconscious and automatic was gradually replaced by the possibility of different ways of relating to others.

It is not uncommon for patients to experience their therapists as feeling superior to them. Some writers have recognized that the interaction between therapist and patient can contribute to such experiences. Greenson (1972), for example, pointed out that persistent interpretations of the patient's unconscious conflicts can cause the patient to feel diminished. Interpretations can seem to originate from a superior stance on the part of the therapist— a privileged perspective regarding the centrality of feelings that the patient had seen as peripheral or the presence of feelings the patient had never suspected:

> It is one of the vocational hazards of psychoanalysts to fall into the trap of habitually committing one-upmanship with one's patients. The overriding importance of interpretation tends to blur our awareness that by constantly confronting the patient with our discoveries of his unconscious distortions we may be repeating a damaging part of the patient's past relationship to his parents. As the patient's transference neurosis often makes him excessively submissive, he may yield to our interpretations rather than cope with them. (p. 216)

When the therapist recognizes the potential for such unintended results, it is possible to explore aspects of the therapeutic relationship that might otherwise be overlooked. This also makes it possible to evaluate the results of general methods and specific interventions in a continuous "feedback" process. On the other hand, if technical conditions for conducting treatment are regarded as "silent" or standardized, the variance introduced by the current situation can be mistakenly attributed to the patient.

Greenson's paper, which generally illustrates the value of noninterpretive interventions, concludes with a cautionary comment:

> Admitting technical errors or apologizing for lapses in behavior can mislead a patient into believing the analytic situation is one between two equals. Some may construe this to mean that we are now friends in the conventional social sense. It then becomes necessary to point out that, however equal we may be in some ways, in fact the patient may be my superior in some, nevertheless, in the psychoanalytic situation he is the patient and relatively unknowing and I am the expert, my errors notwithstanding. (p. 216)

This is not an uncommon view. The danger presumed to exist in the patient's imagining the therapist to be his equal or his friend is that it may obscure the interpretation of transference distortions or otherwise serve defensive purposes. A patient's efforts to recognize the therapist's limitations, to arrive at his own assessment of his strengths and weaknesses, to feel as important or valuable as the therapist, or to feel closer to the therapist can be mistakenly interpreted as depreciating or defensive reactions. Unrecognized mirroring needs of the therapist can be mistakenly construed as idealizing needs of the patient, and an avenue for growth can thus be inadvertently foreclosed.[3]

REFERENCES

Atwood, G., & Stolorow, R. (eds.). (1984). *Structures of Subjectivity: Explorations in Psychoanalytic Phenomenology*. Hillsdale, NJ: Analytic Press.

Brandchaft, B. (1985). Self and object differentiation. In R. F. Lax, S. Bach, & J. A. Burland, eds., *Self and Object Constancy: Clinical and Theoretical Perspectives*. New York: Guilford Press.

Brenner, C. (1969). Some comments on technical precepts in psychoanalysis. *Journal of the American Psychoanalytic Association*, 17:333–352.

Brenner, C. (1976). *Psychoanalytic Technique and Psychic Conflict*. New York: International Universities Press.

Gill, M. (1954). Psychoanalysis and exploratory psychotherapy. *Journal of the American Psychoanalytic Association*. 2:777–797.

Greenson, R. (1972). Beyond transference and interpretation. *International Journal of Psycho-Analysis*, 53:213–217.

Kohut, H. (1977). *The Restoration of the Self*. New York: International Universities Press.

Kubie, L. (1950). *Practical and Theoretical Aspects of Psychoanalysis*. New York: International Universities Press.

Loewald, H. (1960). On the therapeutic action of psychoanalysis. *International Journal of Psycho-Analysis*, 41:16–33.

Menninger, K. (1958). *Theory of Psychoanalytic Technique*. New York: Basic Books.

Schafer, R. (1980). Narration in the psychoanalytic dialogue. *Critical Inquiry*, 7:29–53.

Schwaber, E. (1981). Narcissism, self psychology and the listening perspective. *Annual of Psychoanalysis*, 9:115–131.

Schwaber, E. (1983). Construction, reconstruction, and the mode of clinical attunement. In A. Goldberg, ed., *The Future of Psychoanalysis*. New York: International Universities Press.

Stolorow, R., Brandchaft, B., & Atwood, G. (1983). Intersubjectivity in psychoanalytic treatment. *Bulletin of the Menninger Clinic*, 47:117–128.

Stone, L. (1961). *The Psychoanalytic Situation: An Examination of its Development and Essential Nature*. New York: International Universities Press.

Waelder, R. (1960). *Basic Theory of Psychoanalysis*. New York: International Universities Press.

Wolf, E. (1976). Ambience and abstinence. *Annual of Psychoanalysis*, 4:101–115.

3. See Schwaber (1981), who notes that, when patients with a fragile self experience the analyst as imparting his own point of view rather than understanding their perceptions (such as the view that "what they are perceiving is a defense against their *real experience*"), they may overtly comply but show signs of experiencing renewed injury to their inadequately developed sense of autonomy.

13

Archaic Selfobject Transferences in the Analysis of a Case of Male Homosexuality

SANFORD SHAPIRO

The widening scope of psychoanalysis has resulted in increased effectiveness in the treatment of perversions. "We have learned that some preoedipal problems do yield to analysis and that the manifestations of oedipal and preoedipal pathology can be intertwined" (Solomon, 1982). We have also learned that paying attention to self-pathology can add another facet to the understanding of those cases that have been stubbornly resistant to psychoanalytic therapy (Kohut, 1979; Kohut & Wolf, 1978).

Our theoretical understanding of homosexuality began with Freud's description of the relationships between infantile sexuality, perversions, and neuroses and the role of the castration complex in the formation of many of the perversions (Freud, 1905). An addition to this understanding was the appreciation of the significance of the aggressive drive and its role in the development of the concept that a narcissistic object choice can be a defense against destructive wishes toward the object (Arlow, 1954).

The psychology of the self has further expanded our understanding of these issues. Goldberg (1975) has described how a perverse erotic experience can serve to master painful affects and Stolorow and Lachmann (1980) have described how perversions can serve to stabilize fragmenting self and object representations.

In the clinical field the technical handling of many perversions has been enhanced by the understanding of archaic idealizing and mirroring selfobject transferences (Kohut, 1971). In this chapter I would like to illustrate how the emergence of these transferences, the reactions to empathic failures, and the working through and resolutions of these transferences allowed for the successful analysis of a case of male homosexuality.

The case to be presented is that of a 47-year-old professional man, highly accomplished in his field, consulting me because of homosexuality of 30 years duration. Married, with three children, his homosexuality had been confined to discreet, long-term relationships with younger men, his wife ostensibly knowing nothing about it. He was now experiencing a change in his pattern. His youngest child, now grown, had left home and he found himself feeling distressed. He took out an ad in an underground newspaper, which led to his first casual affair with a stranger. In turmoil, he did not understand this change from discreet relationships to casual affairs. He did know, however, that if this behavior were to continue, the best that he could hope for would be to get VD and the worst would be discovery leading to the ruin of both his marriage and his career.

I had been acquainted with this man for some 8 years prior to this consultation. His middle child, a daughter then 15 years old, had been referred to me because of school difficulties, running away from home and the use of drugs. I treated the daughter initially with psychotherapy but within a few months recommended family therapy. I worked with the mother, father, and daughter as a unit for 2½ years with a successful result. The daughter stopped running away, was able to stay at home, and stopped using drugs. She graduated from high school without further incident. My assessment of the father at that time was of a rigid but warm individual who found it hard to tolerate dissension. He was the peacemaker of the family, the middle man. The wife impressed me as cold, rigid, and angry. It was hard for her to show emotional warmth to either her husband or her daughter yet she expected a great deal of them.

Six months after termination of the family therapy I was again consulted, this time for the younger son, then 14 years old. His grades were deteriorating, he was interfering with other children in school and he was about to be expelled. I saw the boy in psychotherapy for approximately 6 months with a good result. Six months later I was again consulted, this time about the oldest child, a son now aged 24 who was having marital problems. I counseled the father, in effect, to stop interfering and to allow the son to work out the problems with his wife on his own. At no time had I any inclination of his homosexuality.

Another year and a half went by before he again consulted me, this time for himself. He said, "Do you treat homosexuals?" I was amazed.

This analysis, which lasted 5 years, began with an idyllic story about his happy childhood. He was an only child. He described an idealized relationship with his mother, stating that they were very close. And, in fact, they wrestled together until he was 12. The father was described as passive, quiet except when drinking and largely unavailable.

He felt hopeless about his homosexuality: he felt he was born that way and nothing could be done about it. He said he knew all about Freud and psychoanalysis. He considered it a bunch of mumbo-jumbo, but he was desperate. He saw his behavior now becoming self-destructive and he felt out of control. His attempts at self-cure had failed. Since homosexuality was something ingrained, he saw no way that working with me could change it, but the alternative was suicide, so he felt he had nothing to lose.

The analysis can be summarized in three phases. The first phase, lasting about a year, was characterized by his struggle with our developing relationship. As the therapeutic alliance began to develop and we began to work together, he feared becoming attached to me and depending on me. With the clarification of his fears of being hurt and disappointed he allowed himself to gradually come more often. We started meeting on a twice a week basis and, after several months, increased to three times a week. A few months later he began coming four times a week but it was a year before he could use the couch.

Over time, as the relationship with me became important to him and he felt safer, he could allow himself to miss me. This feeling opened him up to memories of early experiences of being alone and isolated, feeling helpless, vulnerable, and in danger of falling apart, of disintegrating. His mother had been afraid that if she picked him up or held him when he cried she would spoil him. He had been expected to be a "little man," not to cry or be "needy." His childhood dilemma was that when he felt frustrated and alone with no available support, any expression of this frustration or annoyance caused his mother to be anxious, and to complain that he was hurting her. He came to believe that feelings of frustration were damaging to others, a sign of abnormality or defect, and shameful. As a result, he learned at an early age to divert his attention from such feelings, and to present a compliant, false self to the world. Thus he came to feel dead and empty inside, his spontaneous, true self having been buried.

My first interpretation was to make a connection between his upsurge of homosexual fantasies, which occurred over weekends and periods of separation with the underlying feelings of longing and aloneness of which he was only barely aware. He was amazed to see that a homosexual fantasy such as sucking a penis could serve to protect him from the fear and pain associated with the aloneness. Fellatio could provide a sense of contact, a feeling of relief, comfort, and reassurance, a sense of integrity that momentarily relieved the fear of fragmentation. In his relationship with me he began to feel that it was all right to have longings and frustrations. He came to see that I would not ridicule and humiliate him for these normal and expected human emotions.

My countertransference reactions during this period were to be pleased and impressed both with the patient and with myself. I saw him as bright, conscientious, and highly motivated. As he began to idealize me, he experienced my interpretations as revelations. He grasped their meanings quickly and found himself beginning to change. He brought in dreams with productive associations and found my interpretations impressive. He was further impressed with my intuitive capacities and my cleverness. I looked forward to our sessions. He made me feel good.

He then began to worry about being dependent on me, especially when he became aware of feelings of longing or missing me during separations.

These made him feel like a failure; he would become discouraged, and feel hopeless. He began to withdraw from me and to complain of feeling sleepy. My initial response to this was to feel pressured. I felt I was not doing a good enough job, and found myself trying harder. I became more active and made more interpretations. Then I realized that I was responding to, rather than interpreting his disappointment.

I had begun to treat him as fragile and unable to tolerate disappointment. Then I realized that this was his self-image. His sense of strength depended on being allied with a strong figure, in this case, me, and our separations left him feeling vulnerable, weak, and helpless. It also became clear that he was feeling under pressure to sense my needs, please me with his cleverness and perceptiveness, as if he expected that I would lose interest in him if he didn't make me feel good about my cleverness and perceptiveness. He feared that I would withdraw leaving him alone and helpless. He saw in me all the attributes he felt lacking in himself, and he felt safe only as long as he could be sure that he was close to me, so he did all that he could to insure that there would be no disruption in this alliance.

As we came to understand that the idealization was a reexperiencing of a phase of development when one normally is small, weak, and relatively helpless, the patient began to feel stronger and to see me more realistically. This understanding allowed him to recall new memories. He remembered how his mother would leave him feeling alone and helpless when he didn't comply with her expectations. He told me of an incident when he was 3 and he told his mother to "get lost." Mother became upset and punished him by saying she was going to leave him. She hid in the closet and he became frantic, searching everywhere for her in a panic. He was terrified and felt doomed. Mother then stepped out from the closet to his enormous relief. From then on he was preoccupied with fears of losing her. He became sensitive to her every move, learning very quickly how to anticipate her reactions so as always to do "the right thing" and keep her happy. During this time he also recalled longing to be close to his father, but remembered how mother would withdraw and ignore him if he showed any interest in his father. Father, too, was intimidated by Mother and did whatever was necessary to maintain peace. The patient now began to see his mother in a more realistic and less idealized light. He began to refer to her, somewhat affectionately, as "the barracuda."

The end of the 1st year of analysis revealed a clearer picture of his early development. For several years his grandmother had lived with them. She was a warm, affectionate person with an ample bosom who loved to pick him up and hold him. He could only allow this when Mother was not around for if she saw, she would become upset. An uncle, A, also lived with them briefly. A was a young man very much admired by the patient. Memories included their sleeping together with very warm, secure feelings. When the patient was 7 years old, A moved away, as did his grandmother.

The loss of his grandmother was a crushing blow, leaving him feeling bewildered and devastated. His personality underwent a change as he attempted to protect himself from any further such loss. Whereas he had been assertive and outgoing, something of a "hellion," he now became a "goodie-two-shoes." He became fearful and withdrew from playing with other boys. At age 12, when his mother found him playing with paper dolls, she quickly engineered his joining the Boy Scouts. He found himself attracted there to a senior patrol leader, a boy 2 years older who reminded him of A. He was ecstatic when they could sleep in the same tent.

His first overt homosexual experience occurred at age 17, shortly before leaving home for college. He slept with his good friend, B, a young man several years older. He recalled the incredible feelings of warmth and comfort he experienced while they held and fondled each other, an intensity that he never experienced subsequently with women.

He went to college and graduate school, doing very well both academically and in sports. His first heterosexual experience, at age 23, was described as unsatisfactory. At 25, he was inducted into the Army and sent to Korea where he had occasional heterosexual experiences with prostitutes. Returning home, he tried to resume a homosexual relationship with B, but felt that there was something wrong with him and that the cure would be to get married. At age 27, he met his wife to be, decided she was the right person for him, and in 6 weeks they were engaged and subsequently married. Eight years later, following the death of his grandmother, he began a 7-year affair with a young man, who was 16 years old when the affair began.

The middle phase of the analysis, lasting about 2 years, was characterized by somatic complaints including headaches, stomach aches, and diarrhea. The patient took frequent medications including an aspirin and phenobarbital compound for relief.

These somatic difficulties were worse during periods of separation from me, and I was able to interpret his fears of loss. He came to see that his affair of 10 years earlier had been a defense against mourning his grandmother. After this revelation there followed hour after hour of intense weeping. He recalled the comfort he felt at being held in her arms nestled against her breasts. These soothing feelings could be reexperienced when he fondled the testicles of his lover.

At this time he experienced me as his lifeline. Feeling deficient, he worried that he could not get along without me, yet he feared being trapped in our relationship. He reported a dream in which he was sucking a man's penis and swallowed the semen. "It was a lot to swallow," he said. Associations led to the interpretation that if he swallowed what I told him I would be in control. At the same time he feared my not being in control. In another dream he reported being in a 1955 Buick. A Jewish man in a bathrobe had his foot on the accelerator, "but I wasn't afraid," he said. Nineteen fifty-five was the year he attempted to resume his affair with B;

now he was turning to me. He anticipated that I would be upset with him when he revealed his feeling of need for me, but when his fears were not realized, he felt more secure in our relationship. I interpreted these fears as related to his dependence on his grandmother for strength and support. We understood that he had felt strong and confident with his grandmother, and had never developed a sense of his own strength. I had become his current source of strength and comfort. As this block in his development began to be resolved, his self-confidence began to grow. He then had his first heterosexual dream, which signaled to him that there was hope.

On the couch he responded strongly against being cut off from me visually. It made him feel terribly alone and isolated, and he became preoccupied with wanting to please me, with wanting to avoid disagreement for fear of a disruption between us. My sitting behind him also stirred up fantasies of my penetrating him anally. This both frightened and excited him. He recalled memories of sodomy experiences in which he felt like a "woman."

Conflicts about money now came to light. He was controlling about finances and resentful of the checks he wrote me. He remembered how his father turned his paychecks over to his mother and let her handle all the finances. He tearfully recalled that his father did at least always have money for him. He was shocked at the realization that his father, for all of his absence and passivity, actually did give him a great deal.

In the transference he was now starting to worry about my becoming bored. Now that he was developing a sense of his own ideas, he struggled with fears of expressing them, especially when he suspected I might not agree. He anticipated that I would think he wanted to manipulate me and that I would become contemptuous and critical. Any comment that I made at this time was experienced as proof of my contempt. If, instead, I backed off and waited, it was proof that I was bored and didn't care about him. I did indeed begin to feel controlled and manipulated. I said to him that I could now appreciate how hard it was for him to feel that he had a right to express his own ideas and be taken seriously, especially if he anticipated any disagreement. He said that Mother always had to be right. Rather than acknowledge his efforts to develop his own ideas, she would put him down, subtly ridicule and humiliate him. He now could see that she had been very manipulative.

He looked desperately to me for responses or acknowledgment and when they were not forthcoming he felt cheated and short-changed. "You just sit on your ass and don't do anyting," he would complain. He would then become preoccupied with fantasies of going out and finding young men to sleep with. He explained that he knew how to satisfy a young man and that would be certain to bring the response and acknowledgment that he so desperately craved and could not get from me.

I pointed out that he experienced my lack of response as coldness and abandonment; he felt humiliated by me as he had felt by his parents when little. I said that the coldness and humiliation, the lack of acknowledgment that he experienced when little, deprived him of the opportunity to develop trust in his own abilities, to become able to acknowledge himself. He was stuck at the level of development when one needs outside sources of acknowledgment in order to feel competent. Gradually, feelings of humiliation and rejection by me were replaced with feelings of being understood. During periods when I was silent, he could feel that I was still with him: this was a new experience for him. This, coupled with these new understandings, allowed him to feel even more secure in our relationship and to feel better about himself. He could now begin to feel some confidence in his own ideas and trust in his own judgment.

As a result, his personal and professional life began to change. As he became able to complain and to assert himself, he became more effective in relations with colleagues and with family. He also became able to realize and to express needs with the result that he became warmer with his friends and family.

In the analysis, however, his fantasies toward me became more aggressive and he had desires to penetrate me anally. He became aware of rebellious feelings but was unable to express them while lying on the couch. For a period of several months, he periodically would get up and sit in the chair to face me, tell me his complaints, look at my reactions, see that I wasn't anxious or angry, feel reassured, and go back to the couch. Then, while on the couch, he would analyze his fear of confronting me if he couldn't observe my reaction. As a result of these explorations, he began to feel more masculine, to be assertive, yet still warm, to be more giving, yet still self-sufficient. Around this time he began to enjoy intercourse with his wife.

As the transference neurosis intensified, he expressed great longings to be with me and intense desires to get things from me; these desires were expressed in sexual terms. He complained that he would never get from me what he really wanted: a breast or a penis in his mouth. He wanted me to care about him unconditionally without his having to pay. He spent hour after hour experiencing intense weeping. He felt that I didn't care about him and he threatened to retaliate by cutting down to three times a week. If he couldn't count on me, then I would not be able to count on him. Analysis of this fantasy led to memories of when, at age 9, he found that he was very good at baseball, but could not get his parents to come and watch him play. They remained indifferent. He now began to realize that this was not a reflection on him. Because of his parents' anxieties he could never really count on them. The only sources of support on which he could rely were himself via his homosexuality and on money.

He came now to enjoy feeling dependent on me. He no longer suffered from headaches and intestinal cramps and he was free of all medication.

He began to think about his gains and about leaving me. He was fearful that should he leave me he would lose all his gains and everything would deteriorate. He became discouraged with the therapy; he no longer saw it as magic. Feeling the loss, he became sad and depressed. He began missing sessions, but he was able to do more on his own and with his dreams. He was reluctant to share his insights with me because he expected that I would shoot him down, find fault. It did not occur to him that I might be pleased with his achievements or feel proud of him. He felt he did not have a right to expect me to take pleasure in his accomplishments. He began to do well on vacations and was surprised that he could get along without me. He found himself more independent when away from me and now handled family and professional situations differently than the year before.

The last phase of the analysis, lasting about 2 years, was characterized by struggles with his attachment to me, repeated periods of withdrawal from me, and the further development of a mirroring transference and its resolution. He felt better but also felt stuck. He was afraid to leave me, and he felt doomed to being queer forever. He talked in an obsessional manner, endlessly and without affect. I found it hard to follow him, and to concentrate.

At this point we were both involved in a mirroring selfobject transference and countertransference interplay relating to an early phase of development. It was that phase of development in which a child needs acknowledgment, confirmation, and positive mirroring responses in order to develop and consolidate feelings of self-regard and self-confidence. A child needs to be able to talk about his ambitions and accomplishments to someone who will listen and will understand with a feeling of appreciation. The patient stated that in growing up his parents never listened to him. His father ignored him except to demand "pass the salt" at the dinner table. His mother either withdrew from him or changed the subject and began talking about herself, looking to him for his acknowledgment and admiration of her. His boyhood ambitions were greeted with contempt and ridicule. He was told not to brag, not to be selfish. His need for recognition was seen as a sign of his inadequacy.

I pointed out to him that his being deprived of these mirroring responses resulted in a block in that phase of development whereby one becomes able to provide one's own sense of recognition, one's own sense of satisfaction in achievements. The result was that he continued to depend on external sources of acknowledgment and approval. When these external figures did not come through for him he felt in danger of a disruption. The homosexual erotic experience served to stablilize his fragmenting sense of self.

In the countertransference I initially reacted to his periods of withdrawal as hostility toward me. He responded to my interpretations of his anger by feeling hurt and criticized. He felt accused of not doing what I expected. He felt like a failure and became discouraged. He felt that there was no point in continuing the analysis. I then found myself feeling discouraged and hopeless. Like his mother I, too, had failed to appreciate his attempts to protect a vulnerable, depleted sense of self.

I then began to see his withdrawal as a defense against engaging me; he was afraid of me and needed to keep me at a distance. He experienced this interpretation as an intrusion. He complained that I was cutting him off and he wondered why I was so egocentric that I saw everything as related to me. He felt under pressure from me. He felt guilty that he was not conforming to my expectations. I also found myself feeling under pressure and resolved to myself to be more patient. Instead I became restless and he heard me fidget. He knew that I was bored and not paying attention. His reaction to this was to feel ashamed that he could not be more interesting to me. I found myself feeling paralyzed, worthless; and I withdrew further. I started dozing off in the sessions, which I had now come to dread. We were at an impasse. We were now involved in reliving the original traumatic situation where he was left by his parents and made to feel that it was his failure. He felt it was his responsibility to reengage me.

At this point I came to realize that I was reacting to an archaic, mirroring, selfobject transference in which I was not being related to as an object but rather was being used for a listening function. He would talk *at* me rather than *to* me. I began to realize that he was not giving me any acknowledgment. He was in the room alone treating me like I wasn't there. I was hurt and resentful and the more I tried to engage him, the more he felt frustrated and misunderstood.

When I understood my anger and could limit my interventions to simple confirmations of what he was describing, to show him that I understood what he was experiencing, he felt a renewed sense of vigor, although I often would be left feeling depleted.

A cyclical pattern had evolved. When he felt engaged with me, he was able to talk about his loneliness and disappointment with great feeling. His body would be racked with violent sobs as he verbalized feelings of pain at the loss of his grandmother who held him, his grandfather who shared his music with him, and his homosexual lover who had accepted him and comforted him. He felt close to me at these times and I felt alert and engaged. Next he would become anxious, feel vulnerable, and fear that I would be disgusted with him and ridicule him. He would then withdraw from me, retreat into homosexual fantasies, or talk about daily activities in an obsessional manner without feeling and complain bitterly that nothing was happening. We would then talk about his disappointment, and when he saw that I neither became defensive nor rejected him, he would again reengage me and share with me more of his painful feelings.

The breaking of this pattern occurred as he became able to share his disappointments with me and to work them out with me without having to lose our relationship. This was a new experience for him, and it allowed for the resolution of the mirroring transference. I explained to him that this was a step in his development, an opportunity to learn that he is not responsible for me, rather that I have to take responsibility for myself. As he became able to appreciate this he felt stronger, his omnipotent fantasies diminished, and he was able to be appropriately assertive. He began to trust himself more, to feel less reliant on me and to take more chances especially in reaching out to others. He discovered in himself a natural warmth and was pleased at the response of his friends and colleagues.

Separations from me which usually precipitated a multitude of homosexual fantasies were now accompanied by feelings of loss and sadness. He was pleased with his progress and now looked to me to be pleased as well, to say to him, "good job." When I did not respond in that way, he would again withdraw, obsess, and feel like a failure and I would again lose concentration, become sleepy, and share in his feelings of discouragement. It was hard for him to maintain his own assessment of his progress without constant reassurance from me. When I would realize this and point it out to him, contact would be reestablished.

Disengagement from me was also a way of protecting himself from acknowledging my importance to him. Now that he had changed, he feared that to acknowledge my part in this would give me power and control over him. He was afraid that he would be putty in my hands and vulnerable to humiliation. In addition, he fully expected that I would not acknowledge his gains, that I would not be pleased with his progress but would instead become anxious. By disengaging himself from me he was protected from the humiliation of my dissatisfaction with his achievements, from my pointing out his shortcomings and wanting him to do better as his mother had. He felt safe, but I was left struggling with boredom and sleepiness. When I interpreted these fears, he told me that he had no right to expect that I would be pleased with his progress and be proud of him. He then began to weep. Contact was reestablished and my boredom and sleepiness again ceased.

His wife had mixed reactions to his changes. She liked his increased warmth but was unhappy with his new assertiveness. His relationship with his sons had changed dramatically. Whereas previously he had been standoffish and critical, he now was supportive and compassionate. He could hug his sons and express warmth directly and openly. Yet he worried that should he terminate therapy he would revert. He expressed anger toward me more openly. He didn't like it when I changed his appointments. He became aware of how much he attempted to talk about the right things, to tell me what I wanted to hear. It then occurred to him that maybe he could pursue what *he* wanted to talk about. At this point homosexuality was no longer a concern. His relationship with his wife had taken on new importance and depth. He felt able for the first time to relate to people, both men and women, not just someone he used or someone who used him. He struggled with fears of relating to me as an individual. The mirroring transference was further delineated when he said that it was easier for him to see me as just a sounding board, something he related things to and looked to for some kind of response or answer from time to time. "Just a shrink," he said, "not a person with compassion."

He went through another period of sitting in the chair confronting me, this time trying to see me as a real person. If he could face me directly, he could complain, he could tell me that he wasn't getting anywhere, that he didn't like what was going on. He resented the fact that I wouldn't tell him what was happening. By sitting in the chair and facing me, he could read my face, see that he was getting a response and not have to feel so isolated and alone. He saw me as amused, not devastated as he had imagined. He said, "I'm beginning to feel authentic, not just feeling or thinking something belonging to somebody else."

He experienced new feelings of appreciation for me, feelings that I really meant something to him, that I wasn't just something abstract. However, he also felt his new sense of confidence could only be maintained as long as he was allied with me. He was fearful of leaving me. Separations stirred up insecure feelings that were controlled by fantasies of fellatio. He now could express negative transference feelings and began to recall things I had said in past years that he did not like. He felt his disappointments and dissatisfactions and now he could express criticism.

With this increased confidence he felt less dependent on me. He was able to look back and see more objectively his mother's distress at being confronted with a demanding, unhappy child. He realized that she meant well, but that she had her own anxieties and that her distress wasn't a reflection on him. He talked about his father as being weak in some ways but not in all ways. He now could complete that phase of development in which one develops compassion for one's parents and for oneself.

He realized how much he looked to his wife for mirroring responses, validation, and verification, and how distressed he was when she wasn't there for him. Then he began to see that his wife didn't like him having other friends; she liked his being tied to her. He wondered if she knew his secret, or whether he ought to tell her. How would she respond? Would she blow up and reject him?

After much wrestling with these questions, he finally told her. To his shock, there was no reaction. When he told her that he liked men, she said, "Is that all?" She laughed and said, "You're not going to get rid of me that easily." He felt crushed and humiliated that she didn't take him more seriously. Struggling with feelings of disappointment in his wife, he began to take more responsibility for himself and stop relying on her to perform his errands. He had always seen her as a source of strength, like me, and had seen himself as weak. He had been convinced that he could not function without her, as he had felt he could not function without me.

He felt stronger emotionally and better able to handle hurts and disappointments without fears of falling apart. He had new confidence that he could get over disappointments without turning to men. He began to have dreams about women who were attractive and exciting. He could come late to his appointments without feeling a sense of panic. He wondered whether he really wanted to stay with his wife. He realized that her nonresponse made him feel like he didn't count, and he began to feel he deserved someone who would take him seriously.

He was now ready to resolve his attachment to me. Once, during this time, he saw me outside the office riding a bicycle and immediately felt a sense of loneliness: he saw that I had a life of my own that was independent of him. He was surprised when he realized that his colleagues looked up to him when they asked him to take on new administrative duties at a very high level. Yet the idea of leaving stirred up concerns that he would fall apart without me. "To be myself is to be vulnerable and exposed," he said. "If I could stop apologizing for being me I would be able to stop therapy."

We talked about setting a date for termination. He did well when I was away on vacation but he worried, "Is it good enough?" Although he felt free of anxiety he still wasn't perfect. He wanted to cut down, to try weaning himself from me. We set a date to terminate in 8 months and he cut down to three times a week, not wanting to go cold turkey. He wanted to prove that he could get along without me, since all of his life he had been allied with some expert who allowed him to feel protected.

His struggles now to express anger were getting easier. He was pleased when he could express criticism. He said at this time that the analysis had allowed him to work out his relationship with me and that was the most productive experience. He felt increasingly more confident, more able to do things without me and, although he didn't like the idea of coming less often, he found he was doing more of the analysis on his own.

He began to realize the ways in which his wife was unsupportive. She was now experiencing headaches and having her own thoughts about going into therapy. He wondered if he would be able to leave her and then realized that if he felt able to leave her and to live by himself then he could stay in the marriage. He realized now that he could think of leaving me and feel able to count on himself. He no longer needed her to be there to take my place. He felt confident. However, as the day for termination approached, he worried. Would he be able to continue his self-analysis without me? However, when the time came to stop he said, "Well, it is time to try it on my own."

In summary, this 47-year-old man, struggling not only with his homosexuality, but also with his emotional reserve bordering on coldness, was keeping himself isolated. He felt trapped by his rigidity. He entered analysis after a long introductory period and found that there was a relationship between sexual fantasies and underlying affect states such as longing and loneliness. As he became secure in his relationship with me he was able to undo the idealization of his mother, to get in touch with his frustrations and fears from the past, and to become more aware of his longing for a relationship with his father and his feelings of warmth for his father.

Conflicts came to light in many areas including competitive feelings with castration anxiety, control issues with power struggles, fears of separation with anxieties of loss, and fears of fragmentation with fantasies of fusion. All along there were also constant struggles with an inadequate and defective sense of self, feeling alone and isolated, empty and dead inside, relying on his perversions for the stimulation needed to feel alive and real.

Slowly, as the transference neurosis developed, was interpreted and worked through, he was able to have new experiences via his relationship with me. He could assert himself and see that I wasn't destroyed nor was I about to destroy him. He could express longings without feeling weak and in danger of humiliation and ridicule. He experienced disappointments without having to fear fragmentation. He could feel and express his disappointment in me when I made mistakes or failed to understand him. He said I could tolerate his being angry and didn't fall apart when things didn't go well. His internalization of my tolerance plus his new insight into the past allowed for the formation of new psychic structure, a new self-representation, a sense of inner strength on which he could rely in the face of disappointments. He could complete this phase of his development and now feel a sense of self that was whole and vigorous such that he could now take chances, pursue new challenges with zest and enthusiasm, and show deep affection for both friends and family members. Archaic and primitive ways of looking at things leading to masochistic behavior were replaced with a sense of tolerance and compassion both for himself and for others. Experiences of pain were now supplanted with ones of joy. Feelings of failure at each disappointment were now replaced with a sense of opportunity, the opportunity to learn and to grow.

Finally, we both were aware that he was not alone in his development. I too had learned and had felt my own growth and development. We parted with a real sense of mutual achievement.

REFERENCES

Arlow, J. A. (1954). Perversions: Theoretical and therapeutic aspects (panel report). *Journal of the American Psychoanalytic Association*, 2:336–345.

Freud, S. (1905). Three essays on the theory of sexuality. *Standard Edition*, 7:123–245.

Goldberg, A. (1975). A fresh look at perverse behavior. *International Journal of Psycho-Analysis*, 56:335–342.

Kohut, H. (1971). *The Analysis of the Self*. New York: International Universities Press.

Kohut, H. (1979). The two analyses of Mr. Z. *International Journal of Psycho-Analysis*, 60:3–27.

Kohut, H., & Wolf, E. S. (1978). The disorders of the self and their treatment—an outline. *International Journal of Psycho-Analysis*, 59:413–425.

Soloman, R. (1982). Man's reach. *Journal of the American Psychoanalytic Association*, 30:325–345.

Stolorow, R. D., & Lachmann, F. M. (1980). *Psychoanalysis of Developmental Arrests*. New York: International Universities Press.

14

The Self-Pity Response: A Reconsideration

SAMUEL L. WILSON

Throughout the years I have experienced feelings of anxiety, frustration, anger, and helplessness when dealing with some patients who are commonly described as "difficult." When discussing such cases with others I have discovered that I am not alone in this regard. As a means of self-preservation together with an attempt to understand the dynamics of this situation I have repeatedly attempted to sort out the possible etiology of this phenomenon. In essence, why is it that the difficult patient is so difficult, and why do they so upset us?

After studying and becoming more involved with psychoanalytic self psychology I have gradually become able to shift my focus in a way that allowed me to see and understand elements of my interaction with such people in a new manner. One of the elements that I found to occur with a greater than average expectancy was a behavior that I can best describe as self-pity.

Webster's (1975) defines pity as "The suffering of one person excited by the distress of another." The self is defined as "A person or thing, with respect to his, her or its own person, individuality, or identity." Self-pity might then be defined as: The suffering of a person as excited by its own distress and directed toward its own person, individuality, or identity. While I believe this definition encompasses some common elements of what self-pity is, it does not describe what it does, either as a psychic mechanism within one individual or as an effector of object relations. As I have come to understand it, self-pity is a response to an injury to the self, its purpose is to be self-soothing, reengaging of another, and it is a subtle but potent expression of hostility. The latter is directed both toward the self and the other.

While, like many other psychopathological states, self-pity is a response that everyone has experienced, it becomes a modus operandi or characterological mechanism in those who have experienced significant developmental arrests in what has been described by Kohut (1971) as the narcissistic developmental line. People who have experienced such arrests are included in both narcissistic personality disorders and borderline disorders.

178

In this chapter I am proposing an extension of the concept of self-pity based on my clinical observations facilitated by the work of several authors identified with self psychology. These writers have focused on the vicissitudes of a type of developmental arrest that has added a new dimension to the understanding of clinical situations that had been obscure prior to these discoveries.

As a background, I will touch briefly on the work of others who have contributed to the evolution of the concept of the self-pity response. In attempting to expand the understanding of borderline disorders, Mahler (1971) drew attention to what seemed to her and her co-workers to represent developmental pathology in the rapprochement phase of separation–individuation. She described one such patient who in "grievance sessions" with his analyst would engage in diatribes of self-accusation and self-denigration. This patient's self-accusations were felt to result from the excessive splitting of an integrated self-concept yielding an alternating view of himself as either "good" or "bad." This splitting derived from a similar phenomenon in relation to the world of external objects, which had developed as a result of a fixation at the rapprochement subphase of development. Kernberg (1975) has also written extensively of the relationship between borderline states and narcissistic pathology.

The findings of Kohut (1971) on the nature of selfobject relationships have been elaborated and expanded through the development of the concept of intersubjectivity by Brandchaft and Stolorow (1984). Although the latter authors do not mention the clinical entity of self-pity, the observations of an underlying vulnerability and propensity for disintegration are applicable to the phenomenon. Intersubjectivity as a point of primary focus has been the missing and essential link in the more complete explication of the concept of self-pity.

Intersubjectivity is presented as existing in "a field consisting of a precarious and vulnerable self (patient), and an archaic and potentially failing selfobject (analyst)" (Brandchaft & Stolorow, 1984). In this way the analytic dyad is seen to exist in a constant state of flux. In this field there exists "an intersection of two subjectivities, that of the patient and that of the analyst." Psychoanalysis is not seen as a science of the intrapsychic, focused on events presumed to occur within one isolated "mental apparatus." Nor is it conceived as a science of the interpersonal investigating the "behavioral facts" of the therapeutic interaction as seen from a point of observation outside the field under study. Rather, psychoanalysis is seen as a science of the intersubjective, focused on the interplay between the differing organized worlds of the observer and the observed (Stolorow, Brandchaft, & Atwood, 1983). Taking a position "within this field, rather than from without as an observer, places an emphasis more on introspection and empathy as the method of observation (Kohut, 1959).

It might be said that "good analysts" have always appreciated these aspects of the analytic process and conducted themselves from such a vantage point. I believe, however, that the systematic focus of self psychology on these aspects of the analytic process represents a progression in the evolution of the process that Freud (1905) started when he first described the transference.

Stolorow and Brandchaft (1983) describe the manner in which people who have experienced developmental arrests in the narcissistic sector of their personality, form relationships with others that appear "borderline." They are easily hurt, very sensitive to loss, and are prone to rapid psychotic-like disintegrative processes when they feel rejected. The observation is made by the authors that such borderline phenomena cannot be correctly or adequately understood and treated unless the intersubjective field existing between the patient and therapist becomes the point of primary focus.

I suggest that self-pity, or more correctly, the self-pity response, is a mental state that frequently occurs but has as yet not been adequately explained due to the absence of the necessary theoretical foundation upon which to build. With the contributions of self psychology it is now possible to go further in the understanding and treatment of this phenomenon.

REVIEW OF LITERATURE ON SELF-PITY

The topic of self-pity is largely neglected in the psychiatric and psychoanalytic literature. The index of the *Standard Edition of the Complete Psychological Works of Sigmund Freud* (Freud, 1974), does not list the subject. The only psychoanalytic description of self-pity to date has been that of Milrod (1973). He draws attention to the *continuum on which self-pity and self-comforting responses occur* (italics added). According to Milrod these mental states may be brief, transitory reactions to both internal and external stimuli or they may be so severe as to play a dominant part in one's characterological adaptation.

In his article Milrod describes how self-pity can be a resistance in certain stalemated analyses. He defines self-pity as "an affective state involving a special combination of pain and pleasure in which the self-representation is hypercathected with libidinal energy." He states that after a person passes through the oedipal period, his self-representation will bear the mark of the superego. Milrod points out how the preoedipal child experiences a rise in self-esteem when he or she behaves according to parental standards, and is showered with praise. Later after the superego is more fully formed a person experiences increased self-esteem whenever he lives up to his moral standards. Freud (1921) described this as the feeling of triumph and release that results when some thought or activity of the ego coincides with the standards of the ego ideal. Milrod describes how the empathy that is initially stimulated in the observer gradually sours into disdain.

The particular blend of pain and pleasure encompassed in self-pity originates from a narcissistic wound with subsequent attempts at self-comforting. In Milrod's view this wound may be real, imagined, or self-provoked. Milrod describes how patients so injured often withdraw into a darkened room where in their pain they can savor the gratification of comfort and consolation that they lavish on themselves. He describes this as a "narcissistic orgy tinged with masochism." In this way people with prominent patterns of self-pity convey a self-concept of a victimized innocent.

Milrod's work has added immeasureably to our understanding of self-pity. In not having access to Kohut's concurrent discoveries of the importance of selfobject relationships Milrod was denied the capability of adding those elements of the self-pity response that provide an understanding of its primary motivation. This is its reparative and adaptive potential. He attempts to fit the phenomena into a current metapsychology involving structural and drive concepts. While mentioning the continuum of self-pity and self-comforting responses and the essential part that narcissistic wounds or injuries share in the genesis of the reaction, he is unable to link these concepts to narcissistic vulnerability as manifest in the intersubjective field although he states that it is the *"narcissistic wound or injury that precipitates the reaction"* (italics added). His assertion that this wound may be "imagined, real, or self-provoked" also diverts attention from the subjective experience of the patient in which the wound is always "real," a dangerous trend if empathic resonance is to be maintained. With the addition of the concept of intersubjectivity the focus can be shifted to and maintained on the subjective view of the patient's experience of narcissistic wounding, which precipitates the self-pity response.

In his view of self-pity, Jekels (1930) describes a continuum that exists between object relations and narcissistic relations. While this view prevails in the literature, adherence to its limited focus will obscure an understanding of the adaptive nature of the self-pity response while focusing on other elements of typical defense analysis, which are secondary phenomena. He cites a case of self-pity in which a man would stand before a mirror and tenderly caress his face saying, "You poor, poor thing." Jekels feels that in this instance self-pity is no longer object related. It represents instead a return to a need-satisfying relationship in which both object and subject are within the self. Self-pity is "in other words, a narcissistic regression involving object relationships and the drives."

Kahn (1965) lists examples of how self-pity can be initiated by external factors such as physical deformity. He points out how Soren Kierkegaard, the great Danish existentialist, suffered from a skeletal malformation and used self-pity to affect a "pseudo martyr persona for the purpose of exhibitionistic display."

Another component of self-pity has been addressed by Horowitz (1981). Which he calls "self-righteous rage." Etiologically this is felt to result from an impaired development of the self-concept. Investigation of the family dynamics in these cases often reveals an empathic dissonance in which defects of parental narcissism preclude the consistent empathic resonance that is needed by the child. A capricious shifting of concern occurs. The child is buffeted by inconsistent behavior on the part of the parents resulting in precarious feelings of self-worth. Parental action toward the child cannot be logically attributed to reactions to the child's behavior, rather it appears to be more related to parental states of mind. The child is left in a confused state in which he feels alternatively to be victimized and victimizer.

The authors cited above have all contributed to the delineation of etiologic and phenomenologic elements of what I am describing as the self-pity response.

SELF-PITY: NEW THEORETICAL CONSIDERATIONS

The following is an attempt to explain what I believe is a previously undelineated primary factor in the genesis of self-pity. The self-pitying response is initiated within a narcissistically vulnerable individual following a failure of empathy with someone functioning as a needed selfobject under certain specific conditions. When these conditions are met the response of self-pity is an urgent attempt to counteract feelings of alienation and disintegration accompanying a severe narcissistic wound and to recover selfobject connectedness. In an effort to understand the circumstances that lead to this clinical symptom and its origin the normal narcissistic developmental sequence needs to be appreciated.

In the beginning an infant's cry can be stimulated when an injury to the self occurs (Bowlby, 1980). The cry is a signal of distress that is intended to call forth a soothing response from the mother or caretaker. This soothing response is absoutely essential if the child is gradually to acquire the capacity to sustain narcissistic hurts without suffering varying degrees of damage and eventually to take over its own regulatory functions.

With this sequence as a backdrop it is now possible to explore the phenomenon that I have observed in which a failure of empathic resonance results in severely painful injury and is often accompanied by aggressive-rage responses. A subsequent specific (succeeding) failure of empathy on the part of the caretaker sets the stage for the emergence of self-pity. Such a response may also be ushered in by a deficiency of comforting responses. The rage that is engendered in the subject causes a further deterioration of the selfobject tie and comforting responses that he so vitally needs.

Another aspect of the application of the concept of intersubjectivity, relevant in the genesis of self-pity is contained in the following passage from Stolorow and Brandchaft (1983), "When the psychological organization of the parent cannot sufficiently accommodate to the phase-specific needs of the developing child then the more malleable and vulnerable psychological structure of the child will accommodate to what is available."

When a child must adapt his thinking and behavior in order to maintain the tie to the selfobject a distortion occurs. This results in an organization of affects and behavior around the distortion.

For example, when the child's protest is met with anger rather than comfort by the selfobject, a gradually increasing tendency may develop for the child to turn his protest, or anger, toward himself. This tendency shows up in self-pity as an element of hostility whose purpose is twofold. The attack on the self contains the hope that this will subserve the needs of the selfobject, as they are perceived, and therefore restore the tie. The appeal to the mercy of the selfobject subserves the needs for a comforting response. Unfortunately this reaction is suffused with an overwhelming mixture of helplessness and additional hostility. This provokes the already alienated selfobject into further withdrawal and anger. A situation is established in which the child is left without a way to repair injuries. Subsequently he experiences feelings of being responsible for the failure of the selfobject and unjustly deprived of something essential. The outcome can be a tendency, or when the cycle reoccurs, a repetitive characterological propensity to react with self-pity in the face of rejection and hurt in a continuing, accelerating, and futile attempt to reengage the selfobject with the hope that the normal tie can be reestablished.

Tolpin and Kohut (1980) have described a type of depression that results from chronic states of depletion of the self. They have labeled this state "depletion depression" and have characterized it as an endopsychic state of emptiness, depletion, and helplessness.

In all of the illustrative cases to follow, a strong element of an underlying smoldering depression could be observed. I would hypothesize that at least a part of the depression observed in these patients was due to this depleted state as put forward in Tolpin and Kohut. Although I have as yet not observed a significant enough number of such individuals to make a definite statement, it appears that similar structural deficits may underlie both those who exhibit frequent episodes of self-pity and those who appear to be suffering from depletion depression. Further study is needed to elucidate these ideas.

In these individuals, a continuum seems to exist from transitory states of self-pity to more severe and disruptive chronic depressive syndromes in which depletion becomes more all-pervasive. In the latter case it seems that an unconscious "pact" has been entered into between the individual and his selfobject in which the selfobject is expected to share in the grief. When this does not occur, further depression and/or defenses against it result. These defenses may take the form of various autoplastic or alloplastic reactions. The severely disruptive acting out that occurred in Case 3 below provides an example of the latter.

In this sense the depletion depression may represent a break-down product of repeated failures of selfobject responsiveness to the call for help as manifested by self-pity. Reactions of self-pity that characterize the outside life of the patient will in due time come to structure the selfobject transference as it evolves within the therapeutic setting.

CASE ILLUSTRATIONS

The following cases all involve one or another aspect of the self-pitying response. Many times the exact words spoken by the patient do not by themselves sound self-pitying. I can only ask that the reader accept that the patient's tone and demeanor reflected a sense of self-pity as it has been defined above.

Case 1

A young woman lapsed into a state of self-pity following a severe disappointment when she failed to obtain a job for which she felt well qualified. She felt she could not share her disappointment. She said in a self-pitying tone, "I am not supposed to complain." She explained this conviction by reporting that she had noticed that I reacted more positively or enthusiastically to her successes than to her failures. From this perception she concluded that I could not stand to share her disappointments. Her experience of me in this situation took its meaning from significant experiences in her past. One such incident occurred upon the death of her grandmother. She was in charge of picking up her grandmother's clothes and making all of the funeral arrangements. At first she disavowed her anger at being so put upon. Subsequently she broke down and cried hysterically. Her sister, mother, and stepfather all yelled at her and called her a "stupid bitch." They reacted by being aggrieved at her protest and forcefully asserting that she had no right to put them through this emotional turmoil. She was rebuked for her lack of compassion for her sister who had been arguing with her grandmother when she suffered her fatal heart attack. The self-pitying became increasingly dominant as she complained "I know that something is horribly wrong with me."

Case 2

A young woman appeared for her session looking stunned and upset. She told me in a self-pitying tone that she was not doing well. She recounted how after leaving the last session she felt unsupported by me. She thought I was not taking her seriously. Upon returning home she called a friend who after listening to her for a considerable amount of time told her that she had to leave and go shopping. This triggered a reaction in which she felt tremendously sorry for herself and enraged at her friend. She spent the weekend feeling worthless and deflated. In reconstructing her reactions during the last session we discovered that she felt that I was preoccupied and not interested in her distress. She had called me the night before (unusual for her) to tell me about her fear of being threatened by a known arsonist that she had inadvertently engaged to walk her dog. Upon bringing this up in the session she experienced me as not appreciating how upset she was by this circumstance.

She had noted that I had been a few minutes late in letting her into the consultation room and had seemed "in a hurry" to finish the session. There was some validity in these observations as I had in fact been a bit preoccupied with a professional meeting that I planned to attend shortly following the end of her session. When I was able to listen to her complaints and take them seriously the empathic bond that had been temporarily ruptured was restored. There was a sudden and marked change in her affect and demeanor. The response of self-pity abated. We were subsequently able to go more deeply into an area that had been heretofore obscure. She had exhibited both in and out of the session a characterological lightheartedness interwoven through her disphoric states. This conveyed the message that things were not really as serious as they seemed. This attitude reflected an attempt to minimize her experience and expectation of being misunderstood. The self-pity that remained embedded within and that surfaced intermittently was a veiled attempt at reinstituting the selfobject connectedness that was essential for the growth of her personality. Further exploration of this mechanism illustrated that she had developed this type of paradoxical nonchalance by assimilation of the attitudes of her mother and sister whom she felt regarded her complaints as burdensome and needed her to be the strong, sane member of the family. Conversely this increased her tendency to lapse into self-pitying responses when more ordinary efforts would fail to bring about the hoped for understanding of her emotional needs.

This case also provides an illustration of the analysis of a resistance against the awareness of a selfobject transference in which the patient had to ward off specific feelings of needing me to accept her being "burdensome," without retaliating or withdrawing from her. Her reaction of self-pity was an attempt to keep me connected to her. This reaction would occur in response to failures of varying degree on my part to stay empathically attuned to her affective states. As we worked together in the unraveling and explication of these events, within the transference, both immediate relief and incremental structural change took place.

Case 3

A middle-aged woman left town for her annual visit to her mother's home in a distant state. After a month she again fell prey to her mother's nagging about her past failures. When she tried to assert her own version of past experiences her mother pointed out that since they were in "her" home she must abide by her version of history. This unempathic disavowal of her daughter's experiences began a reaction of self-pity in which she assumed an often repeated stance of the defeated, pitiful victim who, though angry, must submit to a joyless existence. Mixed in with this attitude was the implied accusation that this tragedy had befallen her at the hand of another, who must now set it right. When this response was met with anger and disavowal it led to the disintegrative reactions of substance abuse, manic behavior, and sexual promiscuity, finally resulting in her being hospitalized. In this case the restitutive function of the self-pity response did not occur to a degree sufficient enough to prevent the further disorganization and disintegration of the self.

Upon her return she told me that she had felt that I had implied that she should not go home for the summer, and that I had failed to understand the emotional importance of the trip for her. It was at this point, when she felt that I was unempathic to her need to be with her mother, that the process of disorganization actually began. When she experienced a similar empathic failure at the hands of her mother the self-pitying response was triggered.

If the patient had been in the treatment situation it might have been possible to discover and recognize (as in Case 2) my empathic failure prior to the escalation of the self-pity response. This could have prevented the further disorganization of the self that subsequently occurred.

Case 4

A man in his late 40s became angry, withdrawn, and assumed a "hangdog" self-pitying stance in which he began to withdraw his assertiveness and lapse into an apologetic, self-effacing, and whining mode of speaking. This followed an interpretation that I had made about his acting out his anger. When I inquired as to what might be responsible for this reaction, he told me that he thought I was unable to "put up with" his anger. Consequently he felt that he had lost me as an ally. This was exactly the type of experience he had had with both of his parents on many occasions in the past. This had led to excessive alcohol intake as a way of "feeling whole" again. When I was able to reimmerse myself into the intersubjective field I achieved a new understanding of both the patient's and my own reactions. I could acknowledge within myself the slipping back into previous personal and theoretical positions that I had held in regard to the expression of anger via acting out. The hostile accusatory aspect of this patient's self-pity response had made me want to "fight back" in some fashion, hence the regression to an interpretive stance, which although correct from one vertex, did not focus on the adaptive, reaching-out motive in this patient. The next result of this sequence was that the patient felt attacked.

Without lapsing into a self-indulgent confessional stance, I did acknowledge to the patient that he had correctly perceived my attitude, which was based on previously held views from which I was obviously not yet completely free. My presently developing capacities to place myself within the intersubjective field allowed me to be more aware of both the patient's need to react the way he did together with my original response of easily slipping into a stereotypical "analytic" interpretive stance. I believe it is very difficult and perhaps almost impossible when in such a stance to interpret underlying motives in acting out without actually being guilty of casuistry. He felt relieved at my saying this and was able to gradually reengage the selfobject tie that he had previously felt toward me.

Case 5

A middle-aged woman came to the session looking angry and tearful. It was a familiar sight and portended a gradual, progressive decompensation manifested by a variety of self-destructive behaviors, including alcohol and drugs, which sometimes resulted in hospitalization. She said that she was not doing well and described a situation in which she had angrily berated her ex-husband in front of their son. She realized that this was wrong and said, "Everyone told me I shouldn't do it but I'm tired of things not being fair, and of people saying that life is just not fair. I'm tired of being so understanding of him all the time while he can do anything that he wants to me." Her anger slowly devolved into a gradually escalating state of self-pity in which she became increasingly self-accusatory. The self-accusations, however, were not "pure," that is, there was a distinct feeling conveyed to me that I in some unspoken way was either partly responsible for her situation and/or should do something to make it better.

She continued in a "self-pitying" manner saying that she shouldn't even be allowed to be with their son and perhaps should not be involved with anyone every again. As we began to understand her reactions it turned out that she was also referring to feelings that she had recently experienced with me in the therapeutic situation. She felt that I had implied that she was being too easy on herself and was expecting life to be "more fair" than it actually was. She felt that I was not empathically aligned with the background of deprivation from which her anger emerged. When we were able to elucidate these perceptions of me she was again able to feel a sense of wholeness and to continue on with the analytic work.

DISCUSSION

When, in certain narcissistically vulnerable individuals the subjective experience of being wounded by a person who is vitally important occurs and then is reacted to unempathically a process may be set in motion in which the self undergoes a complex set of transformations in order to maintain the selfobject tie. It is as if, lacking a selfobject connection, a new form of empathy has been discovered, that of the self taking itself as its own selfobject. My own investigations to date have not been complete enough to determine why the self-pitying response occurs in preference to some other form of self-state adaptation. This state of affairs is, however, not unlike other situations in which similar dynamic configurations result in divergent psychopathological states.

Embedded in the self-pitying response may be a component of self-righteousness that registers as a complaint against the person who has triggered the reaction. Each experience of misunderstanding reactivates memory traces of repetitive selfobject failures of acceptance. Such configurations appear widely in patients' everyday lives and are inevitably reactivated in the analytic transference. When this occurs the patient's "self-pity" will become felt by the analyst to be directed in some unclear way toward him. It is as though his value as a therapeutic agent or even as a worthwhile person is being called into question.

The easily felt guilt and impotent anger of the analyst (countertransference) can result in a variety of nontherapeutic maneuvers. He can point out the projective aspects of the process, that is, that it is the patient's unconscious anger that is being incorrectly identified as being caused by the analyst, with whatever transferential meaning this may have. He may also allude to the defensive and passive aggressive nature of the reaction. While these formulations may have validity as components of the self-pitying response, in some instances, to focus on them as primary is in my experience, incorrect and nontherapeutic, in that in both of these instances the most basic cause of the reaction will be missed, therefore increasing the resistances to the analytic unfolding. Such interpretations may also force a defensive identification with the analyst's point of view. It is only with the recognition of the primary empathic failure, which had been reacted against, that a move toward structural change and resolution may occur.

Another aspect of the problem involves a disruption in the development of the capacity to experience a form of normal signal anxiety (Tolpin, 1975). In what I believe to be a landmark paper, Jacobson (1983) has lucidly attempted an integration of the structural theory with representational world concepts. He points out how both models involve a signal function, one activated by instinctual drives and the other by the perceived discrepancy in the representational world. In the latter case the perception of discrepancy and the resulting pain function as a signal for a homeostatic alteration. An example of the latter phenomenon is the infant's 8-month stranger anxiety.

In those individuals who have developed an acute vulnerability to hurt or disappointment it appears that due to repeated empathic failures throughout development the normal phase appropriate structuralization of the signal function has not occurred. That is, under normal circumstances a rescue signal is followed by pleasurable maternal interaction. When this sequence occurs frequently the child has built within itself a "structure" of expectation that his displeasure if expressed in some perceivable way, will be picked up by the selfobject, as a member of the representational world, and will be responded to in a way that brings him a sense of soothing or relief. When this does not occur some distortion of the function signaling rescue ensues.

Here the "rescue signal" has become the self-pitying response. This occurs as a result of a break in empathic union in which the self perceives that it is disliked by the selfobject. The affected one then behaves in a self-pitying way in the misguided hope that he will be pleasing the disjoined selfobject. By such action he hopes to effect a reunion with the lost selfobject. He is, in effect, behaving in a manner consistent with what he feels is expected of him. The goal is to prevent the disintegration that is felt to be imminent if the selfobject is lost.

In these cases it appears that there has been a disruption of the phase appropriate loss of maternal holding functions. Ordinarily these allow the development of ego capacities sufficient to tolerate the awareness of accretions of emotion that are pressing to discharge.

The self-pitying response may then become a chronic, distorted way in which to try to achieve a connection with a needed selfobject. It does not heal the wound produced by the developmental arrest but rather stands first as an emergency measure and later as a manifestation of a disturbed personality structure created in an attempt to maintain a sense of feeling whole. When such states of self-pity occur in the context of the therapeutic process, a breakdown of some aspect of the selfobject transference relationship has occurred.

In the analysis a second chance exists to identify the resistances and defenses against the reemergence of similar anxieties as a type of "acting in" of the transferential relationship. It is possible to identify the reaction, trace out its antecedents in their relationship to the analyst, reconstruct the etiological determinants from the past and in so doing provide an experience in which analytic phase appropriate failures occur with the resultant development of new psychic structure now more capable of enduring the continual disappointments of life.

SUMMARY

The subject of self-pity has been neglected in the psychiatric and psychoanalytic literature. With the exception of the work of Milrod (1973) no psychoanalytic writer has dealt with the topic. His work explores the concept from an object-relation drive psychology point of view. I propose in this chapter that more can be understood regarding the concept by drawing on the insights of psychoanalytic self psychology. Authors identified with this point of view have focused on the vicissitudes of developmental arrests as manifest in the intersubjective field. My clinical observations have led me to conclude that self-pity results from the disjunction of a necessary selfobject union. It is an attempt, albeit in part maladaptive, to reunite with the desired and needed selfobject. Various cases from my psychoanalytic practice are used to illustrate this process. I also discuss how self-pity is related to a faulty development of normal signal anxiety. By proposing a new way of viewing the etiology of self-pity I am suggesting that a different focus, that is, on the selfobject transference within the intersubjective field, can provide benefit to both analyst and patient.

REFERENCES

Bowlby, J. (1980). *Attachment and Loss* (Vol. III, *Loss*). New York: Basic Books.

Brandchaft, B., & Stolorow, R. (1984). The borderline concept, pathological character of iatrongenic myth? In J. Lichtenberg, M. Bornstein, & D. Silver, eds., *Empathy II*. Hillsdale, NJ: Analytic Press.

Freud, S. (1905). A case of hysteria. *Standard Edition*, 7:3–122.

Freud, S. (1921). Group psychology and the analysis of the ego. *Standard Edition*, 18:67–143.

Freud, S. (1974). Indexes and bibliographies. *Standard Edition*, 24.

Horowitz, M. J. (1981). Self-righteous rage and the attribution of blame. *Archives of General Psychiatry*. 38:1233–1238.

Jacobson, J. (1983). The structural theory and the representational world. *Psychoanalytic Quarterly*. 52:514–542.

Jekels, L. (1930). The psychology of pity. In *Collected Papers*. New York: International Universities Press, 1952.

Kahn, E. (1965). Self-pity. *American Journal of Psychiatry*, 122: 447–451.

Kernberg, O. (1975). *Borderline Conditions and Pathological Narcissism*. New York: Jason Aronson.

Kohut, H. (1959). Introspection, empathy, and psychoanalysis: An examination of the relationship between mode of observation and theory. In P. Ornstein, ed., *The Search for the Self: Selected Writings of Heinz Kohut: 1950–1978*. New York: International Universities Press, 1978.

Kohut, H. (1971). *The Analysis of the Self*. New York: International Universities Press.

Mahler, M. (1971). A study of the separation individuation process and its possible application to borderline phenomena in the psychoanalytic situation. In R. Eissler *et al.*, eds., *The Psycholanalytic Study of the Child* (Vol. 26). New York/Chicago: Quadrangle.

Milrod, D. (1973). Self-pity, self-comforting and the superego. In R. Eissler *et al.*, eds., *The Psychoanalytic Study of the Child* (Vol. 27). New York/Chicago: Quadrangle.

New Webster's Dictionary. (1975). Chicago: Consolidated Book Publishers.

Stolorow, R., & Brandchaft, B. (1984). Intersubjectivity: II. Development and pathogenesis. In G. Atwood & R. Stolorow, eds., *Structures of Subjectivity*. Hillsdale, NJ: Analytic Press.

Stolorow, R. D., Brandchaft, B., & Atwood, G. (1983). Intersubjectivity in psychoanalytic treatment: With special reference to archaic states. *Bulletin of the Menninger Clinic*, 47:117–128.

Tolpin, M. (1975). On the beginnings of a cohesive self: The application of the concept of transmuting internalization to the study of transitional objects and signal anxiety." In R. Eissler *et al.*, eds,. *The Psychoanalytic Study of the Child* (Vol. 26). New Haven: Yale University Press.

Tolpin, M., & Kohut, H. (1980). The disorders of the self: The psychopathology of the first year of life. In S. Greenspan & G. Pollock, eds., *The Course of Life* (Vol. 1, *Infancy and Early Childhood*). Rockville, MD: National Institute of Mental Health.

SECTION FIVE

THEORETICAL PAPERS

15

Toward a Pure Psychology of Inner Conflict

ROBERT D. STOLOROW

The centrality of inner conflict in human psychological life has been a fundamental tenet of Freudian psychoanalysis since its inception. In recent years, however, long-held assumptions about the nature and origins of conflict have increasingly become subject to critical reappraisal. Arguments put forth by a number of authors (Gill, 1976; Klein, 1976; Schafer, 1976; Stolorow, 1978) have persuasively demonstrated the extent to which the psychoanalytic understanding of conflict has been obstructed by classical metapsychology and, in particular, by the theory of instinctual drive. Proposals have been offered that would replace the mechanistic imagery of a mental apparatus disposing of drive energies with a psychology of conflict recast in the language of clashing personal purposes (Klein, 1976) and human actions (Schafer, 1976). It is the thesis of this chapter that from a psychoanalytic perspective conflict is to be viewed always and only as a subjective state of the individual person, and that it is the task of psychoanalytic inquiry to illuminate the specific contexts of meaning in which such conflicts take form. I am thus proposing a strictly *hermeneutic* approach to conflict, in line with Kohut's (1982) desire to reframe psychoanalysis as a pure psychology.

The frequently posed antithesis between conflict theory and Kohut's (1977) self psychology is, in my view, an artifact of the embeddedness of the traditional concept of conflict in classical metapsychology and drive theory. When conflict is freed from the encumbering image of an energy disposal apparatus and is pictured solely as a subjective state of the person, then the supposed antithesis between conflict theory and self psychology vanishes. When conflict is liberated from the doctrine of the primacy of instinctual drive, then the specific meaning-contexts that give rise to subjective states of conflict becomes an empirical question to be explored psychoanalytically. The focus of psychoanalytic inquiry then shifts from the presumed vicissitudes of drive to the "intersubjective contexts" (Atwood & Stolorow, 1984; Stolorow, Brandchaft, & Atwood, 1983) in which conflict states crystallize, and to the impact of these contextual configurations on the person's psychological organization. Such a stance holds profound implications for one's *clinical* approach to conflicts that emerge in the psychoanalytic situation, a subject to which I return later.

Another advantage of viewing conflict solely as a subjective state of the person is that it invites a consideration of the developmental origins and, especially, the developmental *prerequisites* of particular conflict states (see Stolorow & Lachmann, 1980). In general it may be said that the experience of the self-in-conflict presupposes that some minimal degree of structuralization of the sense of self has been reliably achieved. Thus, in those disintegrative states in which the cohesion of self-experience becomes significantly lost and immersion in an archaic selfobject tie is required for its restoration, states of conflict between clashing motivational strivings will not predominate in the person's subjective field, because the imperative need to reestablish the required tie is experientially preeminent. When the required tie is reestablished, by contrast, and self-integrity thereby becomes restored, then inner conflict may emerge into prominence—for example, when central strivings and affective qualities of the person are believed to be inimical to the maintenance of the bond.[1] It is in these fluctuating figure–ground relationships between conflict states and archaic selfobject configurations that the experiential meaning of Kohut's (1977) concept of complementarity between conflict psychology and self psychology can be found (Stolorow, 1983).

Observations and reconstructions of self development suggest that it involves at least two overlapping processes (see Atwood & Stolorow, 1984; Brandchaft, 1985; Kohut, 1977; Wolf, 1980): (1) the consolidation of a nuclear sense of coherence and well-being, and (2) the differentiation of self from other and the corresponding establishment of an individualized array of guiding aspirations and ideals. Critical to these structuralization processes is the attuned responsiveness of the caregiving surround to the child's evolving emotional states and needs (Socarides & Stolorow, 1984/1985). The child's needs for such specific responsiveness undergo a series of maturational shifts. Conflicts may arise and become structuralized at any point in this developmental progression. With regard to self-consolidation, such conflicts will center around the child's basic needs for mirroring responses and for connectedness to idealized sources of comfort and strength. With regard to self-differentiation, conflicts will center around the child's need for the continuance of selfobject ties that can serve as a source of affirming, facilitating, and solidifying support for his strivings for self-delineation and for the establishment of individualized goals and values. Under the influence of drive and tripartite structural theory, analysts have tended to interpret these conflicts as originating in oedipal and preoedipal

---

1. A similar conception of the origins of psychic conflict has been formulated independently by Dr. Herbert Linden (1983).

drive fixations and their corresponding superego structures and forerunners. This concept of inevitably structuralized, instinctually derived conflict obscures the contextual configurations in which such conflicts arise, limiting and derailing analytic progress. I suggest that the understanding of emergent conflict is better served by recognizing that, at every phase of development, the structuralization of conflict is determined by the specific intersubjective field in which it is embedded, just as its resolution in analysis is determined by the intersubjective dialogue in which it reemerges.

If parents cannot adapt themselves to the changing selfobject needs of their developing child, then the child will adapt himself to what is available in order to maintain the required ties. This, I believe, is the route by which inner conflict becomes structuralized and by which civilized man continues to exchange "a portion of his possibilities for happiness for a portion of security" (Freud, 1930, p. 115). This thesis will now be exemplified through an examination of the origins of those subjective states that ordinarily are grouped under the heading of "superego conflict."

"SUPEREGO CONFLICT"

Traditionally, the concepts of superego and superego conflict, and the attendant role of guilt in pathogenesis, have been formulated in terms of the metapsychological assumptions of classical drive theory. It is my contention here that the experiential configurations covered by the terms superego and superego conflict originate in the child's perceptions of what is required of him to maintain the selfobject ties that are vital to his well-being. Once these requirements become structuralized as invariant organizing principles of the child's subjective world, he will be vulnerable to painful feelings of guilt, shame, or anxiety whenever his inner strivings threaten to violate them.

Most often the requirements for maintaining needed ties involve the child's having to serve significant selfobject functions for his parents. When a parent consistently requires an archaic state of oneness with a child, for example, then the child's strivings for more differentiated selfhood become the source of severe conflict and guilt. In such instances, the child perceives that his acts of self-demarcation and unique affective qualities are experienced by the parent as psychologically damaging, often leading to the child developing a perception of himself as omnipotently destructive. This self-perception as a cruel and dangerous destroyer, originating in the parent's need for the child as an archaic selfobject, both obstructs the process of self-boundary formation and becomes an enduring source of guilt and self-punishment—the "harsh superego" and "sadistic superego forerunners" of classical theory.

Example 1: An Adolescent Crisis

Sally, a 17-year-old girl, was referred by her former therapist, a woman in her 60s, because the treatment had reached a stalemate. The patient was severely depressed, was relentlessly self-critical and self-attacking, thought frequently of killing herself, and was plagued by recurrent pains in her legs that apparently were of psychogenic origin. The referring therapist conceived of the patient's current intractable state as a manifestation of a "negative therapeutic reaction" rooted in severe masochism and a highly sadistic superego.

Sally seemed to her new analyst to be an attractive and very intelligent youngster, self-reflective to a fault, and acutely attuned to the needs and feelings of others. The imperative that she incessantly please and satisfy others and sacrifice herself to their expectations quickly emerged as the dominant theme in her psychological life, an important element in the transference relationship with her former therapist that had gone unnoticed.

Sally's parents were divorced when she was 4 years old, after which her father became absorbed in an endless succession of short-lived affairs and showed little interest in his daughter. Her mother would frequently speak disparagingly about him to Sally, and the patient herself recalled numerous humiliating incidents in which he let her down—for example, failing to pay her school tuition bills and cancelling scheduled visits with her at the last minute.

The loss of and severe disappointments by her father had the effect of greatly intensifying the bond between Sally and her mother. A central characteristic of this tie was that her mother, who was chronically depressed, had come to require an archaic sense of oneness with Sally as a selfobject— that is, Sally's unfailing, loving responsiveness and continual availability had become essential to the maintenance of her mother's feeling of well-being. Her mother thus experienced Sally's phase-appropriate strivings for individualized selfhood as a profound psychological injury and made Sally feel as if these developmental thrusts were deliberate and cruel attempts to damage and destroy her. Not surprisingly, this pattern had reached crisis proportions during Sally's adolescence, with her mother reacting to her growing interest in boys by dissolving in tears and jealous rages. Sally, in turn, felt unbearably guilty and became increasingly depressed, self-attacking, and suicidal.

Believing that the source of the patient's difficulties was to be found in conflicts over aggressive drive derivatives, her former therapist had begun to offer interpretations of Sally's presumed unconscious aggressive wishes, both in relation to her mother and in the transference. Sally's condition significantly worsened, leading the therapist, who was becoming increasingly alarmed, to make the referral to another analyst. It was reconstructed that the first therapist's interpretations of aggressive wishes were felt by Sally to replicate her mother's view of her as inherently cruel and destructive, and they therefore only exacerbated her guilty self-attacks.

It soon became apparent that because of her mother's archaic enmeshment with her as a selfobject, Sally's strivings for greater self-demarcation had become the source of unbearable conflict and guilt for her. As the analyst repeatedly clarified for the patient how her mother reacted to her thrusts toward more differentiated selfhood as if they were expressions of destructive aggression, and how this was the principal reason for her guilt and self-attacks, her depression and other symptoms lifted, as her stalled adolescent development was permitted to resume. She was able to become involved with a steady boyfriend and to decide to go away to college, though her mother disapproved of both. In the transference she had found a longed-for, idealizable, paternal selfobject who helped extricate her from the web of her mother's archaic needs and who aligned himself with her quest for a more distinct self-definition.

Not unexpectedly, Sally returned to analysis a year after her graduation from college. While the earlier brief course of treatment had helped to free her adolescent development from the grip of her mother's needs, she now found the early pattern of bondage to her mother becoming repeated in her professional and personal relationships. Her wrenching self-demarcation guilt and the corresponding perception of herself as a cruel destroyer (her "superego conflicts") had become structuralized by her early formative experiences with her mother as enduring features of her psychological life that now required engagement in an intensive analytic process.

Example 2: Reactive Depressions

Tom was a 57-year-old man with considerable artistic endowment and, when functioning well, of substantial charm. He had compensated for repeated failures in school by a prodigious regime of self-teaching and thus had acquired expertise not only in cultural and artistic matters, but also in such diverse fields as astronomy, anthropology, and history. He was, however, plagued by recurrent episodes of severe and paralyzing depression, which always followed upon some personal setback. One regular precipitant was the depressive mood of his wife, which he always attributed to some failing of his own. A lack of psychological differentiation was also shown in his reactions to any extended physical separations from her, which produced profound disintegrative changes in his state of mind. To counteract these, he would engage in brief sexual affairs that served to restore a sense of aliveness and fend off frightening feelings of apathy and "deadness." Other frequent triggering events for his depressions were unfavorable reviews of his work or contemporaries being chosen over him for assignments or awards in his field.

In these reactive states he would feel "defeated," find it difficult to get out of bed, and experience a "black cloud" descending over him, along with a nearly complete loss of motivation. He would become beset with intense hypochondriacal worries, feel convinced that his creativity had left him, and brood obsessively about his impending financial demise. He would then sink into an orgy of self-recrimination for his state of mind, alternating with intense and virulent self-pity for the wretchedness of his existence. It soon became apparent that for Tom any trace of depressive affect was a source of severe conflict and ruthless self-attack.

Tom's mother emerged in his memories as an intensely anxious, childlike, and volatile woman, chronically disappointed with her passive and ineffectual husband. From the beginning she was overburdened by the demands of her vigorous first child, Tom, and after 18 months left him in the care of her own inadequate parents, only to reclaim him 2 years later. His subsequent childhood years were marked by frequent scenes in which his mother would bitterly bemoan her fate in getting married and having children, immersing herself in dramatic displays of self-pity, especially when she was disappointed by Tom's maturational lags or failures in school. Often she would fall to the floor in a "dead" faint or retire to her room, pull down the shades, and remain in bed for long periods of time. In consequence of countless experiences such as these, Tom came to believe that his own painful disappointments in himself, as well as his depressive reactions to them, were a source of unbearable psychological injury for his mother.

In the analysis Tom could sustain no positive sense of self in the wake of his recurrent episodes of devitalization, regardless of the successes he had achieved. It became clear that his vicious self-reproaches, in reaction to disappointments and to the depressive moods to which his vulnerability exposed him, completely undermined his resilience and, in circular fashion, further exacerbated his depressive states.

After prolonged, detailed observation it became apparent that Tom consistently, if silently, perceived the analyst to be painfully disappointed in him and in himself whenever the patient felt depressed. Each depressive state was colored by the invariant meanings his moods had come to acquire — meaning structures that now crystallized in the intersubjective context of the analytic dialogue, which revived critical pathogenic elements of his early tie to his mother. These meanings included Tom's belief that he was cursed with a fatal and unyielding defect (his vulnerability to depressive experiences), that he was completely unacceptable and unwanted as he was, and that his depressive feelings were a constant, painful reminder to his objects—now the analyst—of their failures. Thus it could be seen that Tom's need to integrate depressive experiences had been a lifelong source of conflict for him, because of his deeply embedded conviction that the disclosure of such feelings was psychologically damaging to those on whom he relied.

This transference configuration invariably materialized with the first sapping of Tom's vitality. He would try desperately to restore his buoyancy, as well as the analyst's, by offering reassurances, but these would inevitably collapse beneath his (and, he believed, the analyst's) knowledge that he was only attempting to cover up the flaw he had once again exposed. Tom's ruthless self-reproaches (symptoms par excellence of a "harsh superego") now became comprehensible as urgent attempts to maintain his connectedness with the analyst, much as he had found it necessary to do with his mother, when he believed that his state of mind had become a source of unbearable disappointment for the analyst as it had been for his mother. Only by confessing his worthlessness could he in some measure absolve himself and restore the tie, joining the analyst in the latter's misfortune in having him for a patient.

Frequently patients who show symptoms such as these and who seem not to make progress in analysis are assumed to suffer from a basic conflict over depending on an object. It is further widely believed that such conflict originates in the intense destructiveness or envy that dependence mobilizes. Tom certainly experienced enormous conflict over his continued needs for objects and this was an important source of his self-loathing. This conflict, however, was not rooted in an instinctually determined sadism. Rather, it stemmed from two central organizing principles of his subjective life. One was the degree of his vulnerability to separations, rejections, or criticism, a product of his arrested need for confirming and comforting selfobject ties. A second was the extent to which he believed that *he* must accept blame for any disjunctive experience in order to preserve the needed ties. He thus blamed his depressive reactions for the selfobject failures that produced them, with the result that his "hopeless flaws" seemed repeatedly and relentlessly confirmed.

Especially prone to becoming the source of subsequent conflict are those functions, such as affect regulation, whose maturation is impaired by the vulnerabilities and needs of the mother (Socarides & Stolorow, 1984/1985). In the case of Tom, his mother could not tolerate or accept his sadness or disappointments, experiences that therefore could never become integrated or modulated. He was thus unable to acquire the capacity to comfort himself when distressed, and his depressive moods remained a source of unyielding conflict and self-hatred throughout his life, until the pathogenic tie to his mother was reanimated, clarified, and worked through in the analytic transference.

CONCLUSION

When conflict is liberated from the doctrine of the primacy of instinctual drive and is pictured solely as a subjective state of the person, then the specific meaning-contexts that give rise to inner conflict can be illuminated psychoanalytically. Conflict states often arise when central strivings and affective qualities of the person are believed to be inimical to the maintenance of an important selfobject bond. In the two clinical cases presented, structuralized patterns of guilty self-recrimination and self-blame, traditionally covered by the concepts of superego and superego conflict, were found to originate in the patients' childhood perceptions of what was required of them to sustain ties essential to their well-being. When these requirements were revived in the analysis, interpreted, and worked through in their intersubjective contexts, the self-attacking attitudes were significantly alleviated.

ACKNOWLEDGMENTS

I am grateful to Dr. Bernard Brandchaft for contributing importantly to the development of the ideas in this chapter and for providing case material for one of the clinical examples. I also wish to thank Daphne D. Socarides for her invaluable comments and suggestions.

REFERENCES

Atwood, G., & Stolorow, R. (eds.). (1984). *Structures of Subjectivity: Explorations in Psychoanalytic Phenomenology*. Hillsdale, NJ: Analytic Press.
Brandchaft, B. (1985). Self and object differentiation. In R. F. Lax, S. Bach, & J. A. Burland, eds., *Self and Object Constancy: Clinical and Theoretical Perspectives*. New York: Guilford Press.
Freud, S. (1930). Civilization and its discontents. *Standard Edition*, 21:57–145.
Gill, M. (1976). Metapsychology is not psychology. In M. Gill & P. Holzman, eds., *Psychology versus Metapsychology: Psychoanalytic Essays in Memory of George S. Klein* (pp. 71–105). New York: International Universities Press.
Klein, G. (1976). *Psychoanalytic Theory*. New York: International Universities Press.
Kohut, H. (1977). *The Restoration of the Self*. New York: International Universities Press.
Kohut, H. (1982). Introspection, empathy, and the semicircle of mental health. *International Journal of Psycho-Analysis*, 63:395–407.
Linden, H. (1983). *Psychic Conflict in the Light of Self Psychology*. Paper presented at Conference on the Psychology of the Self, Los Angeles, October 7–9.
Schafer, R. (1976). *A New Language for Psychoanalysis*. New Haven: Yale University Press.
Socarides, D., & Stolorow, R. (1984/1985). Affects and selfobjects. *The Annual of Psychoanalysis*, 12/13:105–119.
Stolorow, R. (1978). The concept of psychic structure: Its metapsychological and clinical psychoanalytic meanings. *International Review of Psycho-Analysis*, 5:313–320.
Stolorow, R. (1983). Self psychology—A structural psychology. In J. Lichtenberg & S. Kaplan, eds., *Reflections on Self Psychology* (pp. 287–296). Hillsdale, NJ: Analytic Press.

Stolorow, R., Brandchaft, B., & Atwood, G. (1983). Intersubjectivity in psychoanalytic treatment: With special reference to archaic states. *Bulletin of the Menninger Clinic*, 47:117–128.

Stolorow, R., & Lachmann, F. (1980). *Psychoanalysis of Developmental Arrests: Theory and Treatment*. New York: International Universities Press.

Wolf, E. (1980). On the developmental line of selfobject relations. In A. Goldberg, ed., *Advances in Self Psychology* (pp. 117–130). New York: International Universities Press.

16

Optimal Responsiveness and the Therapeutic Process

HOWARD A. BACAL

Although tacitly accepted as an important element in the therapeutic practice of psychoanalysis, the concept of *optimal frustration* has received little theoretical clarification. The publication of Heinz Kohut's (1977a) landmark work *The Restoration of the Self* established optimal frustration as a central aspect of the curative process viewed from the perspective of self psychology. With one of his critics, Kohut (1977b) recognized the problematic nature of the question "What is optimal?," yet he never arrived at a satisfactory answer.

I intend to reexamine this question in light of the related issue of "optimal gratification." My purpose is, in part, to demonstrate the significance of the latter, which has until recently been regarded with some suspicion as a form of countertransference acting-in, evoked perhaps by the patient's acting-in in the transference; as a manipulation of the transference itself by the analyst deliberately adopting a role (the so-called "corrective emotional experience" of Alexander, 1956); or, at most, as a useful but temporary parameter to be discarded at the first possible opportunity.

I will suggest that any discussion of the concepts of optimal frustration and optimal gratification becomes inevitably entangled in insurmountable theoretical difficulties and endless debate when separated from the more useful and encompassing idea of *optimal responsiveness*, defined as the responsivity of the analyst that is therapeutically most relevant at any particular moment in the context of a particular patient and his illness. Empathy or vicarious introspection is the process by which the therapist comes to understand the patient by tuning in to his inner world. Optimal responsiveness, on the other hand, refers to the therapist's acts of communicating his understanding to his patient.

OPTIMAL FRUSTRATION

The origin of the term "optimal frustration" is not clear. Although he credits Bernfeld (1928) with its first mention, Kohut (1972) appears to have first applied it to the psychoanalytic process. The idea of optimal frustration, however, has always been a cornerstone of psychoanalytic treatment. As early as 1946, Anna Freud wrote:

[As analysts,] we have to play a double game with the patient's instinctual impulses, on the one hand encouraging them to express themselves and, on the other, steadily refusing them gratification—a procedure which incidentally gives rise to one of the numerous difficulties in the handling of analytic technique. (p. 13)

. . . the ego [of the patient] is victorious when its defensive measures effect their purpose . . . and so transform the instincts that, even in difficult circumstances, some measures of gratification is secured. . . . (p. 193)

However, the "measure of gratification" to which Miss Freud referred was not regarded as an aspect of the analytic process, but as one of its results.

While still working within the classical psychoanalytic perspective, Kohut and Seitz (1963) defined optimal frustration as an experience that is intrinsically related to that of gratification in the therapeutic process:

optimal frustrations involve sufficient delay in satisfaction to induce tension-increase and disappointment in the attempt to obtain wish-fulfillment through fantasies; the real satisfaction occurs quickly enough, however, to prevent a despairing and disillusioned turning away from reality. (p. 356)

Kohut indicates that the infantile impulses that have encountered optimal frustration are transformed into neutralizing psychological structure by the internalization of innumerable experiences of optimal frustration, but that "[t]he barrier of defences, on the other hand, which walls off an unmodified residue of infantile strivings, is the result of the internalization of frustrating experiences and prohibitions of traumatic intensity" (Kohut, 1963, p. 369).

In other words, *optimal* frustration of instinctual impulses promotes the development of internal structure comprised of transformed, or subli-mated, instinctual drives; whereas *traumatic* frustration causes a protective barrier to be built up around these impulses, which are left unchanged. Gratification, or "real satisfaction" must be an inherent element of the therapeutic process at some point and in some measure, or else "optimal" frustration will be anything but optimal. Yet, Kohut and Seitz do not sat-isfactorily define what optimal frustration and its associated optimal grat-ification amount to in the psychoanalytic process. Nor, to my knowledge, has this theoretical lacuna been redressed elsewhere.

In *The Analysis of the Self*, Kohut (1971) reiterates his position, still within a classical framework, but focuses now upon the importance of optimal frustration for narcissistic equilibrium rather than for drive mod-ulation:

as continues to hold true for the analogous later milieu of the child, the most important aspect of the earliest mother-infant relationship is the principal of optimal frustration. Tolerable disappointments in the pre-existing (and externally sustained) primary narcissistic equilibrium lead to the establishment of internal structures which provide the ability for self-soothing and the acquisition of basic tension tolerance in the narcissistic realm. (p. 64)

. . . The skillful analyst will assist the patient in keeping the patient's discomfort [vis-à-vis the necessary, i.e., therapeutic, frustration of the narcissistic transferences] within tolerable limits; i.e., he will conduct the analysis according to the principle of optimal frustration. (p. 199)[1]

Further, Kohut (1972) stated that omnipotent objects "become internalized every time the child discovers a flaw in them, providing the discovery is not of traumatic degree but optimally frustrating" (p. 869).

Kohut thus saw optimal frustration as central to the process of transmuting internalization, which he regarded as the essence of the process of analytic cure. As he wrote 5 years later,

Little by little as a result of innumerable processes of microinternalization, the anxiety-assuaging, delay-tolerating, and other realistic aspects of the analyst's image become part of the analysand's psychological equipment, *pari-passu* with the micro-*frustration* [my italics] of the analysand's need for the analyst's permanent presence and perfect functioning in this respect. In brief, through the process of transmuting internalization [via optimal frustration] new psychological structure is built. (Kohut, 1977, p. 32)

Kohut (1977), however, also questions the validity of the view that some individuals with severe psychopathology have had caring mothers who, in attempting to gratify their childrens' wishes, have deprived them of the optimal frustration that would have enabled them to develop a mâture ego. While acknowledging the possibility that these individuals might not have been sufficiently frustrated as children, he suggests that the determinants of their illness appeared to be more complex when viewed from the perspective of an analysis conducted on the basis of self psychology. By way of illustration, he cites his account of Mr. U whose

mother and grandmother had . . . apparently acted out an unconscious fantasy of their own [in] gratifying the child's drive wishes for their own purposes. Fully in tune with his every drive demand, they simultaneously disregarded the boy's maturing changing self, which cried out for a maternal (and later also paternal) confirming-admiring responses and approval [of his own capacities. The boy's fixation on a fetish] was therefore essentially not the result of overgratification but of a specific traumatic absence of maternal empathy for

---

1. In a letter dated a year later Kohut (1972, September 23) also makes the point that "the *drive*-curbing behaviour of the selfobject is in essence experienced by the child as a *narcissistic* injury [and therefore] . . . structure formation is always due to a loss of the prestructural selfobject, not of the drive-curbing true object. . . ."

the healthy grandiosity and the healthy exhibitionism of his forming independent self. (p. 79)

Although Kohut recognizes that insufficient frustration or "excessive gratification" may contribute to psychopathology, he suggests that the pathogenic factor is not the "overgratification" of some instinct, but the accompanying traumatic insufficiency of recognition and "gratification" of a selfobject need. In this context, it is instructive to recall an aphorism that Kohut (1977) introduced in a now-famous passage in *The Restoration of the Self*:

> Man can no more survive psychologically in a psychological milieu that does not respond empathically to him than he can survive physically in an atmosphere that contains no oxygen . . . the analyst's behaviour vis-à-vis his patient should be the expected average one—i.e., the behaviour of a psychologically perceptive person vis-à-vis someone who is suffering and has entrusted himself to him for help. (p. 253)

There is an apparent contradiction between this view and the recognition of the therapeutically beneficial effects of frustration. In order to explore this contradiction intelligibly, it is necessary to consider the difference between "optimal" frustration and "traumatic" frustration, and their relationship to so-called "empathic failure."

Optimal Frustration and Traumatic Frustration

Let me say at once that the notion of empathic failure by parental selfobjects cannot by itself answer the question of what is traumatic, since it is likely that not all empathic failures lead to long-range deleterious effects on the psyche of the child. Indeed, since optimal frustration by selfobjects is regarded as essential to the growth and development of the self, empathic failure by selfobjects in childhood, as well as by the analyst as selfobject at a later stage, should according to this theory be welcomed. The central issue, both developmentally and in analysis, is what will lead to structural deficit or defect and what will be "optimal," in the sense of curative, leading to transmuting internalization of experience that is structure-building or fault-reparative?

The question still remains, however, what is "traumatic"? The earliest conception of trauma focused on isolated events, in particular on sexual seductions. The idea of trauma as the product of ongoing processes and relationships was not recognized before the contributions of such object-relations theorists as Balint, Winnicott, and Masud Khan (1963) with his notion of cumulative trauma. All would agree, however, that trauma involves a degree of intensity that is too great for the ego to master and has far-reaching effects on psychic organization. For example, Kris (1956) distinguished between "shock trauma," the effect of a single powerful experience impinging on the child, and "strain trauma," the accumulation of frustrating tensions. Kris, however, did not emphasize the quality of the relationship, but conceived these events as occuring within a drive–tension–discharge model (Kligman, 1983). Kohut and Seitz (1963) also regarded the quantitative factor as a distinguishing element of trauma, but they also suggested that the qualitative factor was significant:

> The differences between experience of traumatic and optimal frustration are differences in degree. It is the difference between one mother's harsh "N-o!" and another mother's kindly "No." It is the difference between a frightening kind of prohibition on the one hand, and an educational experience, on the other. It is the difference between one father's handling a child's temper tantrum by an equally hostile counter-tantrum and another father's picking up the child and calming him—firm but non-aggressive, and loving but not seductive. It is the difference between an uncompromising prohibition, which stresses only what the child must not have or cannot do, and the offering of acceptable substitutes for the forbidden object or activity. (pp. 369–370)

According to Balint (1969), there are three conditions or phases associated with the occurrence of trauma. In the first stage of the traumatic process, the relationship between the child and the potentially traumatogenic object must be characterized by a certain intensity and be a mainly trusting and loving one. Trauma occurs, in this situation, when the adult does something highly exciting, frightening, or painful, either once and quite suddenly, or repeatedly. This action may involve an excess of tenderness or cruelty, whether or not sexuality is involved, and may result in severe overstimulation of the child or, if the child's approaches are ignored, in rejection and deep disappointment. The first two phases outlined by Balint are necessary but not sufficient to produce trauma. In order for trauma to occur the adult must act with indifference toward the child's experience, whether excitement or rejection.

Balint's thesis goes beyond merely quantitative considerations pertaining to the degree or intensity of traumatic experience (i.e., the field of one-person psychology) to the study of the quality of object-relationship (i.e., the field of two-person or multiperson psychology). In this way, Balint extends the work of Ferenczi (1933) who suggested that the real shock to the psychic organization of the child who is interfered with sexually is the adult's betrayal of the child's trust. The trauma derives from the fact that the child's tender or playful love is mistaken for passion and either responded to or rejected and is not primarily due to the stimulation or frustration of the child's innate sexual drives.

Classical analysis, however, fails to make a meaningful distinction between the pathogenic and the pathogenic that is also traumatic—a distinction, I would suggest, that is of great clinical importance. This failure on the part of classical analysts and current object-relations theorists stems from their attempt to understand the effects of the environment in the context of a theoretical position that is essentially a one-person psychology, where excessive or pathological drives are regarded as the determinants of the psychopathology. From the self-psychological perspective, this is not an issue, as the theory presupposes that psychopathology results from a failure of environmental response to the needs of the child's developing self. Although Winnicott adopted this position quite early, he did not systematically explore its clinical significance. Self psychologists, on the other hand, have only recently adopted the insight of early object-relations theorists such as Balint regarding the specific quality of the relationship between a particular child and a particular parent as the context of pathogenesis, and that between a particular therapist and a particular patient as the context in which pathology is potentially resolvable. In both cases, the relationship is a product of the interaction of two vulnerabilities and two capacities, those of the parent and those of the child and, later, those of the analyst and those of his patient (Stolorow, Brandchaft, & Atwood, 1983).

It has never been our intention, as analysts, to either traumatize or frustrate our patients, however optimally, but to understand them. Consequently the notion of optimal frustration is not tenable as a working clinical concept; however, the idea of optimal gratification conceivably could be. For to be understood can be deeply gratifying and is, perhaps the most important function performed for us by our selfobjects. It is possible that the gratification of being understood by one's selfobject is of central importance in the curative process. If internal structure could not be built and defect repaired through the experience of being understood, the analyst would be wasting much of his time doing good work instead of making calculated errors thought to lead to manageable disruptions between himself and the patient and, thus, to transmuting internalization through the associated optimal frustration and its understanding. This is obviously unsatisfactory, and brings to mind the so-called "corrective emotional experience" of Alexander (1956) in which the analyst adopted the role that he considered to be the opposite of that of the pathogenic nuclear object. This confusion can be resolved if we reflect that no one comes for understanding unless they feel they have not been understood. As analysts, we are constantly confronted with a complex spectrum of varying degrees and kinds of frustrated need for understanding, sometimes of a traumatic order. Our responses must satisfy (a better word, perhaps, than gratify) the frustrated need for understanding of a particular patient or they will not be helpful. We will, as therapists, make mistakes, if only as a result of the analytic inertia that is inherent in our technique and, thus, inadvertently trigger or intensify the patient's frustration. The patient, moreover, will inevitably reenact his frustration with us in an attempt to right the original wrong. In many, perhaps in the majority of instances, if we understand, as and when our patients need us to, frustration will not be a factor in the therapeutic process. We are not analytic machines, however, and upon the not infrequent occasions when we fail, when we are in a state of empathic lapse, or when our responsive understanding is not accurate, we will encounter a patient who is frustrated with us.

The term "optimal" means "a condition, degree or compromise that produces the best possible result" (*Collins English Dictionary*, 1979, p. 1032). Since our approach to psychoanalytic therapy is to do the best we can and we do not, indeed we cannot, set out optimally to frustrate our patients, I suggest that the idea of optimal frustration is really an after-the-fact metapsychological explanation of what happens when the analytic relationship breaks down, retrievably. From the patient's point of view, it breaks down when his selfobject needs are greater than the analyst's capacity to understand and respond at a particular moment.[2] Furthermore, the patient's apparent stubborn resistance, and "negative therapeutic reaction" may not represent an intention to defeat the analyst, but are caused, at that moment, by the breakdown of the analyst's empathy and the patient's incapacity for reciprocal empathic resonance (Bacal, 1979; Brandchaft, 1983; Wolf, 1981). When, however, the "intersubjective disjunction" cannot be resolved, even by an honest scrutiny of countertransference, and a "decentered" (Stolorow, Brandchaft, & Atwood, 1983) perspective on the part of the analyst, it may be useful to consider whether the patient's feeling that he is not optimally responded to, may be attributable to a traumatic injury or frustration that has caused a defect or deficit in the self, that is, whether he has been seriously hurt in a state of extreme vulnerability (Balint, 1968, 1969). I propose that an experience is traumatic to the psyche of the child if it has apparently caused a degree of defect or significant enfeeblement of the self, in our patients, that is not responsive to ordinary interpretative work. This operational definition of traumatic experience can be crucially important as a guide in our treatment of those patients for whom the resumption of selfobject relatedness, after disruption, is especially difficult to achieve, and sometimes impossible to restore by ordinary analytic work—even in instances where both patient and analyst agree they are grappling with the relevant issues.

Freud, "in the social matrix of his time . . . felt constrained to publicly overemphasize restraint and austerity in analytic practice in order to mute criticism engendered by having placed sexuality, and particularly infantile sexuality, at the center of his scientific investigations" (Wolf, 1976, p. 104). While this was an understandable concern in Freud's day, I would agree with Wolf's (1976) assertion that "contemporary psychoanalysts need rather less constraint and more freedom to engage the analysand in the analytic process" (p. 104), because of the increasing numbers of patients whose pathology is the result of serious disorders of the self. The real

2. Stolorow, Brandchaft, and Atwood (1983) have discussed this issue in terms of dissonant intersubjective states between patient and analyst.

"danger" inherent in the analytic situation is not the possibility that the analyst might respond sexually to his patient, as such behavior is governed by moral and ethical principles and cannot seriously be regarded as a valid part of the therapeutic process. The danger is rather that the analyst, by assiduously or rigidly avoiding any interaction with his patient except that of verbal exchange, may mistake a regressively repetitive transference for acting-in and repeat and perpetuate the childhood experience that caused the self defect or developmental arrest in the first place and, in this way, miss the patient's bid for a *creative transference relatedness*.

Freud's counsel to frustrate the patient's wish for libidinal gratification has, unfortunately, often been taken as a directive to block all satisfaction within the analytic situation. As Wolf (1976) noted, "a misreading of this rule of abstinence creates a cold and critical ambience and will result in transference artifacts that are easily mistaken for derivatives òf aggressive drives (p. 113). . . . Ideally the psychoanalytic situation ought to be constructed in such a way as to yield the optimally facilitating ambience for the ongoing psychoanalytic process" (p. 111).

Interpretation and Therapeutic Relationship

Balint (1969) argued that we have "two major therapeutic methods, one of which is interpretation and the other the creation of a therapeutic relationship between the patient and ourselves. Compared with the first, the techniques for the second method have been much less well studied and it is important that we should start investigating them" (p. 435).

The self-psychological understanding of the therapeutic process and its associated analytic technique more closely represents a synthesis of these two facets of therapy, "interpretation and relationship," than the traditional psychoanalytic model. There are, however, contradictions and inconsistencies still to be resolved.

For some time, Kohut was undecided as to whether interpretation or relationship is the fundamental therapeutic component in psychoanalysis. In *The Restoration of the Self*, Kohut (1977, p. 31) held that interpretation and insight are not in themselves what cure the patient, but are the means by which the essential curative factor, the beneficial structural transformation of the self, is effected. For example, Kohut described his work with Mr. M as follows:

> [The analyst's] attention is focused predominantly on the analysand's subjective transference experiences and, on the basis of his understanding of their form and content, [he] reconstructs the experiential world of the patient's childhood during the genetically decisive junctures. . . . In Mr. M's case, the essential psychological fact (the reactivation of the decisive genetic determinant . . .) was that he experienced his mother, and in the transference the analyst, as traumatically unempathic vis-à-vis his emotional demands and as unresponsive

to them. True enough, the analyst might occasionally wish to point out (in order to retain a realistic framework—if, for example, because of the intensity of the frustrations he experiences in the transferences, the patient might seriously consider quitting the analysis) that the patient's expectations and demands belong to his childhood and are unrealistic in the present. And he might at the appropriate moment also wish to explain to the patient that the intensity of his childhood needs may have led to a distortion of his perceptions of the past (in Mr. M's case, to a falsification of his perception of his adoptive mother's personality). The essential structural transformations produced by working through do not take place, however, in consequence of such supportive intellectual insights, but in consequence of the gradual internalizations that are brought about by the fact that the old experiences are repeatedly relived by the more mature psyche. (pp. 29–30).

By reliving these early experiences *with the analyst* the patient transmutes (i.e., converts and assimilates) into his self structure the "anxiety-assuaging, delay-tolerating, and other realistic aspects of the analyst's image" (p. 32)—that is, the function of the analyst as a selfobject. Regardless of whether it is "optimal frustration" or "optimal gratification" that produces this curative process of transmuting internalization, Kohut emphasizes the curative effect of *relationship*.

Although Kohut never explicitly addressed the issue of interpretation and relationship as complementary aspects of therapeutic work, the clinical process in psychoanalytic self psychology illuminates their interacting functions. Let us consider, for example, from the self-psychological perspective, a therapeutic situation in which frustration is not a significant factor in the relationship between the analyst and the patient. In what he judges to be a facilitative ambience (Wolf, 1976), the analyst communicates through interpretation his empathically determined understanding of the patient's inner world. The patient's response, although perhaps a negative one, nevertheless indicates that the intervention has been successful, that is, accurate and useful. If the analyst's intervention takes the form of a transference interpretation, it would also be considered mutative (Strachey, 1934). While some would argue that all interpretation frustrates or irritates in that it causes a degree of narcissistic injury by revealing to the patient something he does not know about himself, at least consciously, I believe that the feeling of being deeply understood is more frequently a rich and gratifying one that relieves frustration and tension.

Since optimal frustration has not occurred here, but understanding and explanation instead, must we conclude that transmuting internalization and related structure building have not taken place and that the apparent therapeutic gain will be shown during the termination phase to be illusory? As I have already indicated, the patient brings *to* the analyst his frustration at not being understood so that any additional frustration caused by the analyst's lack of understanding cannot be regarded as optimal. In this situation, the interaction between the analyst and patient did not generate frustration; rather, the analyst recognized the frustration that the patient brought to him and the patient felt understood by this response. In Wolf's (1981) terms, harmonious or reciprocal empathic resonance took place between analyst and patient: "At the moment that I really understand what is going on in the analysand, I also know that he really understands what I am doing" (p. 7). The accuracy of the analyst's empathic insights is confirmed by the patient's expression of his own empathic grasp of the analyst's psychological activity at that moment. A process of transmutation of the analyst's functions into the patient has begun. The interaction has been optimal from both the analyst's and the patient's point of view and neither need question the appropriateness of the gratification he receives in this way.

As this suggests that frustration is not a necessary condition for transmuting internalization and real structure building to occur, what, if any, is the therapeutic element in the working through of "optimal" frustration? According to the clinical model emphasizing optimal frustration, the patient's reaction to the therapist's supposedly empathically derived communication (or silence) tells the analyst that he has not been attuned to his patient's psychological state. The patient's frustration is manifested in resistance[3] until, under favorable circumstances, the analyst is able to overcome his empathic lag (Bacal, 1979) and perhaps, in addition, achieve an increased awareness of some aspects of his countertransference. Finally, the process of mutative interpretation is completed by a careful analysis of the events that precipitated the disruption and, concomitantly, of the analogous childhood experiences.

In this situation, the analyst believes that his interpretation is empathically correct until the patient's response makes him reconsider its accuracy. Simultaneous with the correction and clarification of the transference disruption, the analyst is able to restore the previous harmonious selfobject relationship with the patient and, in the process, a transmuting internalization occurs.

If both the foregoing processes are therapeutic, what is the common curative element? It is, I believe, the patient's experience of the analyst's *optimal responsiveness*; and the quality of the therapeutic relationship at that moment confirms, for the analyst, that his response is usable by the patient. In the second example, the resumption of the harmonious selfobject relationship is therapeutic, not because the understanding of disruption is therapeutic, but because *understanding* is therapeutic.

Although interpretation is the principal means through which the analyst conveys optimal responsiveness to his patients, it may not be a sufficient

---

3. I understand resistance here as a variety of blockages of communication that are defenses not against drives, but against the anxiety of retraumatization (Wolf, 1981).

or appropriate expression of responsiveness in every case. The continuing controversy among psychoanalysts as to what constitutes a valid addition or alternative to interpretation is due to our failure to evolve a framework for the systematic consideration of the *psychoanalytic* nature of the therapeutic relationship and how it relates to the interpretive process.[4] Acceptance of the importance of *relationship* for the analytic process has until recently been limited to the recognition of the part it plays in the so-called working or therapeutic alliance. Although Wolf's (1976) recognition of an analytic ambience that is therapeutic represents an important advance, most analysts consider the therapeutic aspects of relationship in treatment as a necessary evil, or at best, as a temporary parameter making possible the resumption of the "real" analysis. As analysts, we evade this issue because it raises the spectre of transference and countertransference acting-in. Those of us who have extended the scope of psychoanalytic treatment to include the more serious disorders of severely traumatized people, however, have found an in-depth understanding of the analytically legitimate therapeutic aspects of our relationship with our patients increasingly important.

OPTIMAL RESPONSIVENESS
AND THE DEVELOPMENTAL LINE OF EMPATHY

In his final address to the fourth annual self psychology conference, Kohut (1981) stated that the most important insight contained in *How Does Analysis Cure?* is that "analysis [ultimately] cures by giving explanations, i.e., interpretations. . . . " He maintained that the analyst must proceed from understanding to explanation, from showing that he is attuned to his patient's inner life, his feelings, thoughts, and fantasies, to the next step, interpretation. Kohut (1981) defined the advance from understanding to interpretation as a progression "from a lower form of empathy to a higher form of empathy," and described the analogous development within the individual with the following example:

> a child and the mother are in the park. The child was a young child who clung to the mother. The sun was shining, pigeons were walking around there. All of a sudden, the child felt a new buoyancy and daring and it moved away from the mother toward the pigeons. He goes three or four steps and then he looks back. The general interpretation of that is that he is anxious, he wants to be sure he can come back, to be encased in her arms, cradled, et cetera. That is true, but something more important is true. He wants to see the mother's proud smile; he wants to see her pride [looking] at him walking out now, on his

---

4. There are, in fact, two authors who more or less explicitly address this issue (Gill, 1982; Lichtenberg, 1982a, 1982b).

own—isn't that wonderful—and at this moment, something extremely important had happened: a low form of empathy, a body-close form of empathy expressed in holding and touching . . . is now expressed only in facial expression and perhaps later in words: I am proud of you, my boy.

Kohut (1981) believed that interpretation in psychoanalysis performs a parallel function for the patient as these events in the development of the child. In this process, the "bodily holding" or "merger" phase is superseded by a much higher form of empathy, verbal interpretation, which is a psychological message on a more evolved level of understanding. In the case of the severely damaged patient, this process may be a very prolonged one.

As we have already noted, Kohut was for some time undecided as to whether interpretation or relationship is the therapeutic component in psychoanalysis. Although he maintained at different times that it was not interpretation but the relationship that essentially cured, he still firmly believed in the healing capacity of insight. Kohut's (1981) recent view that progress in the therapeutic process from understanding to interpretation represents a parallel advance on the part of the patient from a lower to a higher level of what he called the developmental line of empathy, integrates the two major methods of psychoanalysis and confirms the intuitive conviction of many analysts that interpretation and relationship are both curative. This is not merely an academic or semantic issue, but has practical implications for the way we respond as psychoanalysts and as psychoanalytic psychotherapists to our patients. Kohut (1981) felt that future research in self psychology should concentrate upon the continuum of empathic stages, "the developmental line of empathy,[5] from its early archaic beginnings to such high levels as barely touching, as barely still having any trace of the original holding that communicates the empathic understanding."

This issue, I believe, can be addressed most effectively in terms of the concept of optimal responsiveness. The analytic attitude that is here termed "optimal responsiveness" is described by Wolf (1976) as follows:

> The decision about a proper response to a patient's demand, be it experienced ever so subtly or directly, must depend upon a proper dynamic understanding of the current analytic situation, its transference implications, and the genetic background. It is thus no different from any other analytic understanding or intervention. Whether to comply enthusiastically or reluctantly, whether to refuse firmly or hesitatingly, or not to respond at all, these decisions belong to the armamentarium of alternative action to be used in accordance with one's total understanding of the analytic process. (p. 107)

Earlier, Winnicott (1967) expressed a similar concern when he stated that the analyst's true function is not to provide the correct interpretation,

---

5. After preparing this chapter, I had the opportunity to read an interesting clinical paper by Charles Coverdale (1983), which deals specifically with this topic.

but to be available to respond with understanding that is appropriate and useful to his patient. In self-psychological terms, the analyst's response must be commensurate with the patient's level of self–selfobject organization or the degree of intactness, defect or deficit within the self.

In the majority of cases this response is communicated largely through verbal interpretation. Changes in the patient population, however, require corresponding changes in the analyst's vocabulary of response. Kohut (1981) recognized the need on the part of analysts for greater freedom to respond to their understanding of their patients in a passage that, because of its controversial nature, has had insufficient attention from self psychologists who are understandably reluctant to adopt a position that might expose them, however unjustifiably, to accusations of engaging in the "corrective emotional experience" advocated by Alexander (1956):

> the more one knows, the less one needs to stick to some ritual anxiously, because one *knows* [my italics] what is appropriate and inappropriate. The question [relates] to treating patients with very severe self disorders who cannot possibly benefit from interpretations for [a very long time, perhaps even] many years. They do need an empathic understanding on the closest level we can muster. It does not mean we cannot naturally move slowly and gradually into higher forms of empathy[6] [the form of optimal responsiveness that we call explaining or interpreting to the patient] much later on.

Kohut (1981) supports this controversial view with a clinical example drawn from the lengthy analysis of an extremely vulnerable woman patient:

> She lay down on the couch the first time she came, having interrupted a previous analysis abruptly and she said she felt like she was lying in a coffin and that now the top of the coffin would be closed with a sharp click . . . she was deeply depressed and at times I thought I would lose her, and that she would finally find a way out of the suffering and kill herself. . . . [A]t one time at the very worst moment of her analysis during . . . perhaps a year and a half, she was so badly off I suddenly had the feeling—you know, how would you feel if I

---

6. I am indepted to Dr. Bonnie Wolfe, who responded to my initial presentation of this material with the following comments: "It seems to me that the important issue is whether and how the analyst's empathy can be conveyed to the patient in a way that the patient can experience *as being responsive to him* [my italics]. Sometimes, the patient can discern the analyst's responsiveness only through gestures, tone of voice, or facial expression . . . [and] . . . attempts at verbal communication are experienced as unempathic and non-responsive to the patient's state . . . I am [here] also reminded of Dr. Basch's nice example of the parent lifting the baby and saying, "U-u-up we go." At a more developed state or stage, the patient may be able to utilize (and tolerate) responses that are more predominantly verbal; although this verbal responsiveness may need to be at a primitive level ("you feel that," "it hurts"). At a more advanced level, you may find responsivity in the reciprocal communication [cf. Wolf's (1981) notion of reciprocal empathic resonance] of abstract ideas about psychological functioning" (Wolfe, 1983).

let you hold my fingers for awhile now while you are talking, maybe that would help. A doubtful maneuver. I am not recommending it but I was desperate. I was deeply worried. So I . . . moved up a little bit in my chair and gave her two fingers. And now I'll tell you what is so nice about that story. Because an analyst always remains an analyst. I gave her my two fingers, she took hold of them and I immediately made a genetic interpretation—to myself. It was the toothless gums of a very young child clamping down on an empty nipple. That is the way it felt. I didn't say anything . . . but I reacted to it even there as an analyst to myself. It was never necessary anymore. I wouldn't say that it turned the tide, but it overcame a very, very difficult impasse at a given dangerous moment and, gaining time that way, we went on for many years with a reasonably substantial success.

Kohut is not alone in responding to his patient in this way. Although few analysts have admitted to similar experiences,[7] Winnicott (1947) recognized the appropriateness in certain situations of this kind of intervention:

> There is a vast difference between those patients who have had satisfactory early experiences which can be discovered in the transference, and those whose very early experiences have been so deficient or distorted that the analyst has to be the first in the patient's life to supply certain environmental essentials. In the treatment of a patient of the latter kind all sorts of things in analytic technique become vitally important, things that can be taken for granted in the treatment of patients of the former type. (p. 198)

The important clinical issue raised by Winnicott concerns what response on the part of the analyst can be considered optimal in relation to the patient's level of organization of his self–selfobject relationships. This level, as one would expect, corresponds to the position the patient has achieved on the developmental line of empathy.[8]

The empty nipple for Kohut's patient was the antithesis of a selfobject that would satisfy her selfobject need (not only drive need) to suck. Other selfobject needs may require a responsiveness for which verbal interpretation will not do and we need to study the significance of these optimal responses for the patient, for example, the warmth provided by the analyst's blanket, or the thirst or faintness that elicits a drink,[9] as well as other needs that may be related to the "psychological survival of the self."

In my opinion, there is no such thing as a "parameter," an extraanalytic, or unanalytic, measure we adopt for a time in order ultimately to return to doing proper analysis in the traditional way. We must respond in ways that enable us to communicate understanding to the particular patient with whom we are working. That is analysis.

7. Freud apparently did the same for Marie Bonaparte (Bertin, 1982).

8. Compare Wolf's (1980) notion of the "developmental line of selfobject relations."

9. Eva Rosenfeld (1966) reported that Melanie Klein gave her a glass of sherry under similar circumstances during an analytic session.

OPTIMAL RESPONSIVENESS AND THE REPETITIVE
AND CREATIVE ASPECTS OF TRANSFERENCE

The concept of transference can be usefully reexamined in light of the idea of optimal responsiveness. As no one simply repeats pathological patterns and distortions, selfobject transferences are better understood as *creative aspects of transference*, since their aim is to forge a link with a selfobject that will be a better version of the old one. This is true of virtually every patient, but particularly significant with respect to severely traumatized individuals in whom the development of the self has been seriously impeded. These patients sometimes create what I have called a *fantasy selfobject* (Bacal, 1981) around a nuclear figure whose archaic idealization or mirroring function has virtually no counterpart in the patient's antecedent experiences.

The creative aspect of transference has to do with the area of illusion, the area of play, and what Winnicott (1951) called "the transitional object" and "transitional phenomena." The experience of this kind of illusion is necessary in order for dis-illusion to not become disillusionment and traumatic frustration in analysis. Then and only then will the inevitable dis-illusion with a new version of the old selfobject, now recognizable as "good-enough" in Winnicott's terms, become associated with the ability to tolerate the fact that one's fantasy may or may not always elicit the response for which one hoped. This, in my opinion, is the only frustration that can be considered "optimal," nontraumatic frustration that alternates and is interwoven with the building of developmentally essential illusion associated with experience of a new responsive selfobject. In this way, confidence in the possibility of a "good-enough" selfobject can begin to develop. In this way, an optimal experience with the analyst can occur in which self defect or faulty self structure is repaired and new self structure can be built. Both analyst and patient should feel that progress is resulting from this process. The patient should feel stronger and be able to deal more effectively with the stresses specific to his particular vulnerability. Similarly, disruptions of such an inordinately painful degree that the patient recurrently feels that he cannot go on with the analysis, should not occur.

These ideas assume that there is a basic tendency toward growth and development in every individual that requires the optimal responsiveness of the selfobject in order to be realized. This is, I believe, the implicit assumption that underlies all psychotherapeutic efforts, whether psychoanalytic or not. The concept of "optimal frustration" mainly serves to give analysis respectability. It "proves" we don't think of ourselves as gratifying our patients when we treat them. Related to this image of the hard path that the patient must travel toward cure is that of fixation points of the libido and the idea that patients will adhere to these positions to which they have regressed unless confronted with reality or with the deleterious effects of their continuing to function in their archaic ways with objects. According to this perspective, unless patients are optimally frustrated and exhorted to progress they will simply be gratified by the understanding, demand more and more, and remain where they are. An even less fortunate outcome of "gratification" is said to be the so-called "malignant regression" (Balint, 1968) in which the analyst's accession to the patient's demands is thought to produce a spiral of negative, resistive, clinging, and increasingly demanding attitudes. In a previous paper (Bacal, 1981), I attempted to distinguish therapeutic regression from malignant regression on the basis of their genesis: therapeutic regression occurs as a result of accurate empathic responsiveness; while malignant regression occurs as a result of catastrophic selfobject failure in patients with particularly vulnerable selves. The latter tend to be those whose selfobjects have been predominantly fantasy selfobjects and who, as children, have been pervasively related to by their significant nuclear figures *as* selfobjects.

An optimal synthesis between the experience of the creative selfobject transference, and the working through of the repetitive transference is necessary. Before he can usefully allow himself to experience the old unempathic selfobject in the new selfobject constituted by the analyst, the patient's self must become stronger as a result of a good deal of positive interaction with this new version of the old selfobject. Sometimes, even where the good selfobject is not of the order of a fantasy selfobject, the analyst may have to be experienced by the patient as a good selfobject separately from the old selfobject and it is countertherapeutic to interpret this self-reparative move as "pathological splitting." Rather, it must be accepted as creative transference relatedness.[10] perhaps for some time. However, the split-off good selfobject in these cases *is* often the good *fantasy selfobject*; and, in this situation, when the experience of the split-off bad selfobject occurs in the transference, the patient may fragment dangerously. At these moments, the analyst virtually becomes for the patient the original traumatically unempathic or unavailable archaic selfobject (Bacal, 1981); and situations of this sort may be just barely retrievable. I believe that Kohut (1977) may have had something like this in mind when he suggested that defensive structures may sometimes usefully be left intact and that analytic working through in these cases will be carried out predominantly in the area of compensatory structures. The criticism that this would be merely supportive psychotherapy is undermined by the recognition that working through in the area of compensatory structures is related to the creative aspect of transference.

10. Contrast this to the Kleinian notion of splitting as a way of protecting the good primordial part-object from one's inclination to attack and destroy it.

RESISTANCE AND COUNTERTRANSFERENCE

A reexamination of resistance and countertransference will throw further light on the relevance of the clinical usefulness of the concept of optimal responsiveness. Resistance in classical analysis refers to the patient's inability or reluctance to participate in the analytic process cooperatively, that is, to free associate. The patient's silence, controlling, acting-in, or acting-out is attributed to his fear of the consequences of expressing his instinctual drives in relation to the analyst. From the perspective of self psychology, resistance to the analytic process is seen as reflecting a fear of retraumatization through repetition in the analytic relationship of traumatic childhood experiences. This fear is sometimes justified by the analyst's countertransference, of which the patient is usually aware, and which the analyst should not only analyze in himself but judiciously acknowledge to the patient. In some instances, in order for the inevitable frustrations of the patient by the analyst to be nontraumatic and even potentially useful by enhancing the patient's trust in the analyst and contributing to the working through process, the analyst will not only acknowledge this countertransference, but respond to the distress it occasioned with an explanation that his patient can manage and assimilate. Of course, the analyst must not burden the patient with his own problems.

The analyst works within the inevitable limits of his understanding and his countertransference. His personality will determine, to some extent, his capacity to provide an optimal therapeutic experience for his patient. An analyst who is committed to providing an ambience of replenishing deficits will not provide a patient who needs to engage in recurrent disruptions with his analyst (in order to repeat his pathological nuclear situations for the purpose of healing his self defects) with the analysis he requires. On the other hand, an analyst who is committed to the working through of optimal frustration (that is, transference disruptions) will provide the patient who needs developmental experience with a new selfobject and an understanding of this experience with an analysis that may be worse than useless. Often, of course, both are necessary for analytic progress. It is important for us to consider what I would regard as the clinical counterpart of Winnicott's (1952) assertion that "there is no such thing as a baby, . . . [there is rather] a nursing couple" (p. 99), the idea that "there is no such thing as a patient, there is only an analytic couple." A good match between the analyst and the patient does not have to be present at the outset. It may evolve as a result of the analyst's willingness to scrutinize the intersubjective context in which his interactions with his patient occur (Stolorow, Brandchaft, & Atwood, 1983), and from his capacity to respond in a relevant way.

The following clinical example may help to illustrate and integrate the central concepts and issues we have been discussing.

In her first analytic session, Dr. M, a psychologist in her late 20s, reported a dream that she had not long after her initial interview with her analyst, which took place a few weeks prior to the beginning of the analysis. She prefaced her account of the dream by what was, in effect, an association to it: she said how much she appreciated the generous gesture of the analyst friend who called the prospective analyst to prepare the way for her referral. In the dream the friend appeared as a taxi driver and drove her to a bridge where he said that he had forgotten the analyst's phone number and address. As she searched in her purse for the directions, the contents, her money, and things she had on her mind, fell out. Her son called "Mommy" to her and, as at home, everything was once again pulling at her.

Although the analyst recognized even then that the dream would have significance for the whole analysis its meaning was only partially apparent at that time. The interpretation reached, although tentative and incomplete, was that, despite her hope that her relationship with the analyst (whom she associated with her analyst friend) would enable her to enter a world in which she might receive the generosity of which she felt deprived by her parents, she feared she would again be caught up in a relationship in which she would be traumatized by being exposed to and emptied by another's limitless needs and demands.

A few months after the analysis started, she began to convey to her analyst her increasing anxiety about her financial situation. Although she earned a very good salary compared to a number of her colleagues, she was having serious trouble maintaining her standard of living largely because of the meanness and vindictiveness of her estranged husband with regard to child support for her three children.

Proud of her ability to manage independently, it was with great difficulty, embarassment and hesitation that she asked the analyst for a small decrease in her fee. He agreed, and there soon followed a second request for a substantial decrease, a request that was associated with continuing anxiety about her ability to cope financially. The analyst was initially reluctant to comply with this second request and the situation was discussed over a number of weeks. Dr. M reacted to her analyst's reluctance with a complex mixture of desperate insistence, anger, increasing tension and anxiety, as well as with a continuing sense of shame at having to make the request. Attempts to analyze the issue led only to a heightening of the tension and the analysis showed signs of breaking down. Finally, the analyst acquiesced, and told his patient that he was acceding to her implied request to pay nothing more than the amount that the national health insurance would reimburse her, until such time as she felt she could pay. He also explained that, while he knew that she was aware only of the economic determinants of her need and he was not denying the importance of these factors, he felt the psychological one to be paramount, although at the moment he was not completely cognizant of its significance.

After this, the impasse disappeared, and analytic work resumed. The unfolding of the significant issues and events of her childhood revealed that when she was 3 years old, her father, with whom she apparently had a close, idealized relationship, left the family and moved to a distant city. Her parents were divorced and she was left with her mother, whom she experienced as deceiving and exploiting her throughout her childhood and young adulthood by repeatedly failing to fulfill implicit and explicit promises to meet her emotional and financial needs. Following the departure of her father, she saw him on only two occasions until her late teens, as he did not visit and would not send her a ticket to come to him. Their total contact was restricted to letters, which they exchanged about every 2 months. She maintained her idealization of him, however, and throughout her childhood, never stopped longing for him to come to her. He remained extremely important to her as a sustaining figure. Except for his answers to her letters, she alone sustained this sense of relatedness to him through her capacity to create for herself, where only the barest basis for such a creation ever existed, what I have called a *fantasy selfobject* (Bacal, 1981).

Within a few weeks of the analyst's accession to the patient's request, the analysis of its meaning also began. This analysis had not been previously possible while the analyst was committed to a method (which might be described as optimal frustration) of not complying but trying just to understand and interpret. It is not possible to fully elaborate here the analysis of this incident of the fees, which extended over months and continued from time to time over years—as, indeed, one may have guessed from the account of the initial preanalytic dream. The most significant meanings, which were focused in the transference, were her need to create a new selfobject relationship with her analyst as both the mother and the father who would respond with demonstrable generosity; her need to have tangible proof of being protected from becoming entangled in a trusting relationship with someone who would only take from her and drain her of all her resources; her need for the analyst to respond by demonstrating to her beyond a doubt that he would share her burden and that she could in this sense exercise some control over him (money had always been a symbol of control in her family). Deeper than her need to know that she would not have to bear all of the burden herself lay the need of the child within her not to have to feel she had anyone to care for, specifically, the analyst-mother-child. As the analysis proceeded, a lifelong, sometimes suicidal, depression lifted. Her shaky self-esteem and self-assertiveness strengthened impressively, her career moved forward, and she was able to show her talented and very creative work to others, including the analyst, for the first time in her life.

Ultimately, the analysis of the patient's request and of the analyst's eventual responsiveness to that request revealed what were perhaps their deepest meanings. The analyst, by responding to her request, provided her with the first incontestable experience in her life of someone considering her interests before their own. More than anything else, it meant that someone believed in her, that she was worthwhile investing in.

In this connection, let us consider Wolf's (1981) recommendations for treatment.

> ideally, the analyst by virtue of his empathy and his theoretical orientation, can recognize the legitimate selfobject needs underlying the archaic and distorted manifestations, manifestations that he experiences often with some discomfort also. This then leads to the next substep in achieving empathic resonance. The analyst explains and interprets the sequence of events to the patient. He corrects his own previous misunderstanding of the patient. Again, it is important to point out, that the disruption, like the preceding harmonious selfobject transference, are not new experiences with a new object for the patient. What is new is that the analyst does not respond in a manner of an ordinary social situation but responds by explaining and interpreting on the basis of an empathically informed understanding. Nor is such an explanation a gratification of a need—neither of a selfobject need, nor of an instinctual wish or need—except for the need to be understood. By again feeling understood, the empathic flow between analyst and analysand is restored. (p. 6)

I am in essential agreement with Wolf except, perhaps, on two counts. The first is that, while the disruption was not a new experience for this patient, the means of its restoration in the regressed selfobject transference was essentially new. Dr. M needed to effect a shift or change in her analyst in order to create a selfobject response that was significantly different from anything that she had previously experienced. Secondly, while there was what *could* be called a gratification of a selfobject need, I would suggest that it was the *responsiveness that was optimal* for the patient at the level of organization of her self–selfobject relationships, in other words, at the level of development of her inner experience of empathic responsiveness in relation to nuclear selfobjects.

Implicit in this understanding of analytic work is the recognition of the therapeutic significance of what I have called the *creative aspect of transference* and its associated archaic selfobject, which can, I believe, legitimately be regarded as a "fantasy selfobject" or as a "transitional selfobject."[11] The transitional selfobject can be viewed as a prestage of the transitional object, in effect, a selfobject created by the patient, partly out of himself (in fantasy) and partly out of a sense of pliable surroundings. It constitutes a necessary intrapsychic stage as a precondition for the apprehending of the concrete transitional object, such as a blanket or a teddy bear. (In a sense, it represents, "I know that I can create that inside me.") The fantasy selfobject is created by the patient when the environment provides almost nothing around which he can elaborate a need for the responsiveness

11. Winnicott described the transitional object as the "first not-me possession" (Winnicott, 1951), that is, something that is experienced as part of the world and yet as belonging to me, something about which it is not to be asked, who created it, me or mother?

he requires. Dr. M's demand for a response to a fantasy selfobject need was responded to optimally, which meant, at this level, that it was "gratified." Far from producing a malignant regression, this enabled the analysis to resume and to deepen.

Although the analyst did not subsequently raise the question of the fees, Dr. M herself brought it up from time to time. She wanted to pay a fee but continued to struggle with her anxiety about paying anything. At the same time, it was evident that she was testing the analyst to see whether he would require her to do so. One day, three years after the analysis began, she reported a "new fantasy" that she felt completed the dream that she had shortly before entering analysis. The fantasy concerned the part of the dream where all her money fell out of her purse and her analyst friend picked it up and returned it to her. She reflected at this moment that she had never paid the cab fare. Apparently, no one paid for the cab ride, which she thought symbolized her need for it not to cost her any more than it had already. She felt that no one took care of her, and remarked, "you can't fall apart when there is no one to take care of you." At that moment, the analyst learned that her disintegration anxiety, with which she was struggling when she needed him to reduce the fees, could not have occurred unless she felt there was a potential selfobject who might respond. She was afraid at that time that she would cease to exist personally, professionally, or in some other sense. She reminded the analyst of the enormous difficulty that she experienced in asking to see him during the recent summer break as she was convinced that he would tell her that he had given her enough, that she was selfish, and that she shouldn't ask for such a thing. On another occasion she referred once again to the part of the dream where all her money spilled out of her purse and her subsequent anxiety about the fee arrangement. The original fantasy underlying the dream seemed to be that if she paid her analyst, he would get all her money and she would starve, and if she didn't pay him, she would survive and he would have nothing. The new fantasy was that she could pay him something at some point and the amount would vary according to what she could afford. She experienced this fantasy as hopeful and accepted the analyst's interpretation that it expressed her feeling that the amount that he would have and that she would have could be regulated. Less than 3 months later, she offered, without anxiety and with a quiet pride, to pay a fee commensurate with her economic situation at that moment.

Kohut has indicated that some patients require a gesture of what he called "preliminary enactment" without which no further analysis can take place. While I would essentially agree that certain patients may need this in a preliminary phase (in this sense, the notion of a "transitional selfobject relatedness" is useful), I suggest that it should not be thought of as a stage to be overcome so that the real analytic work can begin. Rather, it should be regarded as central to analytic work with these patients at the level of the development of their experience of empathy.

Sometimes, for some patients, this need arises as a result of progress, as, to some extent, in the case of Dr. M. She told the analyst that the experience of having both her requests granted, particularly having her wish for an extra session during the holiday break gratified, enabled her to think about his limitations. The knowledge that she was in an atmosphere in which she could make requests combined with the fact that she had grown stronger, enabled her to consider not only what she might ask for but also what she might or might not receive. She felt it was important for her to deal with the analyst's limitations and believed that his tolerance helped her to do so. She estimated his tolerance as falling somewhere between saying yes to one extra session, and refusing altogether. Her initial fantasy was to ask for all of them since the analyst was in town for the holiday, but she decided that he would probably refuse this.

I do not believe that the analyst's accession to his patient's request should be regarded as an "enactment" or a parameter. Although many would claim that it is indeed the latter, this seems to me an unnecessary apology on the part of analysts who struggle within the limits of their countertransference and their hard-won theories toward an intelligible flexibility in analytic work. *Rather, I would suggest that we reexamine the so-called "parameter" as a necessary aspect of the analyst's optimal responsiveness for his patient.*[12] In order to answer the question of what is optimal responsiveness for a particular patient at a particular time, I believe that we need to consider carefully the creative aspect of the selfobject transference. We need to remind ourselves that the selfobject transference is not predominantly a repetition, but rather is mainly an attempt at the creation of a new kind of relatedness with the frustrating nuclear object. *Fantasy selfobjects, fantasy selfobject relatedness*, and the specific examples of this that I think deserve to be called *transitional selfobjects* and *transitional selfobject relatedness*, are instances of the transformation of traumatic (often

12. I am grateful to Dr. Michael Basch (1983) for a number of helpful comments on reading the draft of this chapter. He suggests that a differentiation should be made between "transference of need" and the "transference of solution." "When there is a transference of need, a deficit, then the transitional selfobject relationship is called for; when, however, the patient demonstrates that he is bringing now inappropriate attempts of problem solving into the analysis, then these, I think, must be interpreted genetically, contrasting the analytic to the past situation, rather than taking it for axiomatic that the analyst has made a mistake in his relation to the patient. To use your terms, optimal responsiveness on the part of the analyst is not limited to one or another position. Optimal responsiveness can involve the analyst's functioning as a transitional selfobject at one time, as an interpreter of the patient's past reality at another, and as an interpreter of the analytic or external situation at still another time. This, I think, is in complete agreement with your statement . . . to the effect that there is no such thing as a 'parameter.' "

quite early) selfobject failures into *creative aspects of selfobject transference* by seriously injured patients. While the analyst need not intentionally enact a part different than the significant parent ("corrective emotional significance"), he does have to consider what response will be optimal in relation to the current level of his patient's specific developmental capacity to utilize empathic understanding of his selfobject needs for human relatedness. This will be therapeutic. If, however, the analyst does not wish to or feels he cannot respond to the archaic selfobject demand, no shame should attach to his refusal. Indeed, he may feel that to refuse will constitute an optimal response for that patient's growth. I would suggest, however, that there is less danger in responding to a regressed patient's suggestion as to how he needs to be treated than in refusing on the basis of the unproven thesis that the patient will develop if he is frustrated to the optimal degree.

While frustration is an inevitable part of life, I question whether the analyst can usefully regard it as "optimal" when he is working with his patients. This applies to gratification as well. Neither, per se, are appropriate considerations as part of a therapeutic process. They are legacies of a psychoanalytic morality, an intrusion into the clinical situation of a psyhoanalytic ethic that regards the patient's "real" unconscious and conscious intent to be the discharge and satisfaction of instinctual drives. Responsiveness, rarely perfect, almost always flawed in some way, can be optimal and comprises the legitimate efforts of our analytic work.

What does the analyst do with those patients for whom his kind of responsiveness does not work? As I have suggested, it is important to recognize that some forms of responsiveness that are crucially therapeutic may entail responses that an analyst cannot or will not, for ideological reasons, provide. For example, the necessary response to patient X may be withheld by analyst Y either because he simply does not respond to "acting-in" or because the patient's need gives him countertransference difficulties. From this perspective, what is designated as optimal frustration may sometimes be a rationalization of countertransference inflexibility on the part of the analyst. While the therapist must be himself, he also needs to be flexible to a degree or he will be correspondingly limited in treating certain patients. Kohut understood his concept of an average expectable environment as the "normal human responsiveness" promoting the patient's analysis and growth.[13] I would like to stress that *this will be different for each person.*

CONCLUSION AND SUMMARY

My thesis is that if our analytic responsiveness is optimal (and I would define optimal as relative and specific to the particular patient, not simply

13. Kohut conveyed this notion in a conversation with me in 1978.

a matter of degree as Kohut and Seitz viewed it) then our efforts will be growth producing. Selfobject relationships will mature and the self will become stronger and more free, flexible, and more resilient. An "optimal" frustration can only be optimal when it is optimal for something to be frustrated. It would be interesting to know what this might be. The view that optimal frustration alone produces internal structures is a hypothesis that needs to be challenged. As I believe I have shown, we cannot assume that all internalizing processes occur through frustration. In a good-enough situation, for example, identification and assimilation occur. Similarly the prior internalization of the parent/analyst as a responsive selfobject allows the child/patient to tolerate the former's inevitable unempathic responsiveness when it occurs, and to accept with less disturbance the limitations of the selfobject. This is particularly true in the case of patients whose relations with selfobjects in childhood have been traumatic.

It may well be that transmuting internalizations that occur without engaging transference frustrations are those where deficit (versus defect) is predominantly present, both self deficit and defect being ordinarily encountered together. This would be interesting to research in the psychoanalytic situation.

It is my belief that the notions of optimal frustration and optimal gratification can usefully be replaced by the concept of optimal responsiveness. Optimal responsiveness is an analytic concept that is distinct from the concept of the "parameter" and the "corrective emotional experience," which are devices that are essentially nonanalytic, but deliberately planned and actively initiated by the therapist. The *optimal responsiveness of the analyst* is determined by the position of the patient on the developmental line of his self–selfobject relations, and on his position on the developmental line of internalization of, and capacity for, empathy. It is not simply part of the ambience (Wolf, 1976) or the "frame" (Pines, 1981). Nor is it just an expression of the therapeutic or working alliance. Rather, it is the analyst's job. Interpretation and relationship are only the component aspects of optimal responsiveness in psychoanalytic treatment.

REFERENCES

Alexander, F. (1956). *Psychoanalysis and Psychotherapy: Developments in Theory, Technique and Training*. New York: Norton.

Bacal, H. (1979). *Empathic Lag in the Analyst and Its Relation to "Negative Therapeutic Reaction."* Unpublished manuscript.

Bacal, H. (1981). Notes on some therapeutic challenges in the analysis of severely regressed patients. *Psychoanalytic Inquiry*, 1: 29–56.

Balint, M. (1968). *The Basic Fault*. London: Tavistock.

Balint, M. (1969). Trauma and object relationship. *International Journal of Psycho-Analysis*, 50: 429–435.

Basch, M. (1983). Personal communication.
Bernfeld, S. (1928). *Sisyphos, oder veber die Grenzen der Erziehung*. Vienna: Internationale Vereinigung fuer Psychoanalysis.
Bertin, C. (1982). *Marie Bonaparte: A Life*. New York: Harcourt, Brace, Jovanovich.
Brandchaft, B. (1983). The negativism of the negative therapeutic reaction and the psychology of the self. In A. Goldberg, ed., *The Future of Psychoanalysis* (pp. 327–359). New York: International Universities Press.
Collins English Dictionary. (1979). London & Glasgow: William Collins.
Coverdale, C. (1983). Developmental lines in self psychology: Selfobject empathy and interpretation. In L. Hedges, ed., *Listening Perspectives in Psychotherapy*, New York: Jason Aronson.
Ferenczi, S. (1933). Confusion of tongues between the child and the adults. *International Journal of Psycho-Analysis*, 30: 225–230.
Freud, A. (1946). *The Ego and the Mechanisms of Defense*. New York: International Universities Press.
Gill, M. (1982). *Transference in the Divergent Analytic Schools*. Paper presented at the annual scientific meeting of The Canadian Psychoanalytic Society, June.
Khan, M. (1963). The concept of cumulative trauma. In *The Privacy of the Self*. New York: International Universities Press, 1974.
Kligman, D. (1983). *Psychic Trauma Revisited*. Paper presented to the psychoanalytic extension program, Toronto Psychoanalytic Society and Institute of Psychoanalysis.
Kohut, H. (1971). *The Analysis of the Self*. New York: International Universities Press.
Kohut, H. (1972). Letters of September 12th and September 23rd, 1972. In *The Search for the Self* (Vol. 2, pp. 867–870). New York: International Universities Press.
Kohut, H. (1977a). *The Restoration of the Self*. New York: International Universities Press.
Kohut, H. (1977b). Personal communication.
Kohut, H. (1981). From the transcription of remarks presented by Heinz Kohut at the Conference on Self Psychology, Berkeley, California, October.
Kohut, H., & Seitz, P. (1963). In H. Kohut, *The Search for the Self* (Vol. 1, 1978, pp. 337–374). New York: International Universities Press.
Kris, E. (1956). The recovery of childhood memories in psychoanalysis. *Psychoanalytic Study of the Child*, 11: 54–88.
Lichtenberg, J. (1982a). *An Experiential Conception of What Is Curative in Psychoanalysis*. Unpublished manuscript.
Lichtenberg, J. (1982b). *Transmuting Internalization and Developmental Change*. Unpublished manuscript.
Pines, M. (1981). The frame of reference of group psychotherapy. *International Journal of Group Psychotherapy*, 31: 275–285.
Rosenfeld, E. (1966). Unpublished address to The British Psycho-Analytical Association.
Stolorow, R., Brandchaft, B., & Atwood, G. (1983). Intersubjectivity in psychoanalytic treatment, with special reference to archaic states. *Bulletin of the Menninger Clinic*, 47: 117–128.
Strachey, J. (1934). The nature of the therapeutic action of psycho-analysis. *International Journal of Psycho-Analysis*, 15: 127–159.
Winnicott, D. W. (1947). Hate in the countertransference. In *Collected Papers* (pp. 194–203). London: Tavistock, 1958.
Winnicott, D. W. (1951). Transitional objects and transitional phenomena. In *Collected Papers* (pp. 229–242). London: Tavistock, 1958.
Winnicott, D. W. (1952). Anxiety associated with insecurity. In *Collected Papers* (pp. 97–100). London: Tavistock, 1958.
Winnicott, D. W. (1967). Personal communication.

Wolf, E. (1976). Ambience and abstinence. *The Annual of Psychoanalysis*, 4:101–115.

Wolf, E. (1980). On the developmental line of selfobject relations. In A. Goldberg, ed., *Advances in Self Psychology* (pp. 117–130). New York: International Universities Press.

Wolf, E. (1981). *Empathic Resonance*. Panel discussion to the Conference on Self Psychology, Berkeley, California, October 4.

Wolfe, B. (1983). Personal communication.

17

The Rediscovery of Intergenerational Continuity and Mutuality

MARJORIE TAGGART WHITE

The internalization of a "good" selfobject can reinstate the natural process of the continuity of intergenerational mutuality that Kohut emphasized in the last paper written before his death (Kohut, 1982). That the need for a sense of and belief in the possibility of intergenerational continuity is an essential part of humanness was stressed by Kohut in this paper when he said,

> healthy man experiences, and with deepest joy, the next generation as an extension of his own self. It is the primacy of the support for the succeeding generation, therefore, which is normal and human, and not intergenerational strife and mutual wishes to kill. . . . It is only when the self of the parent is not a normal, healthy self, cohesive, vigorous, and harmonious, that it will react with competitiveness and seductiveness rather than with pride and affection when the child, at the age of 5, is making an exhilarating move toward a heretofore not achieved degree of assertiveness, generosity and affection. And it is in response to such a flawed parental self which cannot resonate with the child's experience in empathic identification that the newly constituted assertive-affectionate self of the child disintegrates and that the break-up products of hostility and lust of the Oedipus complex make their appearance (Kohut, 1982, p. 404).

Kohut, reinterpreting the oedipal myth, stressed that Oedipus was "a rejected child . . . Oedipus was not wanted by his parents and that he was abandoned in the wilderness to die" (Kohut, 1982, p. 404). In contrast to this failure of loving parenting, Kohut cited Homer's story of Odysseus who saved his infant son's life at the risk of his own, thus manifesting intergenerational caring rather than the pathological fear and jealousy, which, in the oedipal story, destroys both generations.

Some years ago, before Kohut introduced his concept of intergenerational continuity but after I had begun to consider some of the problems posed by deficits in self development and Kohut's exciting approach to treating effectively the so-called narcissistic disorders previously regarded as untreatable (Kohut, 1971, 1977), I started seeing a 30-year-old lawyer who consulted me because of marital problems. Although I was challenged enough by Kohut's concept of the need for a cohesive self and the related narcissistic transferences that developed in analysis when such a need emerged, I was still convinced at the outset that this patient presented an obsessive character disorder. His difficulties with his wife, which involved his negative reaction to having children, his perfectionism, obstinacy, inhibited affect, excellent functioning verging on the compulsive, and his argumentativeness, which soon emerged as self-destructive in conflicts with his employers—all pointed toward an obsessive defensive picture against an underlying oedipal problem.

His childhood had been a traumatic one, with his Irish mother dying suddenly from a cerebral hemorrhage when he was four and his English father dying of cancer when he was 12. He had been brought up by an extended family of his mother's Irish relatives and while grateful, he expressed distaste for the poverty of their lives. He clearly regarded his father as an unsuccessful man. He had vague, idealized memories of his mother who had been overshadowed by her own intrusive mother. At first, he showed very little affect about his difficult childhood, largely emphasizing how much of an outsider he had felt as he did menial jobs to work his way through a state university and law school. Then he began to express some guilt that he had survived and was making money while his parents had been poor and died prematurely.

His conscious childhood memories, including his guilt, convinced me that he had a very difficult and painful oedipal problem. It seemed clear that the wrong parent had died first, that his vague, idealized recollections of his mother alluded to a passionate oedipal love for her at four and a terrible sense of loss at her death, along with anger at his father for not having died so that mother could have lived on with Mr. B. These death wishes toward his father, I hypothesized, must certainly have surfaced at the father's actual death when Mr. B was 12 and on the threshold of adolescence. The intensification of what I viewed as his expectable narcissistic defenses against oedipal guilt, displayed in his compulsive need to become a rich and successful lawyer overnight, seemed like further indisputable evidence. His refusal to have a child, which was causing marital problems, seemed like a predictable anxiety reaction against having his long postponed oedipal child by his mother and a defense against the unconscious anxiety of possibly having a son who would want to kill him as he had wanted to kill his own father and, seemingly, had brought it about.

It did not occur to me, despite my interest in Kohut's ideas, that this man's reluctance to have a child could involve his impoverished sense of self as a child, a deprivation he did not want to impose upon any child of his. In other words, what seemed like fear and jealousy about being a father could actually be an act of caring about his unborn child, arising out of his own wish to spare his child the awful sense of inadequacy that he had experienced.

Not long after he started analysis with me, he managed to get himself fired from a promising position, a pattern that seemed quite evident before he consulted me. An intense, long-standing ambition to achieve rapid wealth and success began to surface, leading to an impulsive plunge into launching his own law practice. Despite a diffident manner, his enterprise and his contacts enabled him to attract substantial clients, and it seemed that he was on his way to success.

What had appeared to be an unconscious acting out of resistance to treatment, his phallic narcissistic defenses against oedipal rivalry, now seemed to reflect a positive gain from treatment in the sense of a realistic pursuit of an ego-acceptable activity. While this might have been interpreted as a transference wish to please me, I felt it was premature to introduce this possibility since his ambition had started in early adolescence, presumably after his father's death, but conceivably before. In either case, his compulsive concern with swift success seemed to fit into an acting out of oedipal rivalry, intensified by his father's untimely death.

Despite his initial success with his own firm, he continued his doubts about whether he could be helped and whether he really needed it. One of the symptoms that had brought him into treatment was intense anxiety about his self-consciousness in consultation with clients, courtroom appearances, or any other public occasions. Given my tentative diagnosis of an obsessive character disorder, I again assumed that this was a conflict over exhibitionism, related to underlying castration anxiety. His sudden business success only seemed to aggravate this symptom.

Despite the impressive evidence for oedipal pathology, I became aware that if there were any transference at all, it was a faintly negative one, marked by doubts of my ability to help him, implying devaluation. I also became aware that his legal career had started to go downhill. His impulsivity, shown in his abrupt starting of his own firm, led him to make serious mistakes in handling his clients' cases, mistakes that he said he made against his better judgment.

He brooded increasingly about his self-consciousness, which interfered with making good arguments in court. His fights with his wife over having children intensified, but he refused to explore with me why he did not want them. He mocked any attempt to consider his dreams, which often indicated severe anxiety, from an oedipal standpoint. I saw this as a massive resistance to his castration anxiety, expressed in a self-destructive expiation of survivor guilt. He accepted my interpretation relating to his survivor guilt, but it did not halt his plunge toward business failure.

Apart from his exhibitionistic conflict, the one area he seemed interested in exploring was his compulsive perfectionism, which slowed up his work and led to struggles with his clients. While perfectionism is a characteristic obsessive trait, in conjunction with the peculiar obstructionist but seemingly impersonal transference, the fear of exhibitionism, his indifference to his wife's feelings about having children and his overweening ambition, I began to think that it could all point to the possibility of a disorder of the self, in Kohut's sense.

I decided to test for any indication of a neurotic, object-related transference. A relatively early but a very clear criterion of a transference clue as to whether a patient has a cohesive self, including the ability to experience another person as separate with unique needs and feelings was cited by Kohut as follows:

> Anna Freud, commenting on the present study in a personal communication expressed this line of thought in the following way: "In these cases the patient uses the analyst not for the revival of object-directed strivings, but for inclusion in a libidinal (i.e., narcissistic) state to which he has regressed or at which he has become arrested. One may call that transference; or one may call it a subspecialty of transference. . . . This does not matter, really, so long as it is understood that the phenomenon is not produced by cathecting the analyst with object libido." (Kohut, 1971, p. 205)

I started my transference exploration upon returning from a month's vacation in the second summer of treatment. I said, after listening to his report on the familiar problems with his wife and his business, "Were you aware of any feelings about me while I was away?" He not only said "no" coldly but also expressed his resentment that I would waste his time and money by intruding myself into the conversation that was supposed to be about him. Although I was surprised at his resentment, I was also suspicious from the traditional standpoint that he might be denying any interest in or need for me because of embarrassment or anxiety.

However, I decided not to press the issue of the familiar object-related transference feelings any further and to consider that his denial and resentment indicated a possible narcissistic transference. Given such a transference, he could reject my relevance or importance to him as a separate person and expect that I would be a responsive audience to him with a gleam in my maternal eye (Kohut, 1971), approving his early and later achievements. Obviously, an individual's ability to experience positive mirroring as a reliable response from a mothering person depends on earlier experiences with such a person where responsive attunement was provided to his anxiety over physical or emotional needs. Conceivably, his mother early on was not able to be as attuned as he needed her to be. Or, perhaps she had been fairly attuned and then, with the onset of her brain disorder, had ominously changed into an unresponding mother at the very time when he needed her for positive mirroring to support his proud phallic ambition, including admiration for his body and his bold reaching out to the environment.

Since my question on whether he had feelings about my absence had obviously aroused resentment, I decided to express some precautionary empathy in case he had experienced my intervention as quite insensitive to what he was feeling, that is, as a failure in mirroring. So I said: "Perhaps my question about myself seemed intrusive and unattuned to your feelings about your marital and business problems."

He sighed and said: "Well, I'm glad you're beginning *to listen to me* and hear how upset I've been feeling about my business going downhill and my wife being so depressed. The only ideas you've ever given me about handling my troubles is to tell me I'm punishing myself for guilt over my parents' death. Even if this were so, I don't know what I can do about it."

I felt his resentful remarks could be understood as an expectable response, expressing a negative therapeutic reaction. For instance, I had suggested that he could be unconsciously compelled to fail in his business and his marriage because he felt he did not deserve to live and be happy since he should have, somehow, magically kept his parents alive. I also wondered if his bringing up my interpretations spontaneously was actually a validation of them. Or was it an unusual expression of helplessness in response to my tentative effort at empathy?

Recalling that Freud had said the negative therapeutic reaction "constitutes one of the most serious resistances" (Freud, 1924), I decided that nothing would be irretrievably lost if I focused on Kohut's empathic approach and the possibility that Mr. B was moving into a mirroring transference with me.

If Kohut were right, a regression to a mirroring transference indicated an unmet developmental need that would have to be accepted and worked through by the analyst before a higher level fixation, for example, a negative therapeutic reaction involving superego guilt, could be approached. The affect of helplessness, touched off by my effort at empathy, seemed like a worthwhile self deficit to explore, along with the spontaneous anger at my originally intruding myself into the scene, anger so characteristic of a frustrated mirror transference.

I began to empathize consistently with the blows to his self-esteem, inflicted by his business troubles, focusing on how difficult it must be for him to endure this, especially in view of his long-standing hopes for a quick and smashing success. I realized that, in self psychology, the need for mirroring directly involves not only the failure of the mothering person to support the child's healthy ambition, but also the defensive regression to the infantile grandiose self who feels he has to do it all himself since the parents have failed him.

To my surprise, he began to respond with real affect, indicating that he had had little empathy or interest in his childhood from his insensitive, overworked relatives who had no time or understanding to give, either to his painful loss of both parents or to his compensatory ambitious strivings. The latter, I came to realize gradually, seemed to serve as a compensatory structure against an early self deficit arising from both a paucity of mirroring and inadequate idealization (Kohut, 1977, pp. 3–4). These ambitions needed to be sustained, yet divested of infantile grandiose expectations that already seemed troublesome.

He began to admit how frightened he was of succeeding with his own law firm and that he was terrified of having children because he didn't think he would be able to spend enough time with them or to make enough money to give them a good life. In line with Kohut's concept of intergenerational continuity, he was not afraid that he would lose out with his children, for example, not be able to compete with his son, but rather that he could not care for them adequately just as his father had failed him.

His conviction that he needed to give so much to his as yet unborn child to spare the child the deprivations he had, could certainly have been seen as a reaction formation against his own anger at not having been given what he wanted from his father, namely, a big penis, his mother, and a father he could look up to rather than mourn. This last possibility brought to my mind Kohut's view of the "second chance," that is, the idealizing aspect of the bipolar self. If the child is deprived of enough reliable mirroring to give him a basis for his healthy ambition, at least he may have a chance with his father (or possibly mother or another significant person) to attach himself to the values of one or both people, values that can come to be the guiding stars of a person's life (Kohut, 1977).

For Mr. B, this value seemed to be the goal of being both a loving and a powerful parent who could help a child get on the "right track" and also believe he could make it. This seemed to be an interesting and fertile fusion of both aspects of Kohut's bipolar self, for example, his healthy ambition and guiding ideals. That Mr. B might have received some phase-appropriate mirroring from his mother before she became terminally ill raised a hopeful but also puzzling question about the fate of his infantile grandiosity when confronted with her death.

I felt that some of his survivor guilt might be rooted in his narcissistic rage against himself when he could not prevent his mother's death and the presumably puzzling changes in her that preceded the fatal cerebral hemorrhage. That the child holds himself responsible for the reactions of his-her parents has been well documented (A. Freud, 1960; Kohut, 1977; Mahler, Pine & Bergman, 1975; Miller, 1983; Spitz, 1965, pp. 258–259).

Mr. B's solution to the problem was being the all-powerful parent, giving to his child so that the child could never find a flaw in his own grandiosity arising from the failure of the mother or father. Therefore he would never be at risk for a negative therapeutic reaction.

I tried to catch up some of these thoughts in an interpretation to Mr. B along the following lines. I said: "If you could make any child of yours as happy as possible, then you would never have to experience the awful feelings of the parent who fails the child or the child who feels he should be able to make his sick parents happy and well." This interpretation caught

Mr. B off guard, and he ws silent for a few minutes. Then he said, "Well, I guess that would be a foolproof way of avoiding blame if anyone were foolish enough to think he could always avoid blame."

Mr. B then had a most unusual dream. It had to do with explorers, trying to trace the source of the Amazon River, who suddenly found themselves in a lost world where dinosaurs appeared as if this species had never been extinguished. The explorers were both joyously excited at their find and frightened of the dinosaurs.

It seemed to me, following Kohut's approach to the exciting experience of becoming attached to an attuned selfobject and the fear of psychoeconomic imbalance coming from the sudden release of narcissistic energies, arising from feeling accepted and understood (Kohut, 1971, pp. 229–238), that this dream was a confirmation of my finally having found the attuned approach to Mr. B's problems. The dream showed my orthodox but off-the-track approach to the Amazon's source. The lost world, however, is the real relevant focus of the lost self, with the dinosaurs representing his ebullient but frightening grandiose self.

I recognized the fear of the grandiose self and of the concomitant narcissistic rage against the self for failure, emerging in the confirming dinosaur dream. His associations to the dinosaur dream focused on the explorers' fear of the monsters rather than their joy in discovering their "real find," that a so-called extinct species was still alive. When I asked what was frightening about the dinosaurs, he said: "They seem like evolution gone wrong. They needed so much to be all-powerful that they sort of grew their own armor, and then it almost immobilized them. "Yet," he recalled, "I saw a picture recently, showing a dinosaur mother sort of crooning over a baby dinosaur. So it seems as though there's some evidence they weren't 100% destructive monsters."

I pointed out that there was some joy on the part of the explorers in the dream over finding the lost species alive and suggested that perhaps it represented a hope he had that I would be interested in some hidden aspect of himself which he felt was like a dinosaur—perhaps the need to be all-powerful.

He was silent for a few minutes and then said, "Well, the idea of being like a dinosaur is pretty repellent. Yet when you put it in terms of needing to be all-powerful, it seems more acceptable. I'm beginning to see there were a lot of experiences in my life that would make me want to feel all-powerful even though I feared this would drive people away from me."

I intervened at this point, saying: "You also put a caring aspect of the dinosaur into the dream where the little one is being crooned over by the adult. It seems to show you need to be all-powerful, partly because you need to take perfect care of any child you have."

He smiled warmly, perhaps for the first time in the analysis, and said, "But of course! That's why I want to be a millionaire. Then, any child of mine would never have to suffer. I don't see why you can sense this, and my wife just doesn't understand it at all."

This open acknowledgment of my understanding his need to be all-powerful in order to provide perfect care and protection for his child was a welcome recognition that I was gradually becoming an attuned selfobject for him—one that he clearly never had. His reference to his wife raised the problem of whether I, as an empathic selfobject, should openly side with him against what he experienced as the obtuseness of his wife. His marital discord had been the alleged reason for his starting treatment. Was his reference to his wife now, at the point of his first acknowledgment of a selfobject transference, a test of my empathy?

I realized that I had never explored how his wife had reacted to his wanting to postpone having children until he was a millionaire, because I had assumed that this was a phallic–exhibitionistic defense against his underlying oedipal problem involving fear and guilt over having a child. Whatever his wife's reactions had been, I had felt, from my traditional therapeutic stance, that they were irrelevant to his unconscious conflict. Now I wondered if, given his underlying grandiosity, he had expected his wife as a part of his grandiose self to "know" why he had to become a millionaire in order to have children. So I took the risk of asking him how his wife had reacted to his reasons for needing a lot of money before he had children. He said, a little surprised, "But why should I tell her? She should have known!"

The extent of his fixation on his underlying grandiosity and his need for attuned mirroring by her thus became apparent in this revelation, not of his inability to communicate with his wife, but of his angry, hurt refusal to do so. It suggested an anxiety about expressing either his angry or hurt feelings to anyone close to him, for fear any incomprehension on the part of the other person would arouse in him narcissistic rage as a defense against his feelings of utter helplessness in relation to getting empathy or being adequately mirrored by another person.

This narcissistic rage, of course, had burst forth against me when I had raised the "unspeakable" question of his having any feelings about my absence on vacation. To have such feelings, of course, would be to acknowledge the helplessness that accompanied an unmet need and a fear of the narcissistic rage turned against the self for not being able to fulfill such a need, especially by controlling the needed person as a part of one's grandiose self.

The transferential selfobject problem—particularly the problem of achieving the internalization of myself as the empathic, mirroring selfobject he never had—became the problem of trying to obtain the information from his past, which, like his wife, I "should have known already," and the acceptance of his infantile grandiosity without encouraging its acting-out to a point where his reckless need to prove himself all-powerful could end in actual disaster or misfortunes.

After the dinosaur dream and the revealing associations it led to, including his need for mind-reading and mirroring by a potential selfobject, I decided to go slowly in supporting his grandiosity, while striving to maintain an overall positive tuning in, both on his ambition and his need for empathic mirroring. The result was that he began to gather himself together, closed out his own practice and was soon able to get himself a good position with a well-established law firm.

Gradually, he began to work on his conflicts with authority in the context of blows to his self-esteem that he suffered when he failed to get 100% agreement with his ideas from everyone. When I put it delicately, slowly, and very tactfully in this perspective, he was able to consider his unconscious grandiose need for absolute control (the dinosaur), which also involved his exhibitionistic conflict and the wish to command total admiration from his audience.

It appeared that the unconscious grandiose configurations that underlay his exhibitionistic ambition and his need to command total understanding and appreciation from others revealed an inadequate mirroring experience with his mother. Seemingly, she was not able to separate herself enough from her own narcissistic, dominating mother to encourage healthy exhibitionism and self-esteem in her little son. On the contrary, it seemed that before her cerebral hemorrhage, she had turned to him as if he were her parental selfobject, thus intensifying his fixation on his grandiose self and his consequent narcissistic rage against himself for not omnipotently saving her from her tragic illness and death (Weiner & White, 1982). Certainly, his desire to be a perfect parent partly stemmed from this sense of tragic failure, as well as his own feeling of developmental neglect, including his mother's inability to give him adequate and not grandiose mirroring (Miller, 1981).

In addition to his mother's grandiose expectations of him, interspersed with his own fantasies including getting the *best* doctor to save her, Mr. B's father had shown somewhat grandiose independence after his wife's death by trying to maintain a home for his son, with occasional girlfriends, and fending off the suspect generosity of the mother's demeaning relatives. Conceivably, the father's somewhat grandiose efforts at self-sufficiency, including running a small hardware shop while trying to raise his son, could have inspired that son, Mr. B, toward strenuous achievement of his goal to become a millionaire parent.

It was not clear whether Mr. B blamed his father's unexpected death on the latter's too strenuous efforts for self-sufficiency. Certainly, the father's sudden death seemed to make more difficult the realization of Mr. B's previously mentioned second need of the bipolar self, namely, the chance to develop guiding values through the idealization of a parent after the failure of maternal mirroring. The postmortem criticism of his father, especially by his mother's relatives, further undermined his chances to idealize the father, particularly when Mr. B. was confronted with having to depend upon resentful relatives and to work his way through college and law school because his father was financially inept. He also revealed his anger at the father's girlfriends, condemning his father for his "infidelity" to Mr. B's dead mother.

Under these pressures from adverse life circumstances and developmental needs, his early fixation on his grandiose self became obviously intensified, and its pressure was not relieved by the release of fixated narcissistic energy sufficient for the development of a reliable cohesive self. Mr. B was left, as his father had apparently been before him, with only his perfectionistic, controlling, rageful but very needy grandiose self. It was not until his analysis with me began to focus on his self needs, including the awareness and acceptance of this primitive, omnipotent self that the energies imprisoned in it could become available for his mature goals.

In recalling the shock of finding out that his father had cancer and the subsequent memories of feeling so ineffectual and hopeless in relation to his father's death—memories that brought back similar feelings about his mother's early death, he became aware of a need to protect himself from ever feeling so utterly helpless again. This need, he was able to recognize in treatment, took the form of becoming a self-sufficient millionaire, a goal partly shaped by an uncle on his mother's side who was wealthy and contemptuous of Mr. B's father. My exploration of his anger at this uncle led to a fuller expression and documentation of how alone, criticized, and even ridiculed he felt by his mother's relatives for his aspirations to go to college, become a lawyer and be successful.

Mr. B's grandiose expectations of his wife—and me—"that we should have known" what his feelings were—became much clearer when he could talk about his terrible feelings of isolation and rejection in his adolescence at the hands of his resentful relatives who supported this penniless orphan as an unpleasant "duty."

It would have been natural for a 12-year-old boy to have hoped that his grandmother, aunts, uncles, and cousins would have understood how shocked, frightened, and heartbroken he was at his father's unexpected death from cancer. This was an aspect of his regression to his grandiose self that we can certainly understand in regard to Kohut's concept of aggression as a disintegration product in reaction to an unresponsive environment (Kohut, 1977).

From this standpoint, Mr. B would have hoped, despite his natural distrust, that his relatives, belatedly, would have understood his hurt, his loss, his bewilderment, and especially his trying to pull himself together to become a success and even pay them back for their support. But their failure to empathize with him, their ridicule of his "being too big for his britches" and their refusal to loan him money for even a relatively inexpensive state university only kindled the fires of narcissistic rage that drove his

grandiosity. Nevertheless, it seems possible that the focus of his grandiose
need to succeed took such a respectable and achievable form, to be a millionaire by being a lawyer, as an idealized reflection of his father's need to
care for him by running an independent small business. Having a profession,
the law, is somewhat akin to having your own store.

However, it is conceivable, given Mr. B's tragic early life, his high
intelligence, and his aggressive grandiosity, that he could very easily have
turned to crime. Why he did not seems to me an indication that Kohut's
concept of intergenerational continuity is rich in its potential. Whatever
mirroring care and idealizable values Mr. B received from his sick, prematurely dying mother, from his father, somewhat inept but trying hard,
only to be defeated by cancer, and even from his grudging but still shelter-
providing relatives, brought out of it a perfectionistic goal to have children
who would never want for anything. This is not an aggressive wish for
revenge on all those who disappointed him. It could be seen as a wish to
surpass them, in a kind of loving competition, to show how really to take
care of children; but there is no destruction here.

As he felt more reliably understood by me as an empathic selfobject
and as he became more realistically self-confident through transmuting internalization of me, he spontaneously began to consider having a child right
away, before he made a million. So, shortly before the treatment terminated,
he became a delighted, proud father. It seemed a reliable indication that he
had worked through much of his narcissistic grandiosity, that in the process
he had internalized me as a responsive and trustworthy selfobject and had,
consequently, arrived at a cohesive sense of self and a differentiated level
of object relations that, as a symbolic change, he was able to thank me
warmly at the conclusion of the treatment.

That Mr. B could develop from an isolated, hostile, joyless, success-
ridden person to a warm, responsive, joyful, and loving father in the course
of a self-psychologically oriented analysis was to me an impressive demonstration of the effectiveness of Kohut's concepts, particularly with reference
to the possibility of the recovery of intergenerational continuity. Kohut
concluded in his final paper (1982) that

> The normal state, however rare in pure form, is a joyfully experienced devel-
> opmental forward move in childhood, including the step into the oedipal stage,
> to which the parental generation responds with pride, with self-expanding
> empathy, with joyful mirroring to the next generation, thus affirming the younger
> generation's right to unfold. . . . We believe . . . that in the last analysis we
> are not dealing with an uninfluentiable conflict of basic opposing instincts
> (Thanatos battling Eros) but with, at least potentially remediable, interferences
> that impinge on normal development. (pp. 402–403)

As humankind faces the possibility of total destruction of ourselves,
civilization, and planet earth itself through a nuclear end of the world, it

would seem that Kohut's concepts of aggression as a reversible disintegration product and of the normality of intergenerational continuity both offer a species-rooted preventative for a nuclear holocaust, namely that we are not born to kill.

REFERENCES

Freud, A. (1960). Four lectures on child analysis, given under the auspices of the New York Psychoanalytic Society. (Cited in Spitz, R. (1965). *The First Year of Life*. New York: International Universities Press.)

Freud, S. (1924). The economic problem of masochism. *Standard Edition*, 19:159–170.

Kohut, H. (1971). *The Analysis of the Self*. New York: International Universities Press.

Kohut, H. (1977). *The Restoration of the Self*. New York: International Universities Press.

Kohut, H. (1982). Introspection, empathy and the semi-circle of mental health. *International Journal of Psycho-Analysis*, 63:395–407.

Mahler, M. S., Pine, F., & Bergman, A. (1975). *The Psychological Birth of the Human Infant: Symbiosis and Individuation*. New York: Basic Books.

Miller, A. (1981). *Prisoners of Childhood*. New York: Basic Books.

Miller, A. (1983). *For Your Own Good*. New York: Farrar, Straus and Giroux.

Spitz, R. (1965). *The First Year of Life*. New York: International Universities Press.

Weiner, M. B., & White, M. T. (1982). Depression as the search for the lost self. *Psychotherapy: Theory, Research and Practice*, 19: 491–499.

18

Alterego Phenomena and the Alterego Transferences

DOUGLAS W. DETRICK

Heinz Kohut in his summarizing reflections at the 1981 Berkeley Self Psychology Conference returned to an image that must have been one of his favorites. In discussing one of the many dimensions of empathy, the concept that he placed at the center of his work, he recalled the reaction of the astronauts as they were forced, by a malfunction of their spaceship, to choose between leaving the earth's orbit and forever circling the universe, or returning to earth to what was sure to be a fiery death. Kohut recounted that the astronauts' decision was instantaneous: return to earth and a certain death rather than circle endlessly in the dark void off infinity. His point was at once simple and profound: human beings even in death prefer being surrounded by a human silence and a human darkness rather than by a nonhuman, meaningless void. It is here that we find a fitting symbol for one of the two major aspects of alterego selfobject phenomena: a need for sameness in which the individual is stripped of any personal ambition or need for the all-powerful other and experiences himself as embedded in a human sameness, a sameness that both in life and in death binds us together.

To introduce the other major aspect of alterego phenomena, I would like to utilize a second reference to outer space, or rather, to the world presented to us in Steven Spielberg's block buster movie *E.T.: The Extra-Terrestrial*. There is much in this movie for the self-psychology-informed viewer to ponder. We see the all-too-common phenomenon in suburban America, a 10-year-old child, Elliot, growing up in a family characterized by a harried, overworked mother and the recent departure of his father. E.T., the extra-terrestrial then arrives, surely symbolizing the regressively transformed inner experience of the boy. Rather than experiencing himself as a joyful, growing child, Elliot feels like a charming yet ugly being, left by a cruel fate on a distant planet, far from his own kind. Remember E.T.'s overriding motivation was to reach "home." Among other things we see in the film are the dehumanized and dehumanizing scientists, that is, the faceless fathers who with one exception effect the destruction of E.T., in spite of all their well-meaning efforts. That one exception is the scientist at the end who takes off his helmet, reveals his face, and empathizes with

Elliot's deep need to make contact with E.T. He allows the boy to spend the last few minutes with the seemingly dead alien. It is this act of empathy, symbolized by the human face, that allows for the transformation of E.T., Elliot's nuclear self, from a cold, inert, dead being into an enthusiastic, jubilant, living one. He joyfully proclaims that soon he will be "going home." But now rather than focusing on many other aspects of the film that we could profitably elucidate by our self psychological theories, I would like to focus on just one. All of you should remember the rather poignant scene in which Elliot and his older brother go to the garage, the departed father's workshop, in an attempt to gather together a variety of materials and objects out of which E.T. will be able to fashion a radio in order to contact the by now long-departed spaceship. The radio is a tool and also a means of communication. In the movie we see this tool in its fragmented form, the bits and pieces of a mechanism that needs to be put together before it can function effectively.

Bringing together these two factors, the abiding need for human sameness, and its intrinsic role in the acquisition of skills and tools, and suggesting that these two factors together form a third major selfobject developmental line, was Kohut's final contribution of major import to self psychological clinical theory. Detecting a shift in his approach to the alterego phenomenon in his comments at the 1978 Psycho History Conference in Chicago, I wrote to Kohut to ask him about this. In the letter he sent me in reply he stated,

> You have quite correctly recognized a slight shift in my thinking about the types of selfobject transferences. They correspond to the three parts of the bipolar self (mirroring, alikeness, idealization), and they make good sense experientially. Each of them has its own developmental line, from archaic forms to mature forms, and each can be easily discerned during development and in the therapeutic transference (in which all defects are remobilized and offer themselves to be healed). With regard to the sustaining effect of the presence of human sameness, I have in mind the early security that the baby must have in the mere presence of humans (voices, smells). I also think of the little guy just working next to daddy in the basement or "shaving" while daddy shaves (corresponding to the developing intermediate area of skills and talents), the fact that an inimical environment, even one trying to harm you, is better than an exterminating one e.g., the concentration camp experiences, the atmosphere of Kafka's *The Trial*. (Kohut, 1980)

In this letter Kohut refers to the alterego aspect of sameness and links it with the "intermediate area of skills and talents." What does he have in mind? In effect he is saying that this new major developmental line, the alterego selfobject developmental line, should be seen in the metaphorical space of the bipolar self as occupying the area between the two poles.

In other words those skills and talents that we utilize in the actualization of the nuclear program, those skills and talents that occupy the area of the tension arc allowing for the creative achievements of the self, involve the two aspects of the alterego self–selfobject relationships.

SPECIFIC FORMS AND FRAGMENTATION PRODUCTS

As Kohut points out, the alterego selfobject developmental line begins very early in life. What might some of the varieties of forms be? We must realize that answering this question is more complex than this question regarding the mirroring and idealizing developing lines, because of the alterego developmental line has two different aspects that are intrinsically related: the need for sameness, and the acquisition of skills and talents.

In regard to the first aspect, the need for sameness, the earliest and most basic manifestation of the alterego phenomena are found, as Kohut describes, with the human infant finding itself surrounded by a human environment, human sounds, human smells, and human responsiveness. As the person matures the term "oneness," the one most applicable to early in life, is slowly and selectively replaced by the term "alikeness." By alikeness I mean the realization, not necessarily conscious, of a sameness coexisting in another person with traits that are not the same. As the person increasingly grows older and his individuality becomes increasingly differentiated, the relationships in which the alterego phenomena are active become too numerable to categorize. Relying on Kohut's example and trying to find an evocative phrase that would help clarify the alterego experience of sameness in a way comparable to the mirroring "I am perfect" and the idealizing "you are perfect and I am a part of you," I was unable to think of any sentence. However, I feel the noun *"we"* without the verb included but only implied is the best candidate. By this I mean if the psychological phenomenon we are observing can at least partially be captured by the sentence "we" and the appropriate verb, for example, we like, we are afraid of, we read, and so forth, then an alterego selfobject relationship is in evidence.

What about the other aspect of alterego phenomena, what Kohut has referred to as "the intermediate area of skills and talents"? First, I believe that rather than call this intermediate area that of skills and talents we are better off referring to it as the area of skills and tools. By tools I am thinking not only of the acquisition and consolidation of skill with tools such as a violin, a car, or a tennis racket, but also believe that in the domain of thinking, ideas, concepts, and problem-solving strategies and operations should be considered as cognitive tools. Just a little reflection on what the developmental line might be in the regard to the "area of skills and tools" makes us realize that this is not an easy question to answer. It isn't long in our reflections before we are confronted with and required to provide the solution to such difficulties as the relationship between thinking and action, and a deeper analysis of what Kohut has referred to in *The Restoration of the Self* (1977) as "action-thought." Rather than enter into these both murky and deep waters here I will only add that I believe that if we follow Piaget's cognitive developmental schema: sensorimotor to preoperational to concrete operational to formal operational thinking, we will not be very far off in understanding the second aspect of alterego phenomenon.

What might be some of the fragmentation products characteristic of the first aspect of the alterego developmental line? Perhaps the easiest to ascertain are in the domain of the sexualizations. Some alterego sexualizations are those sexual acts or fantasies that require for the generation of sexual excitement the anonymity of the sexual partner or partners. This represents the sexualization of the healthy selfobject configuration in which the self is surrounded by a humanly responsive milieu. One variant of this would be sexual fantasies or behaviors of engaging in orgies whereby a person is unable to determine with which sexual partner he or she is actually engaging.

The more archaic the deficit in the self and the correlated self–selfobject disturbance is, the more central the alterego features of the sexualization are. In other words, the more archaic the deficit in the self the sexualization covers, the more important it becomes that the sexual partner not give any evidence of personality characteristics of its own. Following this line of thought a little bit further, it would then seem that the fetish, the nonhuman sexual partner, presents the most archaic level of sexualization.

Consider the case of Mr. U that Kohut discusses in the first chapter in *The Restoration of the Self*. Mr. U's mother

> appeared to have been totally absorbed in the child, overcaressing him, completely in tune with every nuance of his needs and wishes, only to withdraw from him suddenly, either by turning her attention totally to other interests or by grossly and grotesquely misunderstanding his needs and wishes.
>
> From the traumatic unpredictability of his mother he had retreated early to the soothing touch of certain tissues (such as nylon stockings, nylon underwear) which were readily available in the childhood home. They were reliable, and they constitute a distilate of maternal goodness and response. The transference material also alluded to the existence of earlier (pre-fetishistic) substitutes for the unreliable selfobject . . . [these] thus creating a psychological situation of merger with a non-human selfobject that he totally controlled. (1977, pp. 55–56).

Although Kohut describes the fetish of Mr. U as being the result of a faulty disturbance in the grandiose self, I think we can see certain aspects of his symptomatology as disturbances in healthy alterego needs, especially as they are manifested in the archaic need for predictability and control of the surrounding environment.

Nonsexualized disturbances in the alterego need to experience human sameness might manifest themselves in patient's descriptions of such feelings of aloneness, isolation, and a lack of relatedness to other people. Often such people at the end of a successful therapy will with obvious pleasure describe how they "now feel like everybody else" or "I'm finally joining the human race."

Fragmentation in the skills and tools aspect of the alterego developmental needs are manifested in a variety of ways, for example, difficulties in learning, and innumerable varieties of reduced effectiveness in thinking. Thought disorders, from subtle and hardly noticeable to blatant and obvious ones should also be seen in this context (Kohut, 1981).

A CASE VIGNETTE FROM THE RESTORATION OF THE SELF

Although not identified as such, Kohut's case of Mr. W in *The Restoration of the Self* (1977) seems to have a description of alterego pathology as it emerged in the psychoanalytic process. Kohut stated that the most characteristic "manifestation of Mr. W's psychological disturbance was the recurrence of a syndrome of irritability, hypochondria, and confusion" (p. 153). He described how initially the sensitivity of Mr. W to actual or impending separations from the analyst was contained in a dream near the end of the first year. The patient dreamed he was on an airplane flying from Chicago to New York "occupying a window seat on the left side of the plane, as he mentioned looking out toward the south" (p. 153). When this discrepancy was called to Mr. W's attention, Kohut reports that "the patient became utterly confused and spatially disoriented to the point that he literally could not tell left from right for a short time" (pp. 153–154). Associations followed tht led Mr. W to recall the key incidents of his adult life and later childhood "when he had become spatially disoriented in unfamiliar places — with a dreadful feeling that he would never find his way back to familiar surroundings" (p. 154). It was with the beginning of the analysis of this dream and the subsequent spatial disorientation that memories emerged of early in life being left with "conscientious people who took care of his physical needs but otherwise paid only scant attention to him" (p. 154). Kohut goes on to say that later in the analysis "a number of childhood memories began to emerge concerning the time when he was first on the farm, when no one paid attention to him, and he was often alone when everyone was working in the fields" (p. 167). In regard to the quality of some of the transference experiences, Kohut noted that "certain phases of the merger-mirror transference, when the analyst was felt to be unresponsive, unpredictable, and of a non-human, stony quality . . ." (p. 160) pointing to a possible very early disturbance in Mr. W's relationship with his mother, prior to his being left with relatives on the farm. Although I am leaving out other details of this case, I believe we can see the breakdown products of Mr. W's healthy alterego needs as the selfobject transferences were disrupted. In particular, I am referring to the breakdown in his cognitive efficiency, that is, spatial disorientation, and the correlated feelings of isolation, aloneness and the experience of the analyst as "nonhuman."

A CASE EXAMPLE

Mr. X, a middle-aged, twice-divorced physician, was an exceptionally narcissistically vulnerable individual whose psychological disturbance was both widespread and deep. His fragile personality was threatened equally by success and failure. Success, such as on the tennis court, would evoke grandiose fantasies about himself that at times he was apprehensive he might actually attempt to implement. For example, when it looked as if he was about to defeat a stronger opponent in tennis, he would begin to entertain fantasies of dropping his business affiliation and become a tennis professional. These ideas were quite threatening to him because he knew they were totally unrealistic, yet he was fearful that he would be carried along by the current of this grandiose view of himself. Later, he also came to see that successes whether in sports or work also led him to experience a painful generation of excitement in himself that he would then use a variety of means to dissipate. Failures, whether a slight rebuff from a colleague or a lack of immediate assent by a patient, would evoke deep anxieties in him and an almost paralyzing inability to attend to even the most mundane daily activities. When in this mental state, he was simply unable to return phone messages or take care of routine aspects of his practice.

Mr. X almost immediately established an archaic merger transference to me seemingly of the idealizing type that lasted approximately 2 to 2½ years. After approximately 3 years this archaic merger transference had slowly resolved and was replaced by a rather easily identifiable mirror transference. A characteristic aspect of this new phase was that Mr. X would come into each session with enthusiasm to report some new insight that he had discovered about himself since he had seen me last. Almost invariably my response to this achievement was not what he wanted, and he felt either ashamed or enraged. The following session is one that occurred at the end of this second phase, the phase characterized by a mirroring transference. This second phase lasted for approximately 6 months to a year and was replaced by a relatively short-lived alterego transference.

The session was the first one following a weekend break. Mr. X entered the session and immediately described how furious he had been over the weekend. He quickly added that he blamed me for all of his problems, although he couldn't say exactly what my role was in his difficulties. He then associated to having also had more than usual to drink over the weekend. His associations then moved to a conversation that he had had with a good friend over lunch earlier in the same day of the session I am now describing. He and his friend had talked about the behavior of school kids and how it had been when they had been in grammar school. Mr. X described how angry he had become that his friend had not been able to understand that when school kids mimic each other, "it is cruel and hurtful," and then he went on to say to me that "It's thievery."

His associations then moved to how earlier in the day he had been enraged at his secretary because she's "so stupid and she doesn't copy *exactly* what I want her to." I stated to him that the two elements that seemed to emerge from his associations were rage at sameness as illustrated by school children mimicking each other, and rage at a lack of sameness, illustrated by his secretary's inability to do exactly what he wanted.

He more or less agreed with my comments and went on to state that during his rages at me over the weekend a saying had come to him that he had repeated to himself over and over again, "Someone has stolen something from me."

At this point I suggested that perhaps the weekend break had caused his feelings of rage, an idea he quickly dismissed with the comment that there had been innumerable weekend disruptions but his rage over this one was caused by something different. In a few moments he then said that he remembered in the prior session he had asked me if I played tennis and that my answer was given in an impatient, "let's get on with the show here" attitude.

I said I remembered the incident that he was talking about and that he had turned to me at that time and asked me if I knew what an American twist shot was. I then added that he had talked often with me about his tennis game and that this was the first time he had ever asked if I actually played. Perhaps that was of some significance.

At this time he became mildly agitated and said "You've screwed up again; I had said American twist serve, not American twist shot, and anyone who knows anything about tennis would have said American twist serve." He went on to add that although now he felt I was not a good player, having made such a *faux pas* in reference to the game, when he had left the previous session he was certain I was a player of far superior skill to him.

A variety of thoughts occurred to me in regard to the significance of his associations and our interaction around them. Because I was so struck by the fact that in the previous session he had actually turned to me directly and asked me a question, a behavior so uncharacteristic of anything that had occurred previously between us, I suggested to him that perhaps the reason he had asked me a question at all was to find out in what way we were the same and in what way we were different. I went on to add that his asking me a direct question was most unusual and that perhaps at this point in the process he was able to risk such a step. After a few moments he responded: He remembered becoming preoccupied with the sentence "sameness is differentness" over the weekend, although he had no idea what this meant, despite this, he felt it had a deep psychological importance to him.

I suggested that in this important area of interest for him, his tennis game, he had hoped, by asking me if I played tennis, to confirm that he and I were very much the same in this particular area. I then added that my response to his question had been quite disturbing to him, although the very fact that he could ask it signaled a shift in his previous vulnerability.

He more or less agreed with my interpretation and then became rather pensive. After a few moments he wondered out loud if there were any response to the question that he had asked me in the prior session that would not have disrupted him in one way or another. I stated that I thought there was and it would have been a response from me that would have allowed him to feel that in this particular area he and I were if not identical, very much the same. He felt this was correct.

Several months after this session Mr. X became preoccupied with a specific image. Actually the visual puzzle had emerged early in his analysis, but it was only after several years that he felt it was imperative for him to understand it. It was the image of a sculpture of a man, a bust. On this bust was a mold, a soft clay-like material that, when dried, one could remove and have the impression of the sculpture remain. Mr. X ruminated regarding this problem: whether the mold was the same as the sculpture, after all it was a direct result of the bust's shape, or whether it was different and actually the opposite. He came to see, and most of the insights were originally his and not mine, that this puzzle represented an important psychological experience for him. It represented an aspect of what he needed to get from his father but was never able. In one moving session he associated to a detail of this image he had never mentioned before. He said that there was a dark line between the bust and the overlaying mold, and that this line represented "the transfer of information." When this thought occurred to him, he stated that he had no idea what it really meant but that it simply had popped into his mind. I thought and expressed to him in an appropriate way that this must be another way of his describing his deficit in the alterego developmental line. That the experience of sameness symbolized by the sculpture and the mold allowed for the transmission of information, learning in a fundamental sense that is experienced by a child as coming from the benign, empathic parent. Mr. X then went on to add that one could never become a person, a real person, if one had never had early in life this kind of experience of sameness. It was only through the experience of empathy, or to use his word, "resonance" that one could eventually allow oneself to become different.

After this session alterego themes were not clearly discernable. Then, approximately 1½ years later Mr. X started a session by reading a letter he had received 5 years before from a close friend who had often given him advice. He read over and over one paragraph in which his friend had described to him an example of his (Mr. X's) psychological difficulties. Mr. X found the description both confusing and contradictory. He wondered if the disturbed thinking in the letter was similar to a vague thinking disturbance in his mother. The possibility that his mother had a thought disorder was suggested by some (rather peripheral) transference fantasies (fears) and the memory of several humorous, seemingly innocuous memories concerning statements his mother had made. Upon closer scrutiny Mr. X became convinced the statements, though humorous, were in fact bizarre.

The other major focus of this session was the patient's belief that the hub of his disturbance was very early in life, "before language is used to communicate." He related how satisfied he had felt earlier in the day when, alone in his office, he had "babbled" sounds intended to convey pure feeling.

The following session began by Mr. X relating that while at lunch he had felt for the first time that "I was deprived of a father." He then associated to the past week, and how good he felt when he was able to aid a more knowledgeable colleague in a particular procedure. Mr. X noted that the best feelings had been evoked when "I was able to anticipate what tool Dr. Y would ask for next."

Then his associations moved to his own son and how proud he was of his growth and achievements. He felt at once sad and good reflecting on how he felt he never really existed for his father, and that he felt himself to be an excellent father for his son.

BORDERLINE STATES AND THE ADDICTIONS

In *The Analysis of the Self* (1971) Kohut states that regarding those people who become addicts

> The trauma which they suffer is most frequently the severe disappointment in a mother who, because of her defective empathy with the child's needs (or for other reasons), did not appropriately fulfill the functions (as a stimulus barrier; as an optimal provider of needed stimuli; as a supplier of tension relieving gratification, etc.) which the mature psychic apparatus should later be able to perform (or initiate) predominately on its own. Traumatic disappointments suffered during these archaic stages of development of the idealized selfobject deprive the child of gradual internalization of early experiences of being optimally soothed, or being aided in going to sleep. (p. 46)

Although in his more recent work Kohut refers to the addictions as serving to cover over deficits in the self, his most lengthy discussion of the addictions is in *The Analysis of the Self*, where he discusses their etiology in early disturbances of the idealizing developmental line. Many of the addictive substances fall into this category. They help the narcissistically vulnerable, anxiety-ridden addict by providing a chemical substance to aid the person in soothing and calming himself. However, following a clue implied by the bipolar nature of the nuclear self, we can specify another major class of addicting substances. They are those that provide the self with not just feelings of a calm well-being, but are energizing. The substance provides the addict with a chemical, nonpsychological equivalent to the "ambitions" pole of the bipolar self. So now we have two classes of drugs, those, such as the amphetamines and cocaine that are correlated with the disturbances in the mirroring developmental line, and those, such as tranquilizers and, I think, to a major extent alcohol, that are correlated with deficits in the idealizing self–selfobject developmental line.

Polydrug abuse, utilizing this approach, is now more understandable. It is well known to researchers on drug abuse how addicts will seek out a variety of drugs in which either to mix into a "cocktail," or to use sequentially. Now, the self-psychology-informed researcher or clinician will be able to get a view into the archaic disturbances of the addicts' self by learning of the specific action of the variety of drugs of the polydrug abuser.

What about the alterego developmental line insofar as it relates to the addictions? Those drugs that reinforce a sense of oneness or communality with others should certainly be prime candidates. Also, the hallucinogens such as LSD, might also be used as a result of a deficit in the alterego developmental line. What I have in mind here is that aspect of the alterego developmental line related to the acquisition of skills and tools. After all, it wasn't so long ago that many of us, at least here in California, were hearing about all the earthshaking insights and the discoveries made by people while on a "trip," that is, an acid trip.

In regard to the borderline states, I believe a new alterego self–selfobject developmental line will provide a significant deepening of our understanding. In my view, the true borderline states as differentiated from those exceptionally vulnerable individuals that nevertheless with a talented therapist become analyzable, are best understood as being the result of very archaic disturbances in *both* aspects of the alterego area of the nuclear self.

First let me focus on that aspect of the alterego developmental line characterized by an experience of/or need for sameness. A common complaint of true borderlines as discussed in the psychoanalytic literature of an acute and painful feeling of aloneness is indicative of an archaic disturbance in this area.

Adler and Buie (1979) in an essay titled "Aloneness and Borderline Psychopathology: The Possible Relevance of Child Developmental Issues" described three experiences of aloneness that are the result of three "psychodynamic roots." The first is the result of rage, the second is the result of a primitive mode of internalization, incorporation, in which the object is experienced as eaten or absorbed by a person, and third, grief as experienced as an unbearable sadness over loss. They then go on to describe a fourth more fundamental determinate of aloneness in borderlines.

> We have invariably been confronted with episodes of aloneness which have been the most unbearable, the most hopeless, for the patient. When explored in the context of a good working alliance, we have been told that this particular aloneness feels more basic in their total life experiences, more like a given primary. For example, one patient who expressed this opinion of her most unbearable aloneness, traced the experience as far back as a memory from childhood. Her mother had in fact been unable most of the time to be empathically together with her daughter. The patient recalled lying in her crib pervaded by a desperate aloneness; she did not, however, call out, because she knew no one would come. (Adler & Buie, 1979, p. 84)

Although this can be understood as a severe disturbance in mirroring or idealizing needs, I think this kind of aloneness is *primarily* a function of a more basic, more primitive disturbance, a disturbance in the capacity to experience oneself as a human being surrounded by other human beings. To utilize the first image that I used that of the astronauts being in outerspace, one might view the experience of these borderlines as existing in a nonhuman environment, or perhaps the image of E.T. is a more useful one, that is, a person experiencing himself as stranded on an alien planet, surrounded by other living beings, but not sufficiently similar to allow an experience of relatedness with another and oneness with a human community.

In a chapter in his first book *Borderline Conditions and Pathological Narcissism* (1975), Otto Kernberg discusses a profound sense of loneliness with a correlated experience of a subjective sense of emptiness. These two subjective states, emptiness and aloneness, one would think are interrelated. Perhaps the profound sense of loneliness is related to the alterego needs closer to the idealizing phenomenon, whereas the sense of emptiness represents the alterego need for sameness closer to the mirroring developmental line. Further clinical research is needed here.

The other alterego aspect is the acquisition of skills and tools. What about this in the context of borderline states? Borderline states also represent an archaic disturbance in this aspect of alterego selfobject.

The standard definition of the borderline person from the point of view of psychological assessment is someone who on the so-called objective tests shows no evidence of thought disorder while on the projective tests, especially the Rorschach, there is blatant and manifest evidence of so-called primary process thinking. Supposedly then, the borderline does well in structured situations, like the objective psychological tests, but decompensates in unstructured situations such as that offered by the Rorschach test. On the one hand this is much too much behavioristically oriented, while on the other it does not allow for a more sophisticated theoretical understanding of the varieties of thought disturbances, especially in the area of concept formation and reasoning found on the Rorschach. Be that as it may, the testing does show in true borderlines, a deep disturbance in cognition. The relationship between borderline thought disorder on the Rorschach and the disturbance in the borderline nuclear self requires consideration of the relationship between the brain's capacity for symbolization of specific relationships with that of the supraordinate self symbol, the self-concept. A metapsychological approach is most likely required to deepen our comprehension of borderline states in this area.

However, to state it differently, I believe the true borderline has the two poles of the nuclear self, yet the so-called intermediate area, that of the alterego developmental line, has its core missing. To put it another way, although a tension gradient has been set up, a tension arc that allows for the nuclear program to grow and mature never develops.

A NOTE ON THE INTERPRETIVE PROCESS

Kohut saw the interpretive process, and for that matter every specific interpretation, as having two aspects. There is first the understanding phase and then the explaining phase. The understanding phase is directly related to the placing of empathy at the center of the psychoanalytic process, and must be counted among Kohut's most important contributions. The understanding phase can be seen primarily as an aspect of one of the alterego needs, the alterego need for sameness. After all, is not the empathic process, at its core, the finding and experiencing of a sameness in another individual's experience? It is this aspect of the interpretive process that I like to characterize as in some way indicating to the patient that you know *what* they are experiencing. The second interpretive phase is the explaining phase. I like to characterize this as telling the patient *why* they are experiencing what they are. Usually this, of course, is explaining to the person what the particular selfobject need was that was either disrupted or gratified that then led them to a particular feeling, action, or response. This explanatory phase can be conceived of as giving the person a particular cognitive tool. By this I mean that they are given a word or concept or language by which to describe first to others, and then to themselves, both what they are experiencing and why (Basch, 1981). The alterego self–selfobject relationship is at the center of *both* phases of the interpretive process! In this sense I think that the alterego selfobject relationships are more fundamental than either the mirroring or the idealizing. Sometimes their role needs to be brought into sharper focus by an interpretation. Sometimes this is not necessary. In any event, it is the experience of empathy or sameness that then allows for the remobilization of the split-off or defended against mirroring and idealizing wishes.

I also think that we can add another dimension to our understanding of the curative process. Kohut's comments in an excerpted draft of *How Does Analysis Cure?*: "the functional yield that we expect to result from the expansion and firming of the psychic structures of the self is threefold: (1) the capacity to make efficient use of selfobjects should be increased; (2) at least one sector of the self, from the pole of ambitions to the pole of ideals, should be enabled to function effectively; and (3) the patient should now be in a position to devote himself to the realization of the nuclear program that is laid down in the center of his self" (Kohut, 1984, p. 152). In a successful analysis, we can further understand the dynamics of the cure by imagining that the so-called intermediate area of the bipolar self, the area of the alterego developmental line, is always expanded. By this I mean that the area between the ambitions and ideals in the metaphorical space of the bipolar nuclear self is expanded. One is reminded of Freud's metaphor, referring to the final great scene in Goethe's *Faust*, of the draining of the Zuider Zee (Freud, 1933, p. 80). The ground claimed from the sea that then can be used for cultural progress is, not as Freud felt, the ego expanding its domain over the id, but the increasing expansion of the alterego domain, at the expense of the archaic mirroring and idealizing needs.

GROUP DYNAMICS, LEADERSHIP, AND THE GROUP SELF

In the context of Freud's (1921) contributions to group psychology, it would seem that self psychology, with its central theoretical concept of the self–selfobject unit, would require a radically new theory of group dynamics. After all, Freud's group theory dealt with *individuals* that come together to form a group whereas it is fundamental to the concept of the self–selfobject unit that another person is experienced as a part of our self. At the very least, from the point of view of self psychology the sharp distinction between the individual and the group is lost.

In regard to the dynamics and structure of the group self, Kohut (1976) suggested that the group self is analogous to the self of the individual. He stated "We are then in a position to observe the group self as it is formed, as it is held together, as it oscillates between fragmentation and reintegration, as it shows regressive behavior when it moves toward fragmentation, etc. . . . " (Kohut, 1976, p. 838).[1]

Undoubtedly, it is the work of Bion that describes the observation of group behavior that can be utilized to realize a self psychological theory of group dynamics. Bion (1959) introduces the concept of a "group mentality." He suggests that there are two major components to the group mentality, one of which may be ascendant at any particular time. The first is called the "work group." This work group is the group mentality characterized

---

1. However, elsewhere Kohut (1972) states that "group cohesion is brought about and maintained not only by an ego ideal . . . but also by their shared subject-bound grandiosity . . ." (p. 658).

by cooperation, effort, and some degree of sophisticated skill in the individual members. According to Bion, this level of group cooperation is voluntary (p. 12).

The second general type of group mentality Bion calls the "basic assumption group." He describes three distinct types of basic assumption groups; the dependent, the fight–flight, and the pairing.

In regard to the basic assumption group called dependent, the group mentality is such that the assumption is that the group has organized itself around a leader who can fulfill its needs. According to Rioch (1975),

> The central air of the basic assumption dependency group is to attain security through and have its members protected by one individual. . . . The members act as if they know nothing, as if they are inadequate and immature creatures. Their behavior implies that the leader, by contrast, is omnipotent and *omniscient*. (p. 24)

The second basic assumption group is organized around the idea that the group has met to flee from something or fight something. According to Bion, "the accepted leader of a group in this state is one whose demands on the group are felt to afford opportunity for flight or aggression" (p. 18). This is referred to as the fight–flight basic assumption group.

The third basic assumption group is the pairing group. Rioch (1975) states:

> Here the assumption is that the group has met for purposes of reproduction to bring forth the Messiah, the saviour. Two people get together on the behalf of the group to carry out the task of pairing and creation. The sex of the two people is immaterial. . . . [The group members] listen eagerly and attentively to what is being said. An atmosphere of hopefulness pervades the group. No actual leader is or needs to be present, but the group, through the pair, is living in the hope of the creation of a new leader, or a new thought, or something which would bring about a new life. . . . (p. 27)

In Bion's discussion of the basic assumption groups we have a clear example of the variety of group regressive processes and fragmentations. All the basic assumption groups are easily observed in small groups[2] when the leader or expected leader refuses to comply with the group expectations put upon him and instead does nothing except interpret the group's behavior to itself.

Although Bion does not suggest it, the various basic assumption groups may be ordered hierarchically. The dependency group is that closest to the work group insofar as it is the first indication of group fragmentation as a function of a loss of leadership. As the group further fragments it organizes itself around the affects of either anxiety, as characterized by the flight

---

2. See Colman and Bexton (1975) for a detailed description of the Tavistock group relations approach.

group, or rage as characterized by the fight group. The pairing basic assumption group should be seen as an attempt to resurrect out of the regressive group process a new leader (idea) by which the group can then reconstitute, that is, form a work group.

However, the hierarchy of the three basic assumption groups is only very grossly true and breaks down under close scrutiny. The dependency basic assumption group that Bion describes is one form of a group experience that ranges from a healthy, vital work group to a unproductive "depressed" group with an identified, yet ineffective leader. Whatever the state of the group vitality, from enthusiasm to depression, the bond to the work group leader is not lost. Its various forms are *regressive* in nature.

In contrast, the fight–flight group is the result of group *fragmentation* in which the goals of the work group are lost and replaced by a leader–group dynamic organized by either anxiety (flight group) or rage (fight group). Because the group self is organized (structured) by the alterego experience, it is natural to expect that the level of the most intense affect is the one to which the group regresses. This phenomenon makes understandable Bion's observation that in leaderless groups it is often the most disturbed member that emerges to become the new leader.

What about the *structure* of the group self? Just as the concept of the individual's nuclear self is essential, so too is the concept of the group's nuclear self. Kohut implies that the group nuclear self would be analogous to the individual nuclear self, one pole of ambitions and the other of ideals (see Kohut, 1976, footnotes on pp. 837–838). However, I believe we should see the group nuclear self as *reciprocal* to the individual's nuclear self. Whereas the individual nuclear self is *bipolar* and is constructed of the ambitions at one pole and the ideals at the other pole with the skills and talents mediating between these two, producing the nuclear program, the group nuclear self is *unipolar* with the alterego dimension of experience central and essential to group cohesiveness and the group boundary. The motivational core of the group is the experience of sameness as a function of the group process as it realizes (is directed by) the ambitions or ideals of the leader.

Basically there are only two types of leaders. We may designate them *a posteriori* as the charismatic and messianic types. There are two basic group nuclear selves, correlated with the two types of leaders. The messianic group nuclear self (i.e., the group) is motivated in the pursuit of its productive goals by the direction-setting, calming certainty of the leader. The charismatic group nuclear self is motivated in the pursuit of its productive goals by the direction-setting, stimulating enthusiasm of the leader.

In sum, an inspection of the small group processes in the light of Bion's findings is most helpful in describing a self psychological theory of group dynamics and the group self. Much of the work that has built on the pioneering efforts of Bion and the Tavistock tradition, has the concept of the group boundary as the center of both theoretical and practical considerations (e.g., Lawrence, 1979). The alterego concept brings a depth psychological, psychodynamic meaning to the essentially metaphorical idea of the group "boundary." The experience of *sameness* gives us an empathically based definition of a group and its boundary.

SUMMARY AND CONCLUSION

The foregoing considerations applied the concept of the alterego selfobject developmental line to a variety of subjects. Its clinical manifestations were noted in a vignette from *The Restoration of the Self*, as well as in a case sample from my own work. On the level of clinical theory the alterego concept was brought to bear on such different phenomena as sexualizations, addictions, and borderline states. The interpretive process was also elucidated from the point of view of alterego phenomena. Finally, a preliminary attempt to add to Kohut's considerations of the group self was undertaken. The concept of the group nuclear self was suggested, along with a deepening of the ideas of Bion by applying self psychological theory to his most valuable observations.

However, this essay should be seen as a prolegomenon to a broader study. The clinical material presented was barely able to substantiate Kohut's observation of the *two* aspects of the alterego phenomena. What about clinical data that do not seem to support this view?

The role of alterego issues in the addictions and borderline states was not discussed in the depth it deserved, especially in regard to the latter. The discussion of the interpretive process was only in the most general terms, and the possibility that alterego phenomena, from the point of view of clinical psychoanalysis, are on a more basic level than either the mirroring or needs was also not given a full discussion.

A discussion of the relationship between the alterego transferences and the twinship transference was not attempted here. It is my belief that the twinship transference is a specific subspecies of the alterego transference and that we should not follow Kohut in using the terms alterego and twinship as synonyms.

I am most regretful that the application of the alterego selfobject concept to group dynamics could only briefly be described. It is in this domain that I believe Kohut's ideas regarding alterego phenomena will gain their greatest significance. It seems most fitting that all of us that were touched by this great scientist's ideas and his vision try to apply his final contribution of major import to the area he himself would have undoubtedly turned to had he not been taken by an untimely death.

REFERENCES

Adler, G., & Buie, D. (1979). Aloneness and borderline psychopathology: Developmental issues. *International Journal of Psycho-Analysis*, 60:83–96.

Basch, M. (1981). Psychoanalytic interpretation and cognitive transformation. *International Journal of Psycho-Analysis*, 62:151–175.

Bion, W. (1959). Selections from: Experience in groups. In A. Colman & H. Bexton, eds., *Group Relations Reader*. Sausalito, CA: Grex.

Colman, A., & Bexton, H. (Eds.). (1975). *Group Relations Reader*. Sausalito, CA: Grex.

Freud, S. (1921). Group psychology and the analysis of the ego. *Standard Edition*, 18:69–143.

Freud, S. (1933). New introductory lectures on psychoanalysis. *Standard Edition*, 22:5–184.

Kernberg, O. (1975). *Borderline Conditions and Pathological Narcissism*. New York: Jason Aronson.

Kohut, H. (1971). *The Analysis of the Self*. New York: International Universities Press.

Kohut, H. (1972). Thoughts on narcissism and narcissistic rage. In P. Ornstein, ed., *The Search for the Self* (Vol. II). New York: International Universities Press.

Kohut, H. (1976). Creativeness, charisma, group psychology. In P. Ornstein, ed., *The Search for the Self* (Vol. II). New York: International Universities Press.

Kohut, H. (1977). *The Restoration of the Self*. New York: International Universities Press.

Kohut, H. (1980). Personal communication, December 6.

Kohut, H. (1981). Personal communication.

Kohut, H. (1984). *How Does Analysis Cure?* A. Goldberg, ed., with P. Stepansky. Chicago & London: University of Chicago Press.

Lawrence, G. (1979). *Exploring Individual and Group Boundaries*. New York: Wiley.

Rioch, M. (1975). The work of Wilfred Bion on groups. In A. Colman & H. Bexton, eds., *Group Relations Reader*. Sausalito, CA: Grex.

Index

exhibitionism and voyeurism, 71–
73, 76–78
sibling rivalry, 71–73, 76, 77
unresolved oedipal complex, 71,
73, 76, 78, 79
empathy, 77
mirroring, 75, 77
overinterpretation and emotional
attack on patient, 82
primacy of self-preservation, 76, 77,
79, 80
retention by patient of defensive
constellations, 81, 82
scientific objectivity, 19th century,
69, 70
hypnosis, 69, 88, 99
surgeon–abscess model, 69, 80
versus 20th century, empathy, 69
self–selfobject matrix, 81
thwarted development of self, 70,
74, 76, 77, 81, 82
Deformity, physical, and self-pity, 181
Deidealization, 26
Denial, psychotic, 38, 39
Depression
husband's, reactive to wife, 198
and self-pity, 183, 184
Development, child, 213 (*see also*
Alterego, selfobject
development line and
transference; Interpretation,
developmental model)
Diarrhea, 110, 111, 113, 115, 117,
120, 121, 133 (*see also* Bowel
control)
Disavowal (Freud), 53
Distance, need for, 84
Dream interpretation, Kohut, 16, 17,
22–26, 28, 29, 98
Drive-defense and ego-defense
interpretations, 46–48, 54, 73,
74, 78–80, 82
anal retentive eroticism, 71–73, 76,
78
exhibitionism and voyeurism, 71–
73, 76, 77, 78, 137, 141, 143,
230
inner conflict structuralization, case,

193–195, 200, 201
and optimal frustration, 203, 204,
211
and self-preservation, 84, 85
sibling rivalry, 71–73, 76, 77
unresolved oedipal complex, 71, 73,
76, 78, 79
Drug addiction, 248, 249, 255

E

Eichorn, August, analysis of Kohut, 6
Eissler, Kurt, 6, 10, 44, 61*n.*
Eissler, Ruth, analysis of Kohut, 7
Empathy, 77, 170, 205, 231, 232 (*see
also* Intergenerational
continuity, case; Interpretation,
understanding and explaining,
empathic vantage point; Optimal
responsiveness)
developmental line, 212–215
failures, 65
Kohut discovery, 12
versus objectivity, 33, 36, 37, 39,
41, 69
resistance and countertransference,
optimal response, 221, 222
and self-pity, 179, 182, 185
as vicarious introspection, 202
Encouragement, interpretive, 20, 22
Envy and interpretation, 64
Exhibitionism, 71–73, 76–78, 137,
141, 143
and self-consciousness, conflict, 230
Explaining (*see* Interpretation,
understanding and explaining,
empathic vantage point)

F

Family therapy, 165
Father, (*see also* Intergenerational
continuity, rediscovery, case)
conflicts with, 150, 154, 157
criticism, 157, 158
distant and faceless, 240, 241